USE HISTORY LIKE A TOOL

AN UNCONVENTIONAL GUIDE TO READING THE PAST AND MANAGING THE FUTURE

STEVEN LEVI

SILVER LAKE PUBLISHING
LOS ANGELES, CALIFORNIA

Use History Like a Tool
An Unconventional Guide to Reading the Past
and Managing the Future

First edition, 2003
Copyright © 2003 by Silver Lake Publishing

Silver Lake Publishing
3501 Sunset Blvd.
Los Angeles, CA 90026

For a list of other publications or for more information, please call
1.888.638.3091. Outside the United States and in Alaska and Hawaii,
please call 1.323.663.3082. Find our Web site at **www.silverlakepub.com**.

Library of Congress Catalogue Number: Pending

Levi, Steven
Use History Like a Tool
An Unconventional Guide to Reading the Past
and Managing the Future
Includes index.
Pages: 298

ISBN: 1-56343-774-0
Printed in the United States of America.

For all the students who take a history class and ask, *Why do I have to learn this garbage?*

Author's Note

History bores many people. Any history class. Any era. Western civilization, American, Asian, African...whatever. And particularly the "survey" classes—the ones required to graduate that cover 10,000 years in 10 weeks. Those classes are often so bad that, if they weren't required subjects, no one would take them.

A neater subject is chemistry, where you can learn how to make things blow up. Then there's math where every equation has a correct answer. Other useful subjects include, economics, business, real estate and finance. You can walk out of an Economics 101 class and see the basic laws at work in your neighborhood—even if you live in Des Moines. You can watch sociology in action at your local mall and if you are of the devious type, you can use textbook psychology to manipulate your friends, enemies and parents.

But what most people fail to realize is that history is *the most important academic* subject. Why? Because knowing history allows you to see into the future. If you know the past, you can predict the future with a lot more accuracy than you can with a crystal ball, deck of Tarot cards or leg of a newt. The problem is that most history instructors do not teach students to read the future like a book; they teach them how to win fame and fortune on the gameshow *Jeopardy*. When was the Battle of Hastings? Who was Joe Stilwell? What was the Essex Junto? Get all three and win a trip to Jamaica! If all you want out of history is to be scintillating at a cocktail party, memorize a few names, dates and places. Then let everyone assume you know what you're talking about.

But if you really want to use history as a tool in your day-to-day survival, you must understand the underlying principles of history and how to use those principles for your own survival.

Doing this requires you to see history differently—as something other than names and dates. You need to see history as motion. In other words, people and countries...armies and economies...move through time toward goals. These goals can be political, philosophical, religious, economic or anything else. In this book, we'll consider the various kinds of historical motion.

History as motion isn't a unique notion. Other historians—notably, Frederick Jackson Turner and more recently Daniel J. Boorstin—have discussed similar ideas. But this book takes a more practical approach.

This is not a scholarly book. It is not a work of philosophy—historical or otherwise. Rather, it is a practical work specifically designed to be readable and understandable so that even someone who *hates* history can read the future like a book. You don't need a Ph.D. to understand the basic laws of history, just the ability to let your mind leap the gap between academic study and real life. This book is designed to teach you how.

—Steven Levi
Anchorage, Alaska
August 2003

Contents

"History Repeats Itself"

When you take a Western history class just about anywhere, it's a virtual guarantee that you will have a final essay question on the rise and fall of the Roman Empire. It's nearly cliché. First semester Western Civilization classes are geared to studying the Roman Empire—with a heavy emphasis on the fall, not the rise. There may be a quick few classes on the Roman Republic, but by and large, the focus will be on the Roman Empire and its demise.

Class discussions involve the theories of the empire's collapse and Christianity's rise. The declining morals of the Romans. Lead poisoning from drinking goblets. The infiltration of salt into the fresh water table. There are those who will claim the empire got too large to govern and others who believe that the cost of the Roman military became too expensive for the tax base. The point of all this speculation is, of course, that if we knew why the Roman Empire fell, we could stop the same fate from happening to modern civilization.

This is the *worst* way to look at the fall of an empire. Look at it another way: In the United States, every time a plane crashes, the National Transportation Safety Board (NTSB) investigates the accident. A team of experts goes to the crash site and examines the crushed plane's body inch by inch to hypothesize why the plane crashed. And, whether the crash was caused by ice on the wings, pilot error, cracks in the frame, a worn tail elevator or a wing bolt, the NTSB wants to know to ensure the same fate does not befall other aircraft. The thought is that if you get rid of all of the faulty airplane parts, you will have an indestructible airplane (in most cases).

This logic is fine as far as airplanes go. But when it comes to civilizations, the process of getting rid of the faulty parts is a lot more complex. It isn't any one thing that brings down an empire. Typically, there are many causes that have been festering for generations. When a ship sinks, there may only be one hole visible below the water line but the entire hull could be composed of rotting timbers. And, just because the puncture was in the stern doesn't mean that if you fix the stern of another ship it will not sink as well.

The key to studying the collapse of the Roman Empire is to look at its historical roots. Why? Because *no one factor* caused the collapse; several factors contributed to the collapse. Furthermore, by going back to the beginning—to the rise of the Roman Empire—you can see the common roots to those factors. This is particularly important because a culture is not a palpable thing like a piece of wood or barrel of oil. It is every aspect of a civilization.

An American automobile, for instance, is a symbol that personifies America for the year in which it rolled off the assembly line. But simply looking at the car itself only tells a small portion of the story. There are features on a car that tell you about the society that saw a particular car's debut: a rumble seat, cigar lighter, radio, 8-track deck, CD player, DVD player, global positioning system (GPS) or a wet bar are a few examples. But what you can't determine by looking at a car itself is how much the car is worth, how it was paid for, how many service stations the culture had, what the most popular car colors were that year, how many people bought the car, how it was transported to the site where it is now, if leather was an option inside the car, how the plastic parts were made, etc. Five hundred years from now, if some future culture finds six cars in different parts of what is now the United States and each car were from a different decade, archaeologists will have a lot of guesswork before them.

Fall of the Roman Empire

Roughly speaking, there are three pillars on which every civilization rests. They include: religion, economics and politics. And, a change in any one of these pillars will have an effect on the others instantly and dramatically. Thus, the key to pinpointing the factor(s) that led to the collapse of the Roman Empire is to see what termites were at work in these three pillars. In the religious pillar, obviously, was the rise of Christianity. Christians were a rouge cult until the time of Constantine the Great and thereafter became the primary religion. (Constantine I, the first Christian Roman emperor, most memorable for his legalization and support of Christianity, established a "New Rome" at Byzantium, which he renamed Constantinople.)

Early Christians were harassed by Roman officials to the point that they were forced to hold their services underground, quite literally in catacombs. They were unpopular and accused of the grossest of actions—including setting the city of Rome on fire under the reign of the Emperor Nero. They were also considered lazy because they did not work on the Sabbath, disrespectful to the emperor because they did not believe him divine, and as the Roman historian Tacitus noted, "for their hatred of the human race." Nero tortured Christians, crucified them and, once again quoting Tacitus:

> they were additionally made into sports: they were killed by dogs by having the hides of beasts attached to them, or they were nailed to crosses or set aflame, and when the daylight passed away, they were used as nighttime lamps.

Prior to the rise of Christianity, the Romans were primarily thieves of other people's philosophies. Their gods were Greek with the names changed and their mightiest god was the sun. When the Romans adopted Christianity, they melded the two religions making Christian holy days near pagan ones with holidays near the summer and winter solstices and the vernal and autumnal equinox.

But Christianity did not cause a decay of Roman culture. If anything, Christianity strengthened it. Christian philosophy strengthened the family unit, the building block of any culture, and elevated compassion from a human weakness to a core belief.

Economically, the empire was on a downward slide. Beginning with the formation of the Roman Republic, the Roman economy was based on land and production. As the Roman Empire expanded, so did the available acreage of lands—up to a point. Not all land seized was farming land and even the domination of rich farming areas resulted in the importation of products other than foodstuffs. The value of Egypt to the Roman Empire, for instance, was in its gold, not its rice.

The economics of the empire were further restrained by the increase in the size of its army. The larger the army became, the more it cost and less it could be sustained by a tax base in Rome. When the army was in Gaul, it had to forage for food on its own. This meant stealing from the local population, which did not make people welcome the arrival of the Romans. The occasional slaughter of people in the regions did not increase the Romans' popularity.

The increasing number of slaves also hampered economic growth. Slavery has never been a profitable avenue. Over the long run, slaves usually cost more than they produced. Even worse, the Romans discovered in the first millennium, as Southern planters in the United States discovered in the 1860s, that dependence on human labor often leads to a disdain of technological advancement.

If you have a thousand slaves, any labor-saving device means that some of those slaves will have nothing to do. Too many slaves with nothing to do leads to mobs. And the more labor-saving devices, the larger the mobs. So, the Romans shunned inventions that centered on human labor. As well they should have because about one-third of the population of the empire at the time of Augustus were slaves.

Deepening the economic woes, slaves paid no taxes but "consumed" public services and externalities such as roads, bridges, harbors, docks, sidewalks, waterworks, etc., as much as any other Roman. Someone had to pay for these public services so, over the centuries, money was less and less available to prop up the Roman infrastructure. This, in turn, had a negative effect on the culture.

Politically, the Roman Empire was in shambles. With no centralizing and stabilizing authority, what was legal was what was tolerated...and that depended on who was in power. In the final centuries of the empire, emperors came and went with irregularity. Following these same irregular patterns were the different cabals, coteries, internecine struggles, conspiracies and corruptions. There was no political stability so there was no bureaucratic consistency.

Government policy changed at the whim of the man in charge, even if he was emperor for only a handful of months. Then someone else would be in charge but his edicts were suspect as no one trusted he would be emperor in five years, much less five months. In 68 CE and 69 CE, there were four emperors.

Later, the emperors were coming and going even faster. There were five in 260 CE, seven in 261 CE and four in 271 CE. After 395 CE, there were always two, one for the Western half of the empire and one for the Eastern half—centered in Constantinople. There were also two triumvirates and some periods where the emperor might not have been in Rome so there were subservient officials actually handling the day to day business of the empire. With no political stability, there is no economic stability. With two pillars of the three in jeopardy, the entire structure was at risk.

Overall, the causes of the collapse of the Roman Empire can be charted from the creation of the Roman Republic. For a stable empire, all three pillars of the empire must remain strong. They must also be able to withstand the advance of technology and the changing texture of the culture. A culture that cannot absorb and profit from the challenges that present themselves will not survive. Thus, the Roman Empire faded into pages of history.

When it comes to misinterpreting history, historians have led the way. They've made misinterpretation easy by coining the most misleading, yet popular statement about history. It's the adage most likely to be used on the first day of every class of every field of history. It's a one-liner so worn out that it requires no clarification. If you don't know what that statement is, read the title of this introduction again.

In academic circles, this one-liner is so widespread that it has become an answer unto itself. It is so accepted that it requires no proof. The statement says it all and students have been quick to pick up on the versatility of the phrase. If the final exam question is to explain why the Roman Empire collapsed, you might start: *History repeats itself.* Then you could wax for three hours about how the Roman Empire wasn't really that different from any other empire and, as we all know, all empires fade for the same reasons because history, after all, repeats itself. Or you could say that wars are inevitable because history repeats itself. Or that political parties come and go because, as they say, history repeats itself. Or that your ex Charlene is no longer dating your friend Robert because she dumped him the way she dumped George before there was a Robert and before there was you and that just goes to show that history repeats itself.

Although this statement is popular, it is not accurate. History does not repeat itself; only historians do.

If after reading what I've just written, you immediately leapt to your feet, shrieking "What do you mean history doesn't repeat itself! I have seen it happen!" No, you haven't. Those so-called "examples" of history repeating itself are actually just part of the ongoing drama of human existence. History appears to repeat itself because human problems cannot be solved. Crime, poverty, drug addiction, child molestation, prostitution, drunkenness and gambling are all human frailties that have always plagued humans—and they always will. These problems are like perennials; they keep cropping up. Whether you're talking about the ancient Egyptians, Greeks, Renaissance Italians or modern day South Central L.A., the problems are the same and the problems are still with us.

Over and over we have tried to solve these problems—and over and over we have failed. We will always fail because these human shortcomings are imbedded in our DNA. Every generation breeds its quota of thugs, thieves and moral perverts. We can never solve the shortcomings of the human spirit, yet we keep trying, generation after generation, solution after solution, often retrying the same thing that failed two, six or 60 generations earlier. Nothing works because these problems cannot be solved. But we hope for a silver lining, so as humans, we keep trying to solve the unsolvable. Looking back over history, it thus appears that history is repeating itself.

Since the first group of humanoids gathered together in a cave, there were bad people. People broke into food stores, abused children, fouled the water supply, made off with other people's mates, short-changed business transactions and cheated at games of chance. In short, there have always been people who did not follow the rules. And, over the eons humans have tried everything in their power to deal with these transgressors. They have been killed, quartered, whipped, crippled, exiled, tortured, imprisoned and even shipped off to desolate lands. We have put them in stocks, cut off their body parts, taken their wealth, sold their families into slavery and performed lobotomies on them. Sometimes we elect them into public office; other times we make them front line soldiers. Has it stopped their depredations? No. In fact, it hasn't even slowed them down. Nothing has worked. In Charles Dickens's London, as pickpockets were being hanged, their fellows were working the crowd even as the unlucky ones marched to the gallows.

This failure to solve the problem of how to deal with these transgressors has not stopped every culture and every generation from trying to solve the problem of crime. But every attempt will fail and nations will end up using temporary methods that are morally comfortable for that generation: death when the population demands severity and prison sentences when the nation is compassionate. But this is not history repeating itself. It is the ongoing drama of humans dealing with human problems that can't be solved.

There are also other issues that have no solution, often because there is no widespread disagreement as to whether a problem exists or not. Consider abortion, which was a major social issue for the Roman Empire and will continue to be a major social issue for Americans well into the next millennium. The debates over family values, racial inequity, equality of the sexes and the right to seek an independent economic destiny have been around since the pyramids were being built.

Basic human disputes are never resolved because they cannot be— and every generation and culture just finds a different way of coping with that problem. Sometimes they ignore it. Other times they won't even admit that a problem exists, or they'll give lip service to a cure and look the other way when transgression occurs. Prostitution, gambling and drugs are illegal in most parts of America but you would be hard pressed not to find prostitutes, poker games or cocaine in any part of the country—be it a big city or rural town.

❧

Once you understand that history is the never-ending saga of human drama, it is easy to see why history is such a valuable tool. The vast majority of humans will let circumstances dictate their course of action. As the old saying goes, "Not to decide is to decide." If you don't choose to act, circumstances will force your hand; you will allow circumstances to resolve themselves. If you do nothing and simply allow your destiny to be determined by the "natural course of events," then, yes, history does repeat itself. You are being stupid and the same things always happen to stupid people.

Those people, cities, states, nations and empires that do not choose to develop their destinies fall into the historical rut that leads to mediocrity. They will follow the path of least resistance and end in the comfortable ocean of ordinariness. Unfortunately, this describes 90 percent of the human race, individuals from kings to guttersnipe who make no decisions but allow the natural course of events to take their natural course.

This is a blessing. Once you understand the history of a problem, you can predict its outcome. As an example, if you study the history of alcohol you will know that Prohibition in any form doesn't work.

Prohibition

One of the rituals of high school graduation is the senior portrait. Students go to great efforts to make certain that their appearance in yearbook history is perfect; not like Mom's or Dad's picture, which was goofy—not to mention grandma's portrait! And more than one mother or father told his graduating son or daughter, "If you think you're cool now, wait until you hear what your kids say about your graduation picture!"

Ideas, like pictures, lose their appeal with passing generations. Concepts that made perfectly good sense in the 1700s go over like black magic today. Trial by combat or tossing a person suspected of practicing witchcraft into a pond to see if she drowns is considered ludicrous today. In the 1700s when witch trials were raging, the examination of goat entrails to predict the future was considered a ludicrous relic. No age is free of the disease of adopting a bad idea and expecting it to work. In the 20th Century, one of the most celebrated examples of a bad idea gone worse is Prohibition.

The primary problem: people like to drink. Every civilization had its unique form of inebriant, and drunkenness is an affliction indigenous to all cultures. The upside of liquor in any form is that if taken in moderate amounts it has positive health and psychological benefits. The downside is the exact opposite. Just as inebriating elixirs have been around since the beginning of time, so have there been wives, husbands, religious orders and social organizations that have fought the "demon rum" in all its historical forms.

In general, consuming liquor in excess is looked upon as an evil because it destroys the moral fiber of the individual doing the drinking, causes the psychological breakdown of the family, opens the door to a new generation of drunkards, draws money away from the necessities of life to be spent on liquor, causes fights at home and in the streets and, in the era of the automobile, gives a one-ton weapon of destruction to men and women who can't walk a straight line much less drive a car. In 2001 alone there were more than 41,000 deaths in the United States attributed to drinking and driving.

The quick fix to solve the problems of the demon rum has always been to ban intoxicating beverages. It never works. But governments keep trying. The most high-profile attempt was the Volstead Act passed by U.S. Congress in 1917, which described liquor as anything that had an alcohol content of higher than 0.5 percent—except for medicinal and sacramental wines. The actual wording in the act banned the importation, exportation, manufacture, transportation or sale of illegal liquor—but it didn't make *drinking* the liquor illegal.

Though the United States has always been a drinking nation, Prohibition rode the crest of a wave of patriotism. America was entering the first World War and there was real concern that the United States would have to provide not only the food needed to keep its boys in the field fed, but the world as well. Europe had been so devastated by the war before the United States entered the conflict that there was concern that Europe would suffer from famine for at least the next generation. Since liquor came from an agricultural product that could be turned into a food, Americans were asked to sacrifice their liquor for the troops in the field. Americans approved the 18th amendment to the United States Constitution and before the ink was even dry there was a booming trade in illegal liquor in the country.

As liquor was illegal, there were no standards for its manufacture. Anyone making the liquor was free to devise his own recipe. Each vintage had its own colloquial name, often describing its effect. Besides REDEYE and RED DYNAMITE, there was SKULL BENDER, BLOCK AND TACKLE and JOY JUICE, the last being so strong that after consuming three drinks, one could be induced to "save his drowning Mother-in-law." There was also BRAVE MAKER, which would "make a humming bird spit in a rattlesnake's eye." And, testifying before Congress, Judge James Wickersham of Alaska described FORTY-ROD as having the ability to make "a man climb a telegraph pole backwards, run up the side of a house [and] spit in the face of a Kodiak bear."[1]

When it became clear that there was big money to be made in illegal liquor, large scale smuggling operations opened up all across the United States. Liquor was imported from Europe and Canada, stolen from government warehouses and brewed in abandoned warehouses. From there the bootleggers would sell it by the barrel and case to illegal drinking establishments called "blind pigs" and "speakeasies," where it was dispensed by the glassful. Millions of glassfuls were sold in the illegal drinkeries and millions more ended up in hip flasks, hollow canes, bottles hidden in wall spaces and kegs on ocean liners.

By the middle of the 1920s, New York City alone had more than 100,000 speakeasies and even the smallest of cities had at least a handful. There were so few government agents for so many miles of American border and so many speakeasies that the best the government could do was publicize the few victories it had. Elliot Ness and his Untouchables along with the bottle-breaking team of Izzy and Moe made history in their war against alcohol—but few people know that Ness's public career was ruined when he became involved in a drunk driving incident. The "Untouchables" were so-named because they could not be bought or bribed. Far too often in the history of liquor enforce-

---

[1]Anderson, Thayne, *Alaskan Hooch*, Hoo-Che-No Press, 1988, page 60.

ment, the enforcers were given large sums of money to "look the other way." Ness and his crew would take no bribes; they were "untouchable." Izzy and Moe were a colorful team of revenue officers who were the darlings of the media. Often dressing in disguise to bust an illegal operation, they worked in New York from 1920 to 1925 and established an impressive list of arrests—4,392 with a 95 percent conviction rate—along with the confiscation of over five million bottles of illegal liquor.

As with any illegal substance, where there is a demand there always will be a supply. With demand for illegal liquor came more organized crime. Prohibition was a big part of organized crime, but certainly organized crime had been around for a long time. From the importer to the manufacturer of shot glasses and hip flasks, the black market provided for millions of jobs. Crime kingpins like Al Capone, Johnny Torrio and Bugs Moran became multi-millionaires and Joseph Kennedy spawned a dynasty of national political power built on a foundation of illegal liquor. Once organized crime seized on the liquor trade, the associated violence quickly followed. Crime rates took a significant jump in the next decade and the homicide rate nearly doubled. Gangland murders made the streets of large cities unsafe and deaths from bad liquor rose.

But the greatest damage done by Prohibition was that it encouraged Americans to break the law. This they did fragrantly. It was easier to find a speakeasy in 1925 than a gas station today. Police turned a blind eye to the illegal drinkeries and those who drank there. Children drank. Pharmacists wrote prescriptions for medicinals for people who were not sick and sacramental wine production jumped by a factor of four.

By the 1930s there was every reason to believe that Prohibition was a failure. While Americans in general agreed that too much alcohol was bad for anyone, they did not feel that banning the substance was the solution. The passage of the 21st Amendment nullified the 18th Amendment and the love affair with alcohol was legal.

In the opening decade of the 21st Century, the failure of Prohibition is cited as the reason to legalize drugs. Logic seems to indicate that making liquor illegal led to horrendous problems that were resolved by legalizing liquor. This would seem to indicate that the way to bring the drug problem under control would be to legalize their use. Actually, the only lesson America learned from Prohibition was that making a substance illegal opened more doors to organized crime and eliminated government oversight of an industry. The repeal of Prohibition did not mean that anyone could drink any time any where. It simply meant that a substance that was not regulated on December 4, 1933 was regulated on December 6. Every state, county and community has its own liquor statutes and ordinances. There is no universal right to drink and there will probably never be a universal right to take drugs.

The greatest failure of Prohibition, however, was that it *increased* alcohol consumption in the United States. Analysis of American drinking habits in the first two decades of the last century showed a precipitous drop in the gallons of alcohol per person from 1910 to 1921. By 1922, the per gallon rate had leapt significantly. Ironically, had there been no Prohibition, perhaps alcohol consumption in the United States might have continued its decline until liquor would not be the problem that it is today.

No matter what laws a city, county, state or country passes, it is not going to stop one person—adult or juvenile—from drinking. Therefore, being a student of history, you can predict with 90 percent accuracy what will happen if a city goes dry. This will also be true of the banning of other addictive drugs. Outlawing cigarettes will not stop people from smoking and only the death penalty will stop cocaine from being sold on street corners across the United States. Declaring a substance illegal does not stop the sale of the item in question; it just makes it a bit harder to get and more expensive to buy.

Nine times out of 10 you will be able to correctly predict the future, better odds than you will ever get in Las Vegas. This insight, incidentally, is called common sense. Common sense may not be all that common but once you have it, the future will open for you like a book you've already read.

However, there will still be that one-time-out-of-10 when you will be in the dark. It's this remaining 10 percent of human behavior that is unpredictable. Ten percent of human beings are unpredictable. They are labeled clever, sly, devious, shrewd, smart, sharp, ingenious, innovative or quick. It's this "talented tenth," as author and civil rights leader W.E.B. Dubois called them, who set the course for all civilization. These are the men and women who defy the conventions of their moment on earth and produce the technology, art, political innovations and philosophy that alter the course of history. They are driven to overcome the odds regardless of their race, sex, creed, sexual preferences, education, physical condition or religious beliefs. They are the ones on whose back culture will claw its way upward.

The understanding of this talented tenth is critical at this juncture of world history. Never before have the forces of individualism and personality been such powerful determinants of history. With the blooming of cyberspace and staggering speed of communication, all previous limits on individuals have disappeared. While a Napoleon, Caesar, Da Vinci or Van Gogh could alter the destiny of a country or field, their impact was limited when compared to what a new form of timeshare will do to world communication. Old limits have simply disappeared. When you read a Web page, you have no idea if the person on the other end of the line is black, female, crippled, a Moslem or a prisoner on death row. Ancient prejudices are going to disappear within one generation and personality and individual talent are going to move to center stage.

Further, cyberspace is opening doors to this talented tenth so fast that even they are having a hard time achieving even a fraction of the potential available. The time between the development of a book, product or philosophy and its availability to the consuming public has been reduced from decades to the speed of the inventor's fingers. At the same time, cyberspace is allowing such a segmenting of the market that products that would have been lost on the shelves of retail stores five years ago are now available to anyone surfing the Internet.

Two decades ago, television advertising in the U.S. was largely limited to three networks: ABC, NBC and CBS. Today, there are hundreds of cable channels and people with a $19.95 product can get their advertisement on the air. Specialized books and inventions can be found quickly and purchased easily online. We are just learning to crawl in this new electronic era and no one knows what a decade of experience in cyberspace will bring the world.

The only thing we know for certain is that the power of the individual is going to be an ever-greater determinant of history and success in this new age. And, we know this because the one, inalterable reality in human existence is that personality creates destiny. With a dynamic leader, all things are possible. Societies, businesses and nations will prosper under competent leadership. In reality, one person *does* make a difference.

The driving force of history is human individuality. Great men and women use their personalities as a signature of the era. The age of Napoleon meant more than simply a time when someone named Napoleon was in charge. It meant the Napoleonic Code that is still used today, the intense study of Egyptian culture that still fascinates the world today and the formation of the modern nation of France, which still confounds the world today.

1 Movement vs. Motion

One of the most significant stories of the 21st Century appeared in newspapers across the United States in January of 1998. Five scientific groups, including the prestigious American Astronomical Society, and two international teams who were using the Hubble Space Telescope to probe the depths of the universe, gathered in Washington, D.C. to announce their joint finding. What was that finding? They concluded that the universe was going to continue to expand outward forever. Thus, while there had most certainly been a "big bang" that created the heavens, there would never be a "big crunch" that would draw the diverse parts of the universe back into itself.

The Big Bang and the Big Crunch

One of the most perplexing riddles of life is determining where we came from and where we, as mankind, are going. Every culture on earth has its own version, but each attempts to answer these two questions with more speculation than hard fact. Whether the earth was formed from a cooling ball of fire created by Raven—the Tlingt deity that formed the earth (The Tlingt Indians live along the coast of the Pacific Northwest from Oregon to Alaska)—or is flat and balanced on the back of a huge turtle is irrelevant. What *is* relevant is that each of us has 24 hours in a day to make the best of our lives and that our time, as mortals, is fleeting.

The answer to the question about where we are going is open-ended. Though the future is built on the past, it often defies prediction. Mankind is always planting the seeds of future but few ever live long enough to reap the bounty or experience the whirlwinds of disaster. But when it comes to the question about the origin of mankind, speculation is rampant and hard facts are elusive.

In Western cultures, there are several competing theories as to the origins of mankind. A small percentage of the population believes that mankind was originally an experiment created by an alien empire that, with the use of flying saucers, monitors the progress of mankind. Others believe people are the remnants of interplanetary colonists or clones of celestial beings. And there are others who believe that the universe is actually only one of the elemental building blocks of a larger reality and that the atoms and electrons in the elements of the world are actually smaller universes still *ad infinitum*.

The two most popular theories are those of creation and primordial evolution. The first is the belief that God created mankind in his own image, placed a man and a woman in a sumptuous garden until original sin drove them into the wilderness to survive as best they could. The second theory, known collectively as Darwinism, suggests that mankind is part of evolutionary process that began with one-celled organisms in the primordial soup of an ancient geologic age and progressed through thousands of years to today's order of species where humans are at the top. (See page 218 for more about Charles Darwin and his theory of evolution.)

All the theories about the origin of mankind lack hard evidence. Both have their advocates but often the arguments are more rhetorical than substantive. Debate over the origin of the universe, the cradle of all life, as we know it and as yet undiscovered, is less speculative.

It is generally believed that billions of years ago all of matter (as humans define it) was concentrated in a single mass. Then, in one instant, there was an explosion, known as the "Big Bang," which shattered this single mass into billions and billions of shards that rushed away from the focus of the explosion. As this jumble of matter tumbled outward in an ever expanding universe, some pieces were attracted to others, forming galaxies and solar systems.

Along with the Big Bang theory of the universe is the "Big Crunch" theory. If the universe could be created in a single blast of energy, is it possible that there is an outer limit to the universe? Is it possible that the trillions and trillions of shards exploding outward will, at some point, slow and be drawn back toward the center of the universe for the process to begin all over again, trillions of years from now?

The answer is *no*. While it is very likely that the universe began with a Big Bang, the Big Crunch will never occur. This fact was established in 1929 by astronomer Edwin Hubble, the man for whom the Hubble Spacecraft is named. Hubble was aware of a phenomenon known as the Doppler Effect, a theory proven by the Austrian physicist Christian Doppler nearly a century earlier. Basically, Doppler theorized that as sound waves from a moving source approach or move away from the listener, they are compressed or expanded, changing the frequency of the pitch.

In other words, as a sound approaches the listener, its pitch is compressed. When the sound is moving away from the listener, its pitch lengthens and weakens. The classical example is the sound of an ambulance. As an ambulance approaches a listener, its siren grows louder and its pitch changes. When it passes the listener and moves farther away, the pitch of the siren lengthens and the sound fades.

Hubble knew that the Doppler Effect worked for sound, but he wondered whether it would work for light as well. Light, after all, is a combination of colors. This combination of colors spreads itself in a predictable spectrum, like a rainbow, from blue to red. Hubble postulated that since light was electromagnetic, its movement could be charted. Using the Doppler Effect as a starting point, he examined the electromagnetic fingerprint of the galaxies and discovered that all

cial bodies he examined were shifted to the red end of the
That is, they were receding, moving out and away. This so-
ed shift" meant that the universe was still expanding.

Because Hubble and subsequent astronomers have failed to find a shred of evidence that the universe will crunch back, the occurrence of the Big Bang became a "singularity." This is because it is now believed that the bang did and will only occur once.

While scientifically this is speculative because no one can see 30 trillion years into the future, the use of the term "singularity" fits in well with Biblical scripture. The book of Genesis, for example, does not state *how* God created the heavens and earth; it simply states that "In the beginning God created the heaven and the earth." There is no further explanation. Thus, the Big Bang theory now finds support among Biblical scholars as well as scientists.

∽

So why was the story discounting the Big Crunch theory that appeared in newspapers throughout the country in January of 1998 significant? The scientific significance of the Big Bang theory is twofold. First, there is no one definitive theory on how the universe began. Second, there are circumstances that defy scientific law. Sometimes what goes up doesn't come back down. Common sense and theology preach that sayings such as "it is always darkest before dawn" and "as one door closes, another opens" are not always true. Sometimes it's not darkest before dawn and sometimes politics or economics may not allow another door to open when the previous one closes.

Ever since the time of the Greeks, scholars and theologians have based their understanding of man, God and the universe on harmonics. They believed, as we believe, that there is a natural rhythm to all of nature and that everything can be explained by a universal standard. Rules of physics, for example, are based on such universal theories as the following: what goes up must come down (Sir Isaac Newton's Law of Gravity) and that for every action there is an opposite but equal reaction (Newton's Third Law of Motion). So, too, are the rules of economics (Law of Supply and Demand), theology (there is a Supreme Power who judges all men and women, rewarding each for goodness and punishing each for sins), biology (population dynamics) and law (if all criminals are punished properly, there will be no crime). All of these principles lure the unwary into believing that there is a natural order of all things that is self-balancing and that every aspect of human existence has some internal harmony.

None of these theories is true *all* the time. The Law of Supply and Demand, which states that the forces of supply and demand generally push price toward the level at which quantity supplied and quantity demanded are equal, assumes there is always a desire on someone's part to buy.

But, you can't sell a washing machine to a hostage held by terrorists no matter how low the price drops. The existence of a supreme power who punishes evildoers has yet to be proven, and if population dynamics worked, China and India would have half the populations they are now supporting. And when it comes to justice, crime rates rise and fall to their own rhythm, even though there are courts of justice all over the world.

Thus, while the universe and everything in it *appear* to be in harmony, there is no universal harmony because the cosmos are in a constant state of flux.

Mankind has always considered this state of flux a fluke rather than a legitimate part of the real world. It's seen as an exception to the rule and viewed as a "minor consideration" or a "piece out of place." Efficiency is based on removing this fluke. If you are hired to work in an office, for example, on your first day on the job a co-worker may tell you, "we do things in a certain way here and we expect you to adapt to our way of doing things." This is called *corporate culture*. If you stray from this "way of doing things," even if your way is more efficient, you may find yourself out of a job because you don't "fit in" with the corporate culture. Every workplace establishes its own social order and dictates the behavior expected from its employees. If your behavior doesn't match that of the group, you won't be welcome there because you are a threat to the social order of that office.

However, flux is a natural part of the universe and eventually it has to be taken into account. Mathematics is based on the concept that one plus one equals two anywhere in the universe. But mathematics also includes algebra, which is based on the concept that if X plus Y equals four, there are an infinite number of answers. This is an example of acceptable flux. More theoretical mathematical problems, however, are hard to justify by logic. How, for instance, is it possible to multiply a negative number (-5, for example) by another negative number (-5) to obtain a positive number (+25)? Mathematicians justify this by saying that it is a mathematical reality because "it works." It may work on paper but it doesn't always translate to real life.

If you divide five by zero, for example, the mathematical answer is "undefined." But if you have five apples and divide five apples by nothing, you still have five apples.

$$\sim\!\!\sim$$

The concept of flux is often ignored by the mainstream of everyday thinking. The theoretical outstrips the rational. We don't teach our children that math usually works; we teach them that it *always* works. Teachers fail students who suggest that the Law of Supply and Demand might not work *every* time. And we've ingrained this concept of harmonics and "natural balance" in our thought and educational process so much so that anything other than an overall balance of all things is heresy. Even the solid sciences, such as chemistry and physics have bought into this myth.

Picture a cup of water. For most of us, the cup holding the liquid is a solid and mentally visible object, made out of plastics, styrofoam or glass with water from the tap or distilled and from a plastic container.

Whatever the origin or size or shape, each glass of water is different. Tap water, for example, varies from city to city and from utility district to utility district even within the same city. Brands of bottled water also vary from state to state, city to city and even store to store.

Where the glass came from, how the glass was washed, if it was washed or how well it was washed can also affect the taste and the contents of the water. If you poured your water from a filtered container, there are other variables to contend with, like the age of the filter, the buildup of residue in the holding tank, the tastes from other food in the refrigerator that have invaded the water as it sat in a pitcher or icemaker and how well and recently that container was washed—if it's ever been washed—and what was in the packing container that it came in, etc. And there are a whole set of other factors that go into the distilling, packaging and disbursement of distilled or other types of bottled water.

Water is a combination of molecules. Molecularly speaking, water is comprised of two molecules of hydrogen and one molecule of oxygen (hence, H_2O). But, most people think of water in less scientific terms—for example, freshwater, saltwater, vapor, ice and crystal.

The point here is that the term *water* is not universal. When you say the word *water* not everyone will know what you're talking about. The term only exists in a snapshot of time in each individual person's mind. Water's state is constantly changing. Therefore, its definition should always be changing as well. We allow our vocabulary to set artificial limits to our thinking. Rather than understand "water" as a fluctuating concept, we view it in a stable, unalterable state.

The danger of this is evident in our schools. Students are taught to consider the world as an inalterable state of affairs. Art, culture, economics, chemistry and math are viewed as stable. The Renaissance, for instance, is a stable, unchanging period that existed after the Reformation and before the Rise of Modern Europe. In addition, students are taught that ancient Egypt remained unchanged from King Zoser's Third Dynasty to the reign of Xerxes in the late 400s BCE.

This is why history is viewed as a static study. People don't think of history as a subject in a state of flux. They see it a snapshot at a time.

George Washington's Administration is viewed as though it was the same at the beginning of his term as at the end. Even though the same people may have been in the cabinet for eight years, every day of those eight years the cabinet members were forced to deal with new challenges, old opponents, etc. to guide the nation into the future. It was not eight years of the same issues. This is how history is taught— and why most people find history a boring and useless subject. And usually, they're right.

The most important aspect of history, and one that has been ignored for centuries by history teachers, is that history is best studied while it is moving. That's what makes history so useful. Real life is rarely static. Things are always changing. Nothing stands still— your life, your job, your children, politics, economics and the problems before the PTA are constantly moving. Most of the decisions you make in your life are made on the fly, based on a limited amount of information. Sometimes you make decisions without basing them on facts. And like Napoleon Bonaparte, Gonga Musa and Cornelius Vanderbilt, you have to make the best guess possible based on the information before you at the moment the decision is made.

One caveat: Don't mistake motion for movement. *Motion* means that something is happening. *Movement* means that progress is being made. If you work in a busy office, this motion doesn't mean that anything is actually being accomplished. It just means that people are busy, shuffling paper, talking about how hard they are working and how important their jobs are. Motion fills the workday. Movement, on the other hand, means production. Movement means that tasks are being completed and final products are finished.

In both the short- and long-run, the rewards only go to complete projects. No one buys books that are 50 percent complete. An astronaut can't reach the moon in a 80 percent constructed rocket, a 90 percent complete electrical design proposal won't land a multimillion-dollar contract, and half of a signature won't get your check cashed. Movement takes you to the finish. History is made by those who finish.

One of the most popular misconceptions about history in motion is the Rule of the Swinging Pendulum. This theory purports that societies have a tendency to swing from one extreme to the other. A period of right wing witch-hunting, for example, is followed by a corresponding period of left wing hysteria. Or vice versa. Then, as the circumstances of the two periods are understood, the pendulum swings from left to right with decreasing arc lengths until it vibrates to a stop in the center, equidistant from both extremes. In other words, the extremes play off each other until, in the end, a form of stability is reached between the two.

This illustrates the theory of historical motion, not movement. It's also philosophical garbage. While the pendulum may indeed swing right and left and eventually stop in the middle in many cases, it is not because of the countervailing forces from the left or right. It's probably because the population in general wants some form of stability. A society in turmoil cannot feed itself. Stability provides jobs for those who want to work, markets to convert income to food and other household goods, law and order to ensure that what you earn will not be taken from you by force or guile, and a laundry list of other social issues that vary from culture to culture. In the long-run, stability means that businesses will invest money in your neighborhood. This, in turn, means more better paying jobs close to home. Stable countries attract foreign investment; countries on the verge of revolution see money leaving the country as fast as the electronic transfers can be made.

Thus, the swinging of the pendulum is yet another historical myth. Radical periods are not always followed by less intense reactionary periods. Typically, each is followed by a similar period. Violent revolutions are put down by violent conservative forces. A reign of terror on the Left is followed by an equal or more intense reign of terror on the Right. Periods don't calm down successively like the pendulum image suggests. They can get more extreme or keep an intense level of extremity rather than calming down. They go from one extreme to the other, from segregation of black and whites in the South, for example, to affirmative action. Neither is productive; it's just a different group of people that is suffering discrimination. Once the general public realizes that neither segregation nor affirmative action will bring social stability, both will be dumped.

What eventually brings these periods of violence to a halt is a general breakdown of all stability, leaving the combatants to fight over rubble. There is no profit in rubble—the economic reality of what the terror is doing is what eventually brings the period to a close. The end of Nazism in Europe, for example, didn't bring on an ultra-liberal society. But it did bring stability.

End of Nazism—The Road to Stability

When it comes to evil incarnate, every century has its villain. In the last century, Adolph Hitler lead the way with a supporting cast of Joseph Stalin, Benito Mussolini and Francisco Franco. In earlier times it was Genghis Khan, Attila the Hun and even John's incarnation of 666: Nero Claudius Caesar Drusus Germanicus. And, while some of these men had few redeeming features, others had legions of supporters. Why? Simply put, evil, like beauty, is in the eye of the beholder.

However, the villains of the 20th Century have one thing in common: they were all living proof that democracy is a flawed political system. Hitler and Mussolini were elected; Stalin and Franco claimed to be. As Winston Churchill once lamented, democracy is the worst form of government on earth—with the exception of all *other* forms of government that have been tried.

Another way of seeing Churchill's irony is to say that all forms of government work—if you define *work* loosely enough. That is, as long as the people being governed accept the form of government they live under, it "works" for them. But, one form of government may not work for another group of people.

Communism, where no one owns anything individually and everyone owns everything in common, can work in a small community where everyone shares everything. Socialism, where the state owns everything and everyone works for the state, works well with organizations like the United States military because there is a clear, identifiable chain of command and the overall mission, governed by rules, regulations and standards of behavior is the same for everyone. Anarchism, where there are no rules, works well when there are a handful of people on a lush island where there is no shortage of food or water. Otherwise, it's not good at allocating resources.

The perfect form of government, according to the philosopher Plato, is a republic ruled by a council of wise men. The leaders would be incorruptible and the rights of the masses protected. A strong second choice: a wise, incorruptible king. History, however, reveals that there haven't been a lot of wise, incorruptible kings and that wise men are only wise if they are deciding matters of money in your favor. This is primarily because kings and wise men are human—and, being human, they make mistakes and can be corrupted. Just as important, humans can be illogical, irrational, greedy and stupid. History is replete with wars based on the flimsiest of justifications, including gold rushes, witch-hunts, crusades, invasions for plunder and blatant theft of a temple, land, gold or herds of horses.

Because humans are unpredictable and predatory, every government must have the ability to adapt to various circumstances. Even the Greeks, the formulators of democracy, had a safety valve for emergencies. The Greeks, knowing that humans bicker amongst themselves when faced with a crisis could elect a *tyrant*, one man who was in total charge for a period of six months. (Note the verb "election"; this man was chosen by popular acclaim.)

The tyrant had the power of life and death for six months. After that, he would have to be elected again in order to continue his rule. The Greeks also understood that a tyrant could not be trusted to give up absolute power once he had it so they developed a mechanism to rid themselves of an unruly tyrant: the same citizens who had elected the tyrant could vote him into exile. It was as simple as writing his name on a piece of pottery, known as an *ostraca* (the root of our word *ostracize*). If there were 6,000 votes against him, the tyrant had to leave his city-state for a period of 10 years.

In the first half of the 20th Century, Adolph Hitler and his party of National Socialists—the Nazis—ran Germany as a political, social, economic and cultural force. The Nazi party was popular for the basest of reasons: it blamed other people—primarily the Jews—for the Depression that was devastating the German economy *as well as* Germany's failures in World War I. Further, Hitler's philosophy was that Germany was entitled to *Lebensraum* or "living space." The problem? In order for Germany to acquire more land, her neighbors would have to lose it. The Germans, however, saw no problem with stealing others' land and that, in a nutshell, was what started the second World War.

What is surprising about World War II was what it did *not* produce. Usually, at the end of a conflict that devastates a nation—militarily, politically or economically—there is a tendency for the population to shift Left, that is, become more liberal.[1] Generally, the instability that follows a devastating loss compels popular sentiment toward the relative security of communal activity—even communal resources.

---

[1] The terms "Right" and "Left" come to us from the *Estates General* in France in 1789, when Louis XVI convened the *Estates General* to give him the power to make "fiscal reform" (i.e., raise taxes). The people who were going to have to pay those taxes, the merchant class, were seated on the left side of the hall. The rich, the conservatives, who would not have to pay the taxes, sat on the right side of the hall. Generally speaking, those who want to change things are known as liberals or left wingers. Those who want no change are called conservatives or right wingers. People with reforming ideas that have little basis in fact on the left are called ultraliberals, while the most extreme conservatives are known as reactionaries. The term "loonies" are those who are beyond the ultraliberals and reactionaries and are usually referred to as "loonies of the right" or "loonies of the left."

Oftentimes, wild ideas are tested and quickly fail because only those ideas that produce political, economic and cultural stability survive. World War I, for example, generated the short-lived an pacifistic Weimar Republic in Germany and Provisional government under Alexander Kerensky in Russia.

This didn't happen in post-Nazi Germany. The victorious Allied Forces made a specific effort to replace the militaristic Nazis with a moderate republic (at least in the parts of Germany they controled).

There's more than just luck to the post-Nazi history of Germany. The United States took the lead in building the successful government that followed Hitler. And the U.S. was uniquely qualified to do so.

The U.S. is a melting pot of ethnic persuasions, religious alliances and political affiliations. It lacks the sense of nationalism or collective destiny that cripples many countries. Americans are more interested in their individual destinies than in the collective. The only thing Americans share is a desire to make money.

Crude as this may sound, self-interest is the glue that gives the U.S. its stability. Americans don't like extreme politics because it threatens individual prospects. At the end of the American Revolution in 1781, the revolutionaries such as John Hancock and Samuel Adams who had precipitated the war were squeezed out of power quickly. Compare the signatures of those who signed the Declaration of Independence and those who signed the United States Constitution. Then compare the names of both to a list of congressmen, judges, governors and other federal dignitaries for the next two decades. Aside from a few names, the lists are completely different.

Perhaps the single most important lesson to come out of World War II—and one Americans will re-learn with the rebuilding of Iraq and Afghanistan in the 2000s—is that good economics makes for political and cultural stability. At the end of World War II, the armies of the allies stayed in Europe to guarantee law and order. But the greatest impact, given barely a paragraph in most history books, was the Marshall Plan.

Under the Marshall Plan, also named the European Recovery Act, America poured $11.8 billion dollars of raw materials, supplies, goods, services and expertise into the rebuilding of war-torn Europe. At the end of World War II, there were 16 nations with a combined total of 270 million people who were unemployed, starving and had no political or economic future. The Marshall Plan provided the critical cash to get Western Europe back on the road to recovery. This brought economic stability quickly, so quickly that the violent swing to the Left that Europe had traditionally experienced was delayed and lessened in intensity. It may also have eliminated a third World War, at least among the traditional enemies on the European continent.

The significant lesson of World War II is as basic as the Tenth Commandment:

> Thou shalt not covet thy neighbor's house, thou shalt not covet thy neighbor's wife, nor his manservant, nor his maidservant, nor his ox, nor his ass, nor any thing that *is* thy neighbor's.

Whether it's called the urge for *Lebensram,* the lure of nationalism or collective destiny or appropriating someone else's land because God gave it to you, it's always bad form to steal from others. You may get away with it for a generation or two, but sooner or later, the descendants of the people from whom you stole will be back for their property.

Rule of Economic Progression

The myth of the swinging pendulum has obscured the underlying truth: the Rule of Economic Progression. This rule is not a myth. It is the reality that makes a neighborhood, city, state, nation or empire vital to its economy. Just as there cannot be a village without water, there can be no city without an economy. The economy moves and as it does, so do historical forces.

History never stops moving. It is always changing and, as a result, it is directionless. Events do not progress lockstep forward to an inevitable destiny. Depending on the philosophical point of view, these superstitious beliefs are known as meliorism or orthogenesis. *Meliorism* is the belief that with the passage of time, the world gets better and it can be made better still through positive human effort. *Orthogenesis* is the belief that all societies evolve through the same set of circumstances and are unaffected by the environment. The first is rooted in the belief that humans have a spark of divinity that, over time, guides them, collectively, to a better dawn; the second implies that history is cyclical and that every society will go through the same sequence of boom-to-bust cycles without altering the course.

Historical facts do not support either theory. There is no indication that humans are getting any nobler as time progresses. In fact, the opposite seems to be true. Killing has become so efficient that one fool can trigger a nuclear war that will obliterate the world with the push of a button. As far as orthogenesis is concerned, it negates all the advantages of technology. Both theories are in error because they assume that history proceeds in an orderly fashion, marching forward to the steady beat of some distant drum. But, there is no evidence that this occurs.

Consider the invention of the automobile. The average person might assume that cars were inevitable. There were horses and then there were cars. Cars were better than horses so, of course, the car was inevitable. End of story.

Not so. Hundreds of inventors had the idea for the automobile; but only 10 percent ever got the idea to the drafting board. And, only one-tenth of those inventors ever got a prototype out of the garage.

The time also had to be right. Before the auto industry could exist, there had to have been a steel industry and an oil industry and a glass industry and an upholstery industry and a wire industry and a power industry, and so on. There also had to be a pool of available workers that could be trained to do repetitive work and a banking system in place to finance both the plant and the consumer sales. And, even if all these industries were in place, the person in charge of the auto industry had to have business savvy. He had to know how to squeeze every cent out of every dollar, maximize his production with an assembly line and keep his cash flow viable by selling cars at about the same rate the factory was making them.

In this sense, Henry Ford's development of the huge Rouge River factory complex outside of Detroit was as important as his car designs. In 1915 Ford bought 2,000 acres along the Rouge River, intending to use the site to make coke, smelt iron and build tractors; but, over the next dozen years he turned it into the most fully integrated car manufacturing facility in the world. The factory incorporated all of the production aspects of building care—from making steel to painting finished cars. Some teachers simplify this development with the comment that Ford "invented the assembly line." In fact, what he did was more ambitious than that: He decisively took control of all of the elements of building cars. It was a risky...and, ultimately, successful...action. The plant now turns out a car every few seconds.

Today, looking at a successful company like Ford, it's easy to say that the company's success was inevitable. "Everything was in place for Ford to be successful," history teachers say, as if all that it took to be successful was for Ford to be in the right place at the right time.

It is a nice thought but it's never that easy. Henry Ford had a vision and he played his cards right but he also took a big gamble. He succeeded because he was a visionary engineer with consummate business sense. He could have failed at any step in the game in which case we would be marveling at the genius of someone else, say Bernard Swartz of Los Angeles and his Swartzbuggy. Failures are a dime a dozen. Just ask the makers of the Stanley Steamer, Tucker and DeLorean. Henry Ford could have been one of them, but he wasn't.

Opportunities come and go. Ford came close to losing everything he had worked so hard to create when he refused to introduce new models. He continued to produce the Model T long after consumers indicated they wanted something else—but he eventually relented and gave people the different models that they wanted. If he'd continued to refuse to produce any model but the *Tin Lizzy*, few people would know who Henry Ford was.

Edison and the Light Bulb

A more graphic example of this idea of economic progression is the invention of the light bulb. While it is generally taught in schools that Thomas Edison invented the light bulb in 1879, the truth is yet another matter altogether. There were working light bulbs as far back as 1802. Edison's place in history is secure not because he "invented" the light bulb, but because he was able to make a profit on the invention. He managed to capitalize on his product.

While most of what is taught about Edison is true—the light bulb took hundreds of hours to perfect and, in 1879, Edison stayed awake the entire 40 hours that the light bulb burned—there are some things that history teachers do not tell their students. Other inventors created 16 versions of working light bulbs in the years between 1840 and 1879. The inventors were of many nationalities including English, American, Canadian, Russian and French. The filament composition was also varied and included platinum, carbon, platinum-iridium mix. In 1878, the year before Edison's invention surfaced, at least three light bulbs were invented and, in 1879, Edison had three other competitors as well.

If all of these light bulbs were already available, why is Edison's name linked to the invention of the light bulb? The answer is as old as America. Edison knew how to market his invention because he was more than a scientist; he was also a businessman.

Edison is credited for the invention or perfection of several appliances we still use today, most notably the phonograph, light bulb and moving picture camera. But we often overlook the actual reason for why he was so successful. There are a number of geniuses in American history, but only a few stand out. Some of the greatest inventors in American history are barely known today. It is doubtful that many college graduates could identify Nikola Tesla, Elias Howe, Alfred Russel Wallace or Leon Walras, if asked to. But each changed the world immeasurably with an invention. [2]

In retrospect, it is easy to see why Edison was successful. First, he saw the "big picture," pursued inventions that were useful to society. For example, his first invention—and first patent—was for an electric vote recorder. Unfortunately, it was patented in 1869. Corruption was so widespread then, that any movement toward electoral honesty was viewed as political suicide. No one wanted Edison's vote recorder, and no one bought his recorder. It was a good idea, but Edison was ahead of his time; people just weren't ready for the vote recorder's introduction in 1869.

Edison thought like a businessman and not like an entrepreneur. This is an important distinction because today the two terms are often interchangeable even though the definitions of the two are actually poles apart. An *entrepreneur* invests in a momentary niche in the marketplace for a new toy, gadget or service. For example, an entrepreneur might see a need for a unique toy. Seeing this need, an entrepreneur may design the toy himself or find someone with a similar idea and buy the concept from him. The entrepreneur would then make thousands of copies and hit the streets, selling the new toy to distributors and toy stores. The entrepreneur funds the manufacture of the toy, oversees its distribution and handles the advertising and collections. He would also take the lion's share of the profit. And, as long as the toy sold, he would make a percentage of the gross.

An entrepreneur finds an unoccupied niche in the market and fills it. A *businessperson*, on the other hand, finds an unsatisfied need for a good or service and fulfills that need. This is called *marketing*. Marketing is finding a consumer need and fulfilling that demand.

---

[2] Nicholas Tesla invented the alternating current in 1888. Elias Howe patented his lockstitch sewing machine on September 10, 1846, which was the basis for the Singer Sewing Machine. Alfred Russel Wallace was the co-author of Charles Darwin's *Origin of the Species* and Leon Walras postulated the theory of economic equilibrium.

Edison thought like a businessman; he found products that would serve an identifiable sector of the consuming public. If he could not find a demand, he didn't try to invent something for them to buy. He looked for his market share first, then he invented products.

Edison was also a successful businessman because he used time to his advantage. Edison often caught his competitors flat-footed because his products were on the market years before they had a chance to catch up. Lawsuits, copyright infringement battles and corporate difficulties may have plagued Edison's life, but he never slowed when it came to getting his products on the market. He used "lead time" to his advantage. Today, with the technological advancement of the Internet and related communication technologies, lead time for many products is down to weeks rather than years—for others, such as software-oriented products, it's been cut to days.

The most important lesson Edison has taught us: Think backwards. Whether you're considering starting a new business, running for public office, designing a college literature class or restructuring a corporation, it is crucial to do your research. Know what you are trying to do before you start doing anything. Far too often, people jump into situations without a complete understanding of what it is they want to accomplish.

Without a clear-cut concept of what you intend to do, there is no way to measure your advancement. Every enterprise, association and small business venture has a mission statement that encapsulates the steps toward their goals. This is important in order to determine if the organization is on track.

Positive and Negative Cycles

Though most people can't see it clearly, history moves in one of two general directions: in an upward or positive cycle, or in a downward or negative cycle. A *positive cycle*, when things are going well, means that advantage builds on advantage to create a dynamic forward progression. A simple example would be a booming economy where people are spending money. As more and more people make money, more and more people spend money. This in turn stimulates businesses to make more products. These businesses then hire more workers who, in turn, spend more money. Everyone works and spends money. The stock market goes up, the number of products on store shelves increases and prices go down. It's hog heaven if you have cash.

A good example of history in an upward cycle: America in the 1950s. During this period, Americans had a lot of spendable income. Some people bought a new car every year. Technology was opening the door to new products. Color televisions entered the marketplace, the first atomic submarine was built, a nationwide highway modernization was funded, racial segregation in public schools ended, the AFL and the CIO merged, a polio vaccine was introduced, *Sputnik* went up, signalling that the great Space Race was on, and the standard of living climbed.

The 1950s were an exciting time to be alive. It was the end of the Swing and the birth of Rock-n-Roll. World War II and Korea were over and the Cold War created a massive expansion of the federal bureaucracy. That meant nearly everyone was working and spending money. Highways stretched across America and airports sprouted up on vacant land as fast as cities could finance them. Consumer products flooded the market and automobiles were such a status symbol that it was not unusual for families to buy a new car every year. Food was better, fast food was more convenient, medical facilities were closer and the GI bill was allowing millions to college who had never thought about getting a degree.

History texts are replete with examples of how different the booming 50s were from the wartime 40s. Much has been written as to why the 50s were so rich in cash and culture as compared to the earlier decade. But rarely mentioned are the shortcomings that were spawned in the 1950s that remain with us today. Prosperity is not without its consequences and an astute civilization realizes that it is best to prepare for the eventual balancing acts for the history books.

One of the most pernicious effects of the booming 50s was inculcating Americans into believing that prosperity and a rising economy were the rewards of capitalism. Using this misconception as a foundation for the economics of the era, American businesses and the United States government went on a credit binge—and, the American consumer followed suit. The inevitable result was that America became a nation awash in red ink, which still exists today.

Consumer debt is a boon for businesses because the bulk of this debt is for products and services already sold. And, it is also a blessing for the credit industry that makes more money on credit card debt than on actual solid investments. But it is dangerous debt because consumers pay a high premium for goods and services already consumed. This reduces their buying power.

So, while Americans make more money, they spend an ever increasing amount paying off old debt, not buying new products and services. Eventually, this slows the economy. Even more dangerous, the United States government has been running a multi-trillion dollar deficit—$6.668 trillion in July of 2003. Somehow, someday that debt will have to be paid off and when it is, the economic repercussions will be cataclysmic.

Economic Dominance of World Markets

There is an old joke that asks, "Where does an 800-pound gorilla sleep?" The answer, of course, is "Anywhere it wants to." In the 1950s, the United States was the 800-pound gorilla of the world market. Europe and Asia had been ravaged by the war and were making a slow comeback. America's industry, which, relatively speaking, had been untouched by the war, expanded laterally. In addition to making war material for the Korean War and the Cold War, companies expanded their spectrum of civilian goods. Not only were they selling to American customers but they were selling to European and Asian ones as well. "Made in America" meant quality while "Made in Japan" meant mass produced and of poor quality. Energy was cheap and plentiful because the United States was getting it from the Middle East. But what the American businesses did not account for was the growing economic power of the rest of the world.

Japan became a powerhouse for the automotive and steel industry. Arab nations have their hands on the oil spigot and the European Union is so stable that many countries are considering replacing the American dollar with the Euro. The 1950s gave America a feeling of economic invulnerability that is being challenged today. How well we respond to the challenge will determine how long we are in control of our own economy.

Global Military Obligations

Since the United States had the largest dependable army in the world at the end of World War II, it was saddled with being the policeman of the world. During the Cold War, this meant facing off with the USSR when and wherever the threat of communism appeared. In the 1960s, it meant getting involved in brushfire wars like Vietnam. Our troops have been in conflicts in myriad countries including Somalia, Panama, Dominican Republic, Saudi Arabia, Lebanon, Liberia, Haiti, Cambodia, Laos, Thailand, Korea and the Philippines—to name a few. And, while it is certainly true that someone has to be the "policeman of the world," this is not a function that should be shouldered by any single country, particularly with the United Nations in place.

The problem the United States faced—and continues to face—is that its military is a superb organization for combat but it is less than competent when it comes to civilian functions. Further, establishing and maintaining law and order are functions of a police force and court system that is established and paid for by residents. If residents are not involved in both the establishment and the cost for law enforcement, they have no stake in its success. Law and order will only exist with the support of the population.

Lionization of Entertainment

The 1950s also brought about the birth of the electronic industry, and with it, the lionization of entertainment. Television made its debut in American homes and by the end of the decade, having a television was more than a status symbol—it was a necessity. Nightly news programs kept Americans informed and variety shows allowed Californians to laugh at New York jokes. Actors who were only known in New York—where the theater crowds were located—moved to California where the movie industry was making overnight stars of the unknown. The leap from the small screen to the silver screen was not nearly as far as the leap from the stage to the silver screen.

Media exposure became more important than talent. The inevitable result: quality took a back seat to audience size. Since entertainment draws larger audiences than serious subjects, quality presentations had to find an entertainment angle or hook. Inexorably, both the small and silver screen moved toward the lower brow and, with each incremental movement in that direction, more of the high brow audience was lost. The result has been an intellectual wasteland with fewer and fewer redeeming features as time progresses. Just fork over the $10 to see 2003's Ben Affleck/Jennifer Lopez film *Gigli* and you'll see the proof.

The most important historical lesson to learn from the 1950s is that there is a downside to an economic boom. By focusing only on the upside, you expose yourself to the danger of failing to recognize how pernicious the downside can be. To use an athletic adage, "no pain, no gain." An intelligent person recognizes that with each boom in his personal life, there will be a bust as well. The survivor recognizes this inevitability and prepares for the downside. A culture that refuses to account for the price of its advancement will be forever hounded by the consequences of its folly.

A downward spiral works in the opposite direction. If a company is losing money, it may cut back on the quality of its product. This causes fewer people to buy the product and the company makes less money. To meet its new budget constraints, it terminates the research and development staff and this puts the company at a disadvantage when a competitor comes out with a new product. Now the company loses market share to the competition and has to release more people that, in turn, affects the quality of the product that fewer people buy, placing the company in an even tighter fiscal straightjacket. The company doesn't have the money to improve its existing product line and cannot borrow capital to engineer a new one. Once at the bottom of a negative spiral, the best a company can do is wait and hope that the economy turns around.

Negative Spiral of Christianity

One of the shortcomings of Western education is that it compartmentalizes all of human knowledge. American history is a class distinct from economics, mathematics and psychology. Then there are the "hard" sciences such as chemistry and physics, which are separate from the social sciences and health sciences. The word "science" is used freely because the underlying principle of education is that knowledge can be quantified. Numbers can be assigned, statistics applied, cyclical continuums discovered and inexorable consequences predicted for all fields of human knowledge. It's all scientific and the more math that can be involved in a field, the more reputable the field.

In the scope of real life, however, this is tommyrot. Mathematics is an excellent science for examining numbers theoretically but has minimal applications in what many view as the "real" world. Even in an industry like construction, which depends on precise measurement, theory falls to the wayside when architects, general contractors, ground conditions, carpenters, mechanical engineers, electricians and glaziers combine to complete a building project. Anyone who believes that mathematics is a universal science only has to replace a door and its associated hardware to realize just how inexact the term *two and three-quarters inches* is.

Western education also neglects the study of cycles, and instead, shows life as a one-way journey during which one gains knowledge and maturity. This focus does nothing to explain why people keep making the same mistakes over and over again. This is usually because an individual does not understand that there are repeating cycles.

Associations have their own cycles as well—both positive and negative. One of the best examples is that of the Christian Church, primarily because it has been around for so long.

The Christian Church went through a negative spiral in the 1500s. For centuries the Church had been in a slow, downward spiral. Over the previous 1,200 years its influence had spread throughout Europe to the exclusion of all other religions. There had been attempts at exporting Christianity out of Europe, the most notable for this being the Crusades, which failed miserably. Concentrating on its European flock, the Church gradually became corrupt. Cardinalships were sold, simony—the buying or selling of a Church office or ecclesiastical preferment—became a standard practice, there was a brisk trade in indulgences and charlatans made a living through the sale of alleged religious artifacts. Perhaps most significant, at the height of the Christian Church's influence, money from parishes across Europe flowed to the coffers of the pope in Rome. Little of it flowed back.

The top of the Church's most profound cycle came in January of 1077 when Henry IV of Germany stood barefoot in the snow outside the castle in Canossa in Tuscany where Pope Gregory VII was staying. The pope and emperor were at odds over investiture. The pope had declared his right to universal sovereignty and could remove, replace or reinstate any bishop, depose any emperor and be judged by no one. He excommunicated the German Emperor Henry IV. Henry's transgression was that he appointed his own choice of Bishop for Milan, Italy, which infuriated the pope. The pope also accused Henry of being rude and disrespectful.

It didn't take long for the Christian Church to recognize the difficulties in supporting investiture and the mixing of civil and religious authority. In 1122, at the Concordat of Worms, Pope Calixtus II and Henry V, son of Henry IV, agreed to separate the two realms.

But problems remained. The lowest point probably came in April of 1521 at the Diet of Worms in Germany when Martin Luther refused to recant his demand for a reform of the Christian Church. The Christian Church had become used to demands for reform and ignored them. Barely two decades earlier, in 1498, Girolamo Savonarola was hanged and then burned at the stake for heresy for establishing a Christian kingdom in Florence that was separate from Rome.

The Church could not force Martin Luther to recant his demand for the reform of the Church and the Church would not reform. The result was the splintering of the Christian Church. The breakaway Christians were called Protestants while those that remained with the original Church were called Catholics.

❦

Religions are likely to have cyclical shifts because they have so many members. Any one member can bring shame on the entire association, and with it, a positive or negative cyclical shift. Though Catholic priests who are pedophiles make up less than a fraction of a percent of all priests, their actions bring about multi-million dollar lawsuits and shame to the establishment.

The Catholics, however, aren't the only organized religion to have received a black eye in the public's view. Under the guise of religion, America has witnessed atrocities like the Jonestown suicide, the conflagration of David Koresh and his Branch Davidians, Eric Rudolph and a host of self-styled messiahs who convince small bands that they bring the unadulterated word of God. Some of these bands are called cults; others extreme evangelicals.

These cycles, however, can be controled. Once a negative cycle is identified, it can be reversed. The hard part is convincing the people who are profiting from the negative cycle to stop their activities. This is not easy. If you're getting an unjustified tax break, you'll fight to retain your fiscal integrity. A company making millions selling an immoral but legal product is not going to close its doors voluntarily. And even a drunk that understands she is killing herself may not choose to quit drinking.

A negative cycle can be reversed through the force of the person at the top of the administrative food chain. A powerful head of Church can clean up the corruption in his reign. A forceful captain of industry will not only set his company on the right track but serve as a beacon of success for his industry.

Even in politics, a forceful personality at the helm can change the course of history. A good example: The 26th president of the U.S., Theodore Roosevelt. The power of the American presidency had been in decline since the Civil War. The line of presidents had been exceedingly weak while Congress had been strong and growing. In 1901, with the assassination of William McKinley, Theodore Roosevelt, not quite 43, became the youngest President in the Nation's history. Teddy Roosevelt had a dominating presence and a quick mind and cut his own path through history because of his interpretation of the United States Constitution. Earlier presidents had believed that they could only do what the Constitution said they could do. Teddy saw things differently. He broadened the use of executive power, taking whatever action necessary as long as it wasn't forbidden by the Constitution. And, by doing so, he changed the course of American presidential history and opened the door for the reforming era of Progressives.

Any individual or organization that fails to understand, see and adjust its negative cycles is on the road to disaster. The key to success and longevity is not so much being in the right place at the right time; it's to have a leader with a sterling personality who recognizes a negative cycle exists and has a strong stomach for the housecleaning that must follow. In the end, it comes down to the individual, not fate.

By the time of Martin Luther in the first decade of the 1500s, the little creeks of money had formed a torrent rushing their way to Rome. When Luther went to Rome he was appalled by the corruption he witnessed and how the Church leaders didn't see any wrong in frittering away the wealth that flowed into their purses. Church leaders saw money as a commodity that fell from the heavens. Luther saw the money as the lifeblood of thousands of communities.

When Luther tacked up his 95 Theses on the church door in Wittenberg on October 31, 1517, the time was ripe for dissent. The tide of reform was running high. For an institution that had survived 1,200 years without a lasting schism, the end of its monopoly came quickly.

As the Christian Church became more and more concerned with the personal fortune of its prelates rather than remaining true to the teaching of the Bible, there was an exodus of competent individuals away from Rome. The incorruptible departed. This left Rome with only the most venal of Church officials.

As the corruption grew and festered in the Holy See and in the parishes of the Holy Roman Empire, there was growing unrest. Since those who could have reformed the Church usually ended up being burned at the stake many were reluctant to come forward and express a point of view that differed from that of the Church. But this did not mean that there was no dissent. The very foundation of the unified Christian Church was cracking. And, when dissent came, it found a favorable audience. The attempt to reform the Church, however, ended far differently than Martin Luther had intended.

Cycles Within Cycles

Complicating the simple concept of positive and negative cycles, there are ongoing, minor, positive and negative fluctuations at the same time. While the economy of the 1950s was on an upward swing, if you happened to be a black, life was not so rosy. Wages were low for blacks and job opportunities were few. In the 1950s, blacks represented less than 10 percent of the population, were not politically involved and generally were viewed as invisible, as Ralph Ellison so aptly noted in his classic work *Invisible Man*. In terms of race relations, America was on a downward spiral, and would hit bottom a decade later.

Conversely, even though the Christian Church was on a long, downward spiral from the time of Constantine to Martin Luther, it still bred intellectual giants like St. Thomas of Assis, Gregor Mendel, Peter Abelard, Thomas Acquinas and Anselm of Canterbury, among others. The Christian Church did not suffer from a single, ongoing, deep spiral that took it to moral oblivion. Rather, it rode a long, slow downward spiral with bright periods that stopped the descent momentarily. But, for a wide variety of reasons, the institution could not maintain its grip on the upward spiral and, in the long run, the Church followed the inevitable spiral to disunion.

✎

The two obvious questions here are: *Can you sustain an upward spiral forever?* and *Can you stop a downward spiral?* The answer to both is *yes*. Both positive and negative cycles carry with them the ability to change direction. The seeds of destruction grow ever stronger in positive cycles while the spark of resurrection cannot be extinguished even in the deepest, steepest downward spiral.

Let's look at the positive spiral first. While there is rarely any one thing that produces an upward cycle, it may only take one thing to stop it. At the risk of stating the obvious, positive spirals, particularly in complex technological societies, occur when circumstances combine to make it possible. But there is a threshold mechanism. In other words, all it takes are a small number of factors to combine to make the positive spiral possible. Technology will affect the speed of the spiral and the breadth of its effect, but not its generation.

Consider, for example, the so-called "second American Revolution," or the cotton boom in the 1820s—an upward spiral generated by three, mutually exclusive events. In the South, Eli Whitney's cotton gin put a glut of salable cotton onto the market. At the same time in the North, Samuel Slater's textile mill needed cheap cotton. America's shipping industry was in the doldrums because there was little demand for American cargo transport in the world. But, when cheap American cotton could be placed on empty American ships and transported to under-utilized American textile plants, an American economic renaissance was underway. The cotton gin allowed the South to increase the tonnage of salable cotton per acre. The demand for cheap cotton by Northern and later British factories urged Southerners to extend the frontiers of the empire of cotton West as far as Texas. Northern factories produced textiles for use across the United States. The shipping industry boomed as it transported cotton from Southern ports to Northern factories—and eventually to British textile mills.

One of the difficulties in teaching American history at the college level is that by college age, most students firmly believe in things that are more the fantasy of textbook authors than actual fact. Worse, slogans become catchphrases for eras and, for many students, that is as close as they get to understanding the legacy of their own heritage. Take, for instance, the slogan "No Taxation without Representation." The slogan was never meant to imply that taxation was bad; only that the person being taxed should have some say in how that money is collected—and spent. America was not founded on the principle that taxation is bad; it was unified on the basic premise that he who paid the taxes should determine its destiny.

Taxation has always been a hot button issue. From the first moment that some primordial humanoid decided that some kind of a tribute was to be extracted from everyone else's kill, there were complaints. Everyone wanted the benefit of the tax but no one wanted to pay the taxes. Tax dodging is as old as organized society.

Historically, when it comes to taxes, the focus has been on the amount collected rather than on how it is spent. Why? Because every citizen understands how much they make and what kind of bite taxation takes out of his or her paycheck. Every two weeks there is a graphic demonstration of how much government costs and it can be found on everyone's paycheck. Every April every American worries that not enough is taken out during the year to keep the IRS out of their back pocket and checking account.

And, while Americans are quick to note how much they pay the federal government, few actually pay attention to how their money is spent. They trust the United States Congress to spend intelligently in spite of the fact that there is not a scrap of evidence that Congress has ever spent intelligently. Pork barreling is a standard practice and is held in high regard by those tax payers whose United States Senators have been in office for more than 20 years.

Of course, pork barreling is not always bad. What is one man's pork is another's economic development incentive. The importance of pork barreling is that things that would not be considered economic if examined carefully get funded. Sometimes this is good; other times it's not. But money flows and the internal improvements funded change the economic landscape.

While many people are adept at remembering the trivia of the American Revolution, they often forget the importance of the second American Revolution—the combined impact of Whitney's cotton gin, Samuel Slater's textile mill and the expansion of the domestic shipping fleet. Each is a footnote in history. Together they made history.

The second revolution spawned slavery in the South, child labor in the North and abused seamen on the ships between the two. But, without the revolution it is doubtful that there would have been a United States of America by 1840. At best, the Untied States would have drifted into separate mini-nations. The North was so different from the South that it is doubtful there was enough political glue to hold them in a single nation. The West would have remained a frontier for the next century, maybe longer, depending on the advance of technology in Europe.

But, that didn't occur because America became the empire of the entrepreneur.

Whitney and Slater's inventions generated an industrial revolution that took on a life of its own. The North and South prospered economically. But often with prosperity comes difficulty. In the United States Congress, there was a shift of focus and power. At the time of the American Revolution, the power of the colonies was considered in terms of "big" and "small" states with the emphasis on population, not acreage. With the explosion of the second American Revolution, the split was between the industrial North and the agricultural South with a growing power to the west of the Appalachian Mountains.

This adjustment was further complicated by a number of other factors. First, the industrial North was somewhat contained in terms of geography because of the textile industries need for power. Until the discovery of electricity, cotton had to be turned into cloth at a select number of locations—primarily where there was water moving at a velocity sufficient to create power. Moreover, these locations had to be close to docks where the cotton came in so that the looms could be fed an unending supply of raw cotton and the textile bolts could be exported to clothing manufacturers. This limited where the mills could be built.

On the other hand, there were few limitations on where cotton could be grown prior to the 1830s. There was good soil, an adequate water supply and a growing labor supply for the expanding agricultural frontier. Transportation was needed but not confining as the outgoing product only moved at one time of year and could be shipped in bulk. Cotton thrived and it wouldn't be until the westward expansion reached beyond the Mississippi River and slavery became a political issue that the expansion of the cotton empire would stop.

The "Second" American Revolution

Another factor that complicated the impact of the second American Revolution was the debate in Congress over internal improvements. Many issues were debated, including the following: What, exactly, did the federal government owe the states and, for that matter, the private sector? Was the function of government to fund improvements that generated economic development or was that up to the private sector? Who should decide what to build? Congress or the President? What say do the states have in spending money collected within their borders?

The debate rages on to this day. The difference is that today there's more money. But, the basis for the spending remains the same. Funding of internal improvements such as roads, bridges, docks, harbors, tunnels and the like increases the speed of business. Products and services reach the market faster. Business prospers and, in turn, the federal government profits from the income taxes it collects. But the big loser is often the state. Many states do not have a state income tax so they cannot partake of the profitable environment brought about by the internal improvements. Further, even if the federal government pays for the entire cost of a road, for instance, the state is left with the maintenance cost. Thus, what is good for the federal government and the private sector may not be good for the state if it can't be recouped.

Perhaps the most important lesson of the second American Revolution is that internal improvements expand your economic horizon, but they can also harness you to tremendous expenses. Far too often, local and state politicians see federal money—and particularly pork barrel funds—as "free money." They see a road, dock, tunnel or bridge as something that was not there before and now it is. The danger is that once you put money in the driver's seat, you have to go where the driver goes. The solution to this problem is easy, but it's not very popular—rather than simply developing a list of what the state wants, states should develop a list of the things that they don't want, as well. Few states compile such lists. And, even fewer fight to reject a funded project.

The second American Revolution was a success because it was driven by economic forces. Could it have expanded with federally-funded internal improvements like railroad spurs, bridges, roads, docks and tunnels? Probably, but the United States government did not have the money to make those improvements back then. Today, the situation is reversed. We have the money for a wide array of internal improvements, the problem is that pork barreling often creates improvements that benefit few people but cost many people dollars. Until state and local governments develop both wish and do-not-build lists for their legislators, economic development will be a haphazard affair with tax dollars being frittered away in the late hours of the last day of the legislative session.

Examining this spiral even superficially it is easy to see that the combined technologies of the cotton gin and the textile factory started the boom. That's all it took to get the spiral started. Two small events, and local events at that, changed the face of world history. America, which had been slipping into economic obscurity after the American Revolution, was resurrected.

But, the seeds of destruction were resurrected, too. In the rush for profits, slavery became profitable in the South. The demand for cheap workers in the factories of the North led to child labor. The rush for profits in the shipping industry made the working conditions of sailors, longshoremen and stevedores deplorable. The demand for cheap textiles created sweatshops. Unchecked, these conditions proliferated. The failure to eliminate slavery when it became unprofitable led to the Civil War. Child labor continued well into the next century and the plight of the sailors, longshoremen and stevedores only changed with unionization in the early decades of the 20th Century. To a certain extent, textile sweatshops are still with us today. If you don't believe that, visit the garment districts in New York or Los Angeles.

Could the positive spiral have continued forever? No one knows. But it certainly could have continued much longer and, at the same time, changed the course of world history. If the Southern planters and Northern factory owners had realized that they were riding a dying horse, they might well have made the leap from human power to machinery to harvest cotton and manufacture the textile. This would have effectively eliminated the possibility of an American Civil War. It would have also changed the face of the world. One of the largest buyers of Southern cotton *before* the Civil War was England. Since Southern ports were blockaded by Union gunboats during hostilities, England looked to find another source of cheap cotton. They found it in India. By the end of the Civil War, Indian cotton was keeping the textile plants of England humming.

Who knows what would have happened if mechanization of the cotton industry had started earlier. America might be the cotton capital of the world as well as the breadbasket. Synthetic materials such as nylon and rayon might be luxury items only and, with the advances in technology, maybe even space suits would be made of specially treated cotton. The "culture of cotton," as Lincoln described the South, could have dominated American economics. But, from an historical perspective, this speculation is meaningless. The upward spiral of the second American Revolution ended in the Civil War.

Downward Spirals and Disconnects

So, now that you know it's possible to pull out of an upward spiral, what about downward spirals? Is it possible to pull out of a downward spiral? Once again, the answer is *yes*. Even from the vantage point of 500 years after the splintering of the Christian Church, it is hard to understand why there was a split in the first place. While the ceremonies of worship may vary from Protestant church to church, the core beliefs of Christianity, regardless of the church, are virtually identical to the Catholics. But if they are so alike, why did they split in the first place?

The answer is simple: the Christian Church of the 1500s was no longer in touch with its members. The pope was isolated from parishioners and the cardinals were more interested in the worldly aspect of accumulating fortunes than serving the religious needs of the people. The cardinals were isolated from the riff raff of the streets and fields by layers of Church bureaucracy that cared little for reform. This is understandable because any reform might have left Church bureaucrats out of a job. As a result, more emphasis was placed on "keeping what's mine" than developing good public policy. Any empire, church, business, office or city that spends money on the top layer without responding to the needs of the bottom of the food chain is feeding the fires of revolution. Revolution will come in the form of arms, reform or bankruptcy. Consumers vote with their dollars, customers with their feet. In the 1500s, people voted with their offerings and the Catholic Church was the loser.

Could the Christian Church have turned itself around in 1517? Certainly. Martin Luther's demands for reform were not unreasonable—unless you were in the hierarchy of the Christian Church in Rome. In fact, looking closely at Luther's 95 Theses (see Appendix A for the complete list of Luther's 95 Theses), they appear more as the ravings of an irate idealist rather than the cold-blooded demands of a reformer.

Luther was not the first to demand a purification of the Christian Church; but he was the most successful because he hit a nerve in the common man: money. Cash donated to Christian churches throughout Europe was draining into the purses of the Vatican and none of it was filtering back to the local community or local church. The nobility of Europe recognized this unfortunate circumstance and applauded silently what Luther stated publicly. But the nobles didn't want to reform the Church; they just wanted to adjust the direction of the flow of cash through their own pockets. Luther made that possible.

What doomed the Christian Church of the 1500s to a schism was that the people in charge—and the key word here is "people," as in individuals, not the faceless bureaucracy that ran the Holy See—were locked into their own mentality. They believed their own myths. They erroneously believed that the money coming into their coffers was their reward from God for doing His work. This was what doomed them to follow the downward spiral to its natural conclusion.

Another example of this disconnect is the Vietnam War. President Lyndon B. Johnson and his war hawks firmly believed in a collection of myths that they had created to generate public support for the war. They believed that communism was evil. They believed in the Domino Theory.[3] They believed in "Rolling Back the Red Tide" of communism. Once they got America into the war, the rhetoric and theory proved thin when anti-war demonstrators asked why the U.S. was in Vietnam. Several generations later, that question has yet to be answered.

It is important to note two more reasons downward spirals often continue unabated. The first is how humans think. Regardless of the era, the key to understanding that era is not to concentrate on *what* people thought but *how* they thought. Many people assume that applying today's logic to yesterday's problems serves no purpose other than to imply that "they" were dumb and "we" are smart.

---

[3] At the end of World War II, Americans came to believe that communism was a universal form of government that was the same everywhere. That is, that Russian communism was the same as Chinese communism. This is not true. But because this was the popular perception, American policy was designed to "contain" communism wherever it was. This was a passive philosophy that meant we would not oppose communism where it already was. This policy did not work because of communist incursions out of the contained area—into Greece and Turkey, for instance, where President Truman pumped $400 million to challenge Soviet ambition in the area. The policy of containment later changed to one of "Rolling Back the Red Tide." This was a proactive policy that involved America in what were called *brush fire wars* all over the globe to stop the advance of communism. Fueling America's commitment was the belief in the so-called "domino theory." Nations were looked upon as dominos standing on edge. If one were to topple, it would fall against its neighbor which would, in turn, fall against the next domino and so on and so forth. The core belief was that if one country "fell" to communism, all of its neighbors would be at risk of the same fate.

This, however, isn't true. Today, we have two distinct advantages. First, we have 20/20 hindsight. Because we can see how things turned out, we assume "they" could as well. Since we can see that a particular policy was a failure, we often leap to the conclusion that only an idiot would have made the critical decision in the first place. But, this isn't accurate either. Looking back, all we can really see was the result of one decision. Maybe it was the best of a handful of bad options. We don't know what results the other options would have brought.

History, like life, is not a series of lockstep options where each correct decision brings you closer to a golden age. Rather, it is a blind process where the best you can hope for is to leapfrog social and economic difficulties into an age of prosperity, which will only last as long as politics, world events and human greed allow it.

Further, we are not bound by the myths of the other era. People interact with their realities in accordance with their beliefs of the era. At one time rational men and women believed that God would not allow an innocent person to suffer for a crime she did not commit. Therefore, dunking and trials by ordeal to divide the innocent from the guilty were an accepted legal practice. That's the way "they" thought and thus that era reacted in a logical, rational manner to those myths.

"Good judgment comes from experience," says Alaskan humorist Warren Sitka, "and a lot of that experience came from bad judgment." The problem is that a lot of bad ideas look good from the start.

Life would certainly be simpler if bad ideas were easy to spot. But that's not the way the real world works. Bad ideas are introduced by good people who believe in them. They are also offered by bad people for the vilest of reasons. Regardless of who brings forth the bad idea, the obligation of the community—individually and collectively—is to examine each idea for its merit. Those that are bad should be eliminated as soon as possible

While this is a fine concept for a sociology class, it can be hard to distinguish between the good ideas and the bad ones. It may take years to discover mistakes that result from accepted bad ideas. It took nearly 30 years for Americans to realize that cigarettes and second-hand smoke are dangerous to their health. Sometimes the unintended consequences of a good decision end up disastrously. Asbestos was long believed to be the best possible fire retardant for schools. Today, schools across America are tearing out asbestos because it is believed to be carcinogenic. Bad ideas can sometimes achieve positive results. Consider affirmative action, which has resulted in an altering of the economic dynamics between whites and minorities.

Bad Ideas Can Be Tough to Spot

Usually the worst ideas surface at a time of great hysteria. Perhaps the best known incident of this occurring in American history was the execution of 20 men and women in Salem, Massachusetts on charges of witchcraft in the fall of 1692. On the flimsiest of evidence—if it could be called evidence—these men and women met their fate because the community believed that Satan had stolen their souls.

The sad episode began on January 20, 1692 when nine-year-old Elizabeth Parris and 11-year-old Abigail Williams began to have convulsive fits, scream blasphemies and fall into trances. Several other girls also began to suffer from the same symptoms. The community of Puritans attributed their behavior to the influence of Satan.

Prayers and fasting did no good so magic was used. A local, John Indian, baked a witch cake that included some of the urine of the affected girls. This was supposed to allow the girls to reveal the source of their illness. Now, under pressure to name that source, the girls named three local women as witches: Tituba, a Caribbean Indian slave, and two white women: Sara Good and Sarah Osborne. Good and Osborne denied they were witches but Tituba confessed that she had met the devil who appeared "sometimes like a hog and sometimes like a great dog." She also confessed that there were witches at work in Salem.

The witch-hunt was on. Suddenly every man or woman whose behavior was suspect or not within the mainstream of Salem society was suspect. The list of suspects included upstanding citizens as well as the deviant. As more and more citizens were arrested, there were more and more reasons to suspect there was a coven of witches operating in the area.

The hysteria continued until May 27 of that year when Governor Sir William Phips of Massachusetts established a special "Court of Oyer and Terminer" to examine the cases. Seven judges were assigned to the task. The judges listened to direct confessions, viewed supposed supernatural signs of witches such as "witchmarks" and heard statements from the accused. The first execution took place on June 10, 1692 when Bridget Bishop was hanged. Her last words were "I am no witch. I am innocent. I know nothing of it."

This did not keep people from dying on the gallows and it did not stop the hysteria that infected the populace with the speed of the bubonic plague. Accusations increased and more trials were held. And the hysteria spread. In mid-July, a resident of nearby Andover sought the aid of the afflicted girls to ferret out witches in Andover. The young girls complied and witch-hunt fever spread.

But there was also a growing wave of opposition to the trials. Petitions were circulated and signed in favor of the condemned and at least one member of the community, Giles Corey, refused to participate in a witch trial. For that transgression he was pressed to death on September 19. By October 8, and after 20 executions, the Governor was under pressure to put a stop to the trials. Phips, not wanting to be seen as someone who was soft on witchcraft, chose to end the trials by subterfuge. Rather than demand that the trials end, he ordered that at all future trials, spectral and intangible evidence could not be admitted. As there was no other evidence, there were no further trials and Phips disbanded the special court on October 29.

The importance of the Salem Witch Trials, made immortal by Arthur Miller's play *The Crucible*, is that mob mentality is just one idiot away from the mainstream. Any incident can lead to a period of community insanity, particularly if the cause is unknown. Terrorism is the same way. Terrorism works because no one knows where and when the next act of violence will occur.

But terrorism and hysteria are short-lived phenomena. A community can succumb to a fantasy but sanity will be restored. Usually that sanity is restored by levelheaded people in the community consistently showing the weakness of the poisonous fantasy—and logically showing the root cause of the hysteria. No community can stop a period of hysteria; the best it can do is ameliorate its effects and hope the paranoia does not ruin too many people in its wake.

The importance of understanding witch hunts in the historical context is that they are still with us. Hints of the dark side, dark power, Satanism and similar references to evil infiltrate our culture, including everything from Darth Vader and Scott Peterson to Saddam Hussein and cults.

Every era labors under its own myths. Perhaps a century from now our great grandchildren will shake their heads in disbelief because we employed people based solely on the fact that they were not white males, thought homosexuality was a disease, hypothesized that the greenhouse effect was caused by burning hydrocarbons and thought teletransporting was scientifically impossible.

Downward spirals often continue unabated because of human stupidity. In this case, stupidity is defined as an action that is illogical, irrational and unreasonable at the time it is made. One of our God-given rights as humans is to be stupid and throughout history, we've taken full advantage of this option. Humans in all stations of life, of all races, creeds, sexes, sexual orientation and education levels have made stupid decisions on such a consistent basis that it often seems that stupidity is the norm rather than the exception. Felony stupidity is not a crime. In many cases it is not even embarrassing. One should never underestimate the impact of stupidity when it comes to altering the course of human events.

Prophetic and Cyclical

Once you understand that history is best studied as an object in motion, a whole raft of other concerns arises. One question that surfaces: *If history is a study of people in motion, what drives these cycles?* Good question, but the answer is that we're not sure. Not that philosophers haven't taken a good crack at trying to understand why history works the way it does. In fact, more than a few philosophers have tied the progress of human society to our ongoing need to become more like God.

Early philosophers supposed that life, history and the intellectual process of discovery were a means of humans growing and maturing so we would understand God. This was particularly true in Europe where the influence of the Church was so great that when a scientific fact did not conform to Christian scripture, the scripture was considered correct and science in error.

The belief that human history is powered by divine judgement creates a whole lot of problems. *If God takes an active role in the development of human history, why are we just as corrupt now as we were 30 centuries ago? Why are human vices still around? Why do innocent people suffer injustice and misfortune?* Even religious scholars have difficulty explaining these apparent flaws in the divine intervention theory.

Furthermore, people who refer to themselves as Christians, Jews or Moslems have another historical perspective to include in their worldview. These peoples are prophetic—that is, they base their calendar and religious philosophy on the appearance of a prophet. All three religions begin their calendar on the coming of a prophet—Jesus, Abraham and Mohammed—and run the years in sequence until the prophet returns—Second Coming of Christ, the Return of the Messiah, the Return of Mohammed. Thus, for these religions, history is linear. There is a beginning and an end of time and we live between the two. No one knows for sure where and when the prophets are coming back but until then, God has the right to meddle in human affairs and this supposed intrusion into human affairs is the basis for the philosophical belief that God watches over us all the time. Alexander Pope said as much in his oft quoted *Essay on Man*, "Who sees with equal eye, as God of all, a hero perish or a sparrow fall."

When it comes to understanding history, many people who have a strong prophetic religious base have a tendency to view history as the progress toward a set, inevitable consequence (i.e., meliorism).

In other words, they learn history backwards. They take what they believe to be the inevitable result of history and then work backwards to the present. Since God gave his chosen people the Promised Land, it's perfectly acceptable for them to kill anyone who gets in the way because that's the way God designed the world. Since God gave his chosen people, the Jews, the Promised Land, some Jews feel it's perfectly all right to kill anyone who does not agree with that point of view. This concept is in its most poisonous form when generals, presidents, legislators, and martyrs-in-waiting believe that God speaks to them personally and thus they become the instrument of His/Her/Its divine plan.

☙

Sometimes it's convenient to be on God's side. A good example in American history is the concept of Manifest Destiny. The term itself was coined by John Louis O'Sullivan in an editorial that appeared in the July/August, 1845 edition of *United States Magazine and Democratic Review*. (See Appendix B for the editorial in its entirety.)

Basically, O'Sullivan stated that it was God's destiny that Americans should dominate the North American continent. At that time the only things that stood between the Americans and the Pacific Ocean were a poorly trained Mexican army, a badly armed Indian population and the poverty-stricken Russian-American Company.

Since, as the expression goes, God always sides with the big battalions, there was very little save morality to stop the American advance across the country. That ended when John O'Sullivan's editorial made the stealing of other people's land in the interest of God.

Eastern religions, on the other hand, have been clever in separating God as the central theme in their historical movements. While these religions may have divine individuals, spirits and deities, these spirits generate a "return" in a different manner. Humans die and are reborn, to go through the cycle of life again. A good person is born back in a higher caste; a dirt bag comes back as a worm if he's lucky.

Since, in their cosmos, life is believed to be cyclical, the cycles occur more frequently. You die and you are reborn so many times that there is nothing special about the process. As far as the overall progression is concerned—the process being the equivalent of a religion—since there is no single prophet who symbolizes the beginning of time, the concept of day, month and year is not important. After all, if you believe that your existence is cyclical and that after you die you will be reborn, the year is not as significant as the particular cycle of life you are in. While there are hierarchies of life cycles—if you are evil you will come back as a loathsome animal and have to restart the cycle of rebirths—the end is an extinguishing of the rebirth process. This is more in line with an end to your earthly prison of rebirth cycles rather than changing your form to dwell in the house of the Lord forever. The logical extension of this belief: if it doesn't matter what year it is, there's no reason to be particularly concerned about the rules of history because you won't have to deal with their consequences.

The biggest problem with this belief is that it can't be measured. While it is certainly satisfying to believe that humankind becomes more moral as time progresses, there is no proof that this is the case. Further, there is no way to prove that God has anything to do with any historical event. There is no way to measure any impact. To the contrary, in many cases it appears that God takes no active interest in events at all. While it may be true that God works in mysterious ways, God's work is not memorable enough to be used to predict historical events.

Economics and Karl Marx

Another school of thought is that economics is the prime mover of historical events. According to this theory, individuals, races, nations, cultures and societies are driven by the need to "make a buck"—to trade goods and create commerce—and their collective actions are what we call society. Thus, history is the ongoing saga of the struggle of individuals, races, nations, cultures and societies to advance their own economic position.

What makes this particular body of philosophy so popular is that many historical events have economic roots that can be quantified. In other words, we can find numbers to explain historical changes. The stock market crash of 1929 brought on the Great Depression, for instance.

The leading proponent of this theory is Karl Marx who proposed that human society would progress through a series of forms with communism being the highest and last stage. Simplifying the last three steps, Marx reasoned that humans would find that capitalism does not work and that socialism is a more reasonable form of government. Then, as the weaknesses in socialism are discovered, humans will recognize that communism—where everyone owns everything together—will be the most beneficial form of government.

The biggest problem with believing that economics drive history is that the proof is inconsistent. While it is certainly true that economics has a great deal to do with making people happy, there is no proof that good economics makes a civilization long lasting. Nations with sound economies collapse—Mussolini's Italy, for example—while nations with ungodly economic problems survive for decades—like North Korea, Libya, Iraq, Iran and China in the 20th Century.

One reason economics has been given so much credit as a determiner of history is that economics generates numbers that can be loaded into computers and analyzed. Wall Street is a good example. Statistical analyses can be run and stockbrokers can babble on about earnings per share, liquidity and stock splits. But just because economics generates numbers does not mean those numbers mean anything at all. A stockbroker can tell you all about the financial state of the Disney Corporation, how many films it has in its vault, what's on the plate for the next year and how successful its CEO has been. But that stockbroker cannot tell you anything about how well Disney stock will do even tomorrow. Stock prices are a reflection of so many variables that affect one another that no one can accurately state what any stock is going to do the next day.

Well, if no one can predict with accuracy what is happening on the stock market, an industry driven by numbers, how can economics predict historical events? It can't. Economics is a good indicator of what *could* happen and that's about all you can say about it.

Life Is a Craps Shoot

Then there is the school of thought that historical events are the consequences of random occurrences that have little relation to one other. Humans make decisions based on information they have—or don't have—and the result is unpredictable. In street talk, "life is a craps shoot." Men and women of all levels of society make the best possible decision they can with the information they have and have very little concept of the long-term consequences of their actions.

This school of thought goes even farther, suggesting that great events are simply the accumulation of lesser events that rise in importance because of their relation to one another. This is called *synchrony*, a circumstance in which two or more events occur at the same time and the combined impact is greater than the sum of the two events individually.

A good example of synchrony is the Soviet Union's launch of the first earth-orbiting satellite, *Sputnik*, in October of 1957. Americans, fearful that we would be left behind in the Space Race, began a crash program for space exploration that culminated in our landing on the moon in 1969. There was an explosion of interest in the hard sciences and space became the "New Frontier" and has been in a growth pattern every since.

Sputnik and the Space Race

On October 4, 1957, the most frightening word in the American vocabulary was one that had not been in the American vocabulary the day before—*Sputnik*. *Sputnik* was a 184-pound satellite that the Russians launched into an orbit around the earth, making them the first nation in space. Although *Sputnik* was small and, in retrospect, not a very significant achievement, nevertheless, in 1957 it sent shockwaves across the country.

The reason for the shock was quite simple. The United States viewed itself as nose-to-nose with what President Ronald Reagan later called the "Evil Empire." The previous year, Soviet President Nikita Khruschev had interrupted a speech in the United Nations by banging his shoe on his desk and was then widely quoted as saying, "We will bury you!" [4]

Though only a few Americans had a solid idea of what *Sputnik* was, most Americans assumed that "we" were coming in second place behind the Russians. Americans were shocked; they weren't used to being second. The launching of the Soviet spacecraft had as much of a national impact as Pearl Harbor because there was a widespread fear that the Russians were looking down on us from the one point of the compass from which we had no defenses.

---

[4] The actual translation of what Khrushchev said was, "We will outlive you." But the "We will bury you" made better press so it has become the catchphrase in history classes.

President Dwight Eisenhower and Congress were just as surprised as the rest of America but they weren't as worried as the man in the street. That was because they had intelligence photographs of the Russian launch facilities that had been obtained by U2 flights. No one in authority envisioned an imminent military strike, but everyone could see the shadows of the future beginning to fall—we were behind in what could be a nuclear war with bombs raining down from overhead.

The hysteria over *Sputnik* was exacerbated when the translation of the word was made public. The translation was "fellow traveler," the term used by the FBI for Americans who were unwittingly and unknowingly supporting the Communist agenda.

The impact of *Sputnik* was a sudden, dramatic, national shifting of priorities from domestic issue to space. Suddenly the Soviet threat was as real to the corn farmer in Kansas and the elementary principal in Portland as it was to the solider on the front line of the Cold War in Korea. As a result, the American schools were attacked by politicians and newspaper editors for not concentrating enough on the hard sciences and colleges immediately beefed up their offering of anything and everything scientific that had to do with space exploration. The space race was on!

The national psyche was given a second shock when the Soviets sent up a *Sputnik 2*. This craft was substantially larger than the first *Sputnik*, roughly 1,100 pounds, and carried a live dog, Laika. The Space Race news got worse when America's first attempt at leaping into the atmosphere exploded on the launch pad. The *Vanguard*, about the size of grapefruit, was immediately labeled as *Kaputnik*.

There was no scientific reason for the United States to be "behind" the Soviets when it came to space exploration. In terms of technology, we were ahead. America "acquired" a team of German rocketry experts from Nazi Germany. Headed by Werner Von Braun, they were extending the reach of the rockets and increasing the size of the capsule so instruments could be sent aloft instead of a dog.

There were also very real political considerations that slowed America's space program. In 1957, we had the capability to send a satellite up 700 miles at a speed just 1,000 miles slower than orbital speed. But President Eisenhower did not want to orbit a satellite that would pass over the Soviet Union. America was already surreptitiously spying on the USSR from above with U2 flights and a satellite overhead would increase that chances that a U2 or the satellite would be shot out of the sky. (There was good reason to be concerned. On May 1, 1960 a U2 was shot out of the sky and its pilot, Francis Gary Powers, spent two years in a Soviet prison before being traded for Col. Rudolph Abel, one of the most dramatic exchanges in American— and possibly Soviet—history.) There was also bickering among America's armed forces as to which department should head the program and what the ultimate goal of space travel was supposed to achieve.

Sputnik strengthened American resolve to leap into space. The satellite's vapor trail was still cooling as America leapt to action. Before the end of the month, the United States had created NASA, the National Aeronautic and Space Administration and the ARPA, the Advanced Research Projects Agency. NASA was to lead the space exploration effort—with the support of all branches of the military— and ARPA was established to research new space travel-oriented technologies that were too advanced or too costly for the private sector.

The culminating piece of the space race puzzle was announced by President John F. Kennedy shortly after his inauguration: He wanted an American on the moon before the end of the decade. Though he was slain in November of 1963, his dream was achieved in the summer of 1969 when Neil Armstrong became the first human to walk on the moon.

The significance of *Sputnik* is not so much that America was unprepared—because we were—but that the outcome collimated so well with the economic and cultural direction America had to travel anyway. The 1950s were a time of great economic growth but America's wealth was in consumer products. Because the money was in consumer products, the focus of education was on business. Even though the economic future of the private sector was clearly in the sciences, Americans were more interested in making money than looking at test tubes. *Sputnik* changed our national focus and generated a stampede into the hard sciences.

Whether your future lies in the hard sciences, social sciences, service industries, education or manufacturing, you can be assured of one reality: things will change. They will change cataclysmically or slowly, but they will change. You may even have to change the angle of your occupational sail to ride the currents the way they are going, which may not be the way you want to go. With the boom of the telecommunications industry, the spreading popularity of the Internet, the expansion of terrorism, the shrinking of the world market and increasing human population, there is no reason to assume that the world we live in today will be the same in a decade. *Sputnik* could have been anticipated but our national focus was elsewhere. Remember: It's important to remain aware of trends even if they are not in your industry. There is no substitute for being informed and no excuse for being caught flat-footed by technology.

Looking back on *Sputnik*, it was a very modest first step into the space. Only the fact that Soviets took it first was important. Americans were worried that the Soviets would "bury" us, as Khruschev was misquoted. Feelings of being behind combined with *Sputnik* as a symbol of the Soviet's supposed technical superiority—which was not necessarily true even in 1957—created an explosion of enthusiasm for space travel in the United States.

Complicating the theory of historical movement being the result of random acts is the reality that human beings are not so similar. Cultures are segmented by race, education, income, IQ and sexual orientation. There is no typical Russian, Czech or African. Society is always changing and these days, the impact of technology is splintering cultures into more and more diverse units. Blacks, Native Americans, immigrants and Mexicans with greencards think differently than Italian Catholics, Cajuns, Eskimos and yuppie lawyers in California. Interracial marriages further splinter these ethnic categories. Each of these categories is also segmented by age, education, income, IQ, and sexual orientation—to name just a few. A rich, black executive is going to think differently from a black drug pusher on an inner-city street corner. One middle class Eskimo may go to a professional football game while another goes to the opera. An aging Italian Catholic hippie may be smoking marijuana while another of the same age is driving across town drunk.

Technology further minces these classes. With the advent of cyberspace, even individuals with similar mentalities can find themselves on different cultural paths. Two 50-year-old electrical engineers might be surfing the Web, one looking to find a chat room on existential philosophy and the other searching for pornography. A gay writer may be selling his memoirs on a Web page while his life partner is designing an interactive Web page for automotive repair.

Even without adding such factors as a personality bent toward criminal activity, willingness to take risks, dedication to excellence and perseverance into account, it is easy to see that there are many contributing factors to human existence and that trying to develop a comprehensive philosophy of why human society changes is impossible. All that is accurate is that human society and the story of its existence—otherwise known as history—will change and that change is the consequence of millions of factors.

Gradational and Cataclysmic Change

There is one thing we do know for sure. Change is inevitable and most of the change in our future is unexpected. The good news is that most change is gradational. That is, it comes slowly and predictably. We return to our hometown after 10 years and find it is basically the same with a few new buildings here and there. Or, we work in an office for 10 years and other than the personnel changes, the work remains pretty much the same. Expressions like, "I've seen it all," and, "Here we go again," are good indications that the change in store is really nothing new.

Far more dramatic is cataclysmic change. That's when everything changes unpredictably overnight. The bombing of Pearl Harbor was a cataclysmic change. After December 7, 1941, America and the world would never be the same again. Some historians call it a loss of innocence, others call it the inevitable consequence of ignoring the warning signs of impending disaster. Which historian is right doesn't make any difference. World War II changed the face of the world forever. So will the war on terrorism. For the United States, December 7, 1941, was a cataclysmic day. There was nothing gradational about the change from December 6, 1941 to December 8, 1941.

Bombing of Pearl Harbor and World War II

It was during the darkest days of World War II. The blitz devastated London night after night and Winston Churchill plotted strategy at the White House with FDR. It was late in the evening and FDR's staff needed a bit of information from Churchill. After searching the numerous rooms they came across the Prime Minister "dressed in a Martini." As the aides were mumbling their apologies for catching him in such a state of undress, Churchill waved them inside and said wryly, "The British Empire has nothing to hide."

That may have been true of the British Empire but it was not true of the United States government.

Courtesy of the Freedom of Information Act (FOIA) and a distinguished scholar, the truth of what really happened at Pearl Harbor is finally coming to light.[5] Contrary to high school textbooks, the United States was not, in the words of FDR, "suddenly and deliberately at-

---

[5] Stinnet, Robert D., *Day of Deceit: The Truth About FDR and Pearl Harbor*, The Free Press, 2000.

tacked by the Empire of Japan." In reality, the attack on Pearl Harbor was a long-anticipated event that the United State had precipitated.

Even without the documentation provided by FOIA, an examination of the political events prior to Pearl Harbor could have led to no other conclusion. First, usually mentioned as a footnote to history rather than a critical aspect of American history, in his early career FDR was the Undersecretary of the Navy, the same position his relative, Teddy Roosevelt had held decade earlier. Like TR, FDR understood that America's maritime greatness meant moving product and military might into the Pacific. That was where the future lay and FDR, like TR before him, wanted to make the Pacific an "American lake."

But on that lake, there was one other contender: Japan. The Japanese had a Navy that rivaled that of the United States and was moving aggressively to seize ports, markets and natural resources on the western edge of the Pacific Rim. Like the United States, Japan was isolated from the rest of the world by thousands of miles of ocean that gave her the isolation she needed to pillage China. Eventually, there was going to be a confrontation between Japan and the United States, if not over commerce then over military supremacy.

In the years leading up to Pearl Harbor, FDR sought to achieve three goals. First, he wanted to force Japan to attack the United States so he could use that as an excuse to declare war against Japan and her allies Germany and Italy. Second, he wanted to break the military strength of Japan in the Pacific. Third, he wanted to provide security for American interests in the Pacific by acquiring or controling acreage that could be used by the United States military—and specifically the United States Army Air Corp to provide air coverage of the commercial routes. (There was no United States Air Force yet.)

As all three could be achieved simultaneously, according to military documents released under FOIA, the United States began a policy of quiet antagonism of the Japanese. The weakness in the Japanese rush to empire was in the fact that the home islands of Japan had few natural resources. Everything that was needed for her war machine had to be imported: oil, gasoline, steel, rubber, glass, wire, gunpowder, etc. Even more important, all of these products depend on oil, either to get the raw materials to Japan or to manufacture the products there. Cutting off the supply of oil to Japan was done easily; the United States pressured its allies in the Pacific to refuse to sell oil to Japan. The United States intensified the pressure by refusing to sell Japan any more steel. Now Japan had a choice, stop expanding its empire or take on the United States.

Japan chose the latter course. Thereafter, the biggest problem was keeping the United States military on Hawaii blissfully unaware of the impending attack. According to records released under FOIA, in spite of ongoing warnings from the command structure in Pearl Harbor, nothing was done to safeguard the American Navy personnel and its ships. Thus, when the Japanese Navy struck, it appeared that the United States was unprepared for the attack.

❧

Pearl Harbor was a devastating loss to the United States in terms of human life and material. More than 3,000 Americans were killed at Pearl Harbor along with numerous battleships. But the key word in the previous sentence was "battleships." What were not lost at Pearl Harbor were America's three aircraft carriers: *Enterprise*, *Hornet* and *Yorktown*. Even though the *Yorktown* was badly damaged, it was repaired and participated in the Battle of Midway the next June.

The aircraft carriers were critical to the war in the Pacific. With the aircraft carriers there was air coverage for the American fleet. With the aircraft carriers and the land-based planes on Midway, Wake, Guam, Pearl Harbor and the Philippines, the American Navy had a command of the skies over the Pacific. Thus, the Japanese were well aware of this reality as Japanese Naval forces attacked Malaya, Hong Kong, Guam, the Philippine Islands and Wake Island on the same day as Pearl Harbor. An attack on Midway came a day later.

The key to understanding the circumstances surrounding Pearl Harbor is realizing that FDR and his advisors were horizon thinkers. They planned for the future long before it arrived. Even more important, they were pro-active. They saw the shadows of the future as they began to form and guided American policy. They didn't wait for the future and its problems to arrive, they rushed forward with a plan and a policy.

This is a lesson that one should take seriously. No human catastrophic event arrives unannounced. The best way to solve a problem is to prepare for its arrival. An even better way is to see that you can derive some method of profit from the disaster that is impending. FDR saw an attack on Pearl Harbor as a means of getting the United States into World War II, the Japanese out of the Pacific and the American public behind his programs. It was a successful ploy, the reward for being an horizon thinker.

Conclusion

By now you're probably thinking, "Well, how does history move?" No one knows. There are all kinds of theories but in the final analysis, no one knows for sure. All we do know is that human events move cultures and societies. This book is not meant to delve into why history moves. It is geared to teach you how to use history to like a tool to read the future. To read history like a tool, all you have to understand is that the present is changing even if you cannot see it. This book will help you see those changes and teach you how to take advantage of them. By the time you have finished this book, you have a better understanding of the past, as well as the future.

2 The Laws of Movement

Sixteenth Century French humorist and writer François Rabelais, best known for his novel *La Vie de Gargantua et de Panagruel*, the celebrated satirical story of the giant Gargantua and his son Panagruel, was a master of creative thinking. Once, while traveling far from Paris, Rabelais found himself broke and stranded in the countryside. Undaunted by adversity, he took a room in a local inn and prepared two small packages, labeling them "Poison for the King" and "Poison for the Dauphin." He left the packages where the landlady would be sure to spot them. She did and posthaste Rabelais was arrested for treason and transported to Paris under armed guard. When the packages were discovered to be empty and Rabelais, a personal friend of the King, explained what he had done, the royal court had a good laugh.

And Rabelais never had to pay for his lodging or his trip back to Paris.

History is made by those who finish what they start with competence and ingenuity. *Finishing*, in the classic sense of the word, does not mean "concluding." *Concluding* applies to actions that take place when a project runs out of time or money. It's like buying a car in "as is" condition.

In historical terms, *finishing* is the bottom rung of the ladder of competence. Anyone can begin an endeavor. Millions do. But of the thousands of projects that are started, only a fraction of them are ever finished. Most are abandoned and only a handful are ever finished.

The key to finishing what you've started is movement. Movement is different from motion because something is being completed.

But movement, in the historical sense, means more than simple progress. It means using history to your advantage.

While there are numerous laws of non-movement—which will be discussed in the next chapter—there are only a handful of laws of movement that are consistent throughout history.

A river's course can be charted. But the route of a pioneer over a mountain range involves some guesswork and can only be placed on a map after the ascent has been successful—or finished. Shrewd people figure out how to solve problems in creative ways. Life has too many twists and turns to develop steadfast rules. Competent people know this; they also know that what works today, may not work tomorrow. A successful businessperson knows that no matter how successful she is today, she could be on the street as the result of one wrong move tomorrow. Markets change quickly. Good political connections fade fast. Inside sources may retire or face charges of insider trading. Businesses that appear solid on the outside can be withering—hemorrhaging red ink—on the inside. A flick of a switch can make a good company's product obsolete. Yet, some people remain successful. Why? Because they use history to plan for the future as they live in the present.

The Big Tent

A distinguishing feature of the talented tenth (the ten percent of the population that is unpredictable in behavior and tends to change history) is that they have internalized the Law of the Big Tent, a political expression implying that a political party is like a three-ring circus with many things happening in different parts of the big tent. Everything occurs under the same tent, a big top that is as big as it needs to be to include diverse opinions.

The overall concept is that a political party has many members— some of them strange, others *very* strange—that come together to form one group because they believe in the guiding principles of the party.

However, the Law of the Big Tent extends far beyond the confines of a political party. Roughly translated, the law means that shrewd people don't rule out any source of assistance—even from people they cannot stand—enemies or fools.

A smart leader not only associates with her enemies, she also consults with them frequently. Look at the advisors that surround your local Mayor or Governor. Do they all come from the same party? If they do, you may very well have a leader who is being led by her own vanity. If everyone around the Mayor tells her what a great job she is doing, how will she know if she's *really* doing a great job? The answer is easy—she won't. Many advisors near the center of power are sycophants and as long as they are employed the last thing they are going to do is rock the boat. They're not worried about their place in history, they're worried about their paychecks.

A good leader always has a well-placed opponent in her camp. She needs someone who has the guts to say, "Lady, this is a real mistake" without having to worry about being fired for saying so. Leaders who surround themselves with sycophants find that corruption and incompetence move into their administration quickly. After all, what Republican is going to tell the Republican Governor that her Commissioner of Transportation is taking money from a local teamsters union under the table? But, if she had a highly placed Democrat in her administration, he would gleefully tell the Governor that corruption was making its rounds in the Department of Transportation—and be happy to supply the documentation to prove it.

❧

Opponents are important to rulers, but fools also hold an important place in the world. Historically speaking, one of the great problems medieval rulers faced was that their courts were rats' nests of intrigue. It was this lord against his neighbor; this family against another; the French branch of the family in collusion with the English branch of the family and the Austrian branch of the family against another—all being related at the same time—and each person, family and branch jockeying for position in every imperial court in Europe. Then there was the Queen and her entourage, ministers, courtiers, spies, servants' secrets, inside information from soldiers of fortune, the church and its unique interests and the foreign agents who stirred the pot whenever it served their country's purpose. In this cauldron of plots mixed with cabal, confederacies, schemes, scams and duplicity, there was no one the Queen could trust completely. Everyone had an ulterior motive.

One good example of court intrigue during this time is found in Alexander Dumas's novel *The Three Musketeers*. Dumas, a master of historical research, painted a vibrant picture of the ebb and flow of deceit and intrigue at all levels in the royal palace. At the top was the King, battling the evil Cardinal with the Queen as a pawn between the two powerbrokers. Then there were the Cardinal's men who would fight the King's guard, the Musketeers. Then there were the servants, noble families in the courts of the King of France and the King of England and foreign agents and spies. Written in 1845, the tale of the musketeers has survived 150 years on the bookshelf and 50 years of rewrites as a movie. Variations of the novel appeared as films in 1935, 1939, 1948, 1964 and 1993—not to mention at least one presentation on the small screen and some animated shorts. *The Three Musketeers* is a timeless presentation of human foibles and virtues.

Within the turmoil of the Medieval court, there was one person who had no agenda: the court jester or fool. Hollywood has been partially correct in its portrayal of the court fool as someone who was there to make the royal court laugh. But the jester was more than a clown, particularly to a competent king or queen. As an entertainer, the jester was given the freedom to abuse and poke fun at even the most exalted member of the court—including the king. Many of them did just that and found their way into history's pages. Henry VIII's jester, William Somers, was so famous that a play was written about him. But Somers wasn't the only fool to find his way into history's pages. William I's fool, Golet, saved his patron from an assassination attempt in 1047 because the conspirators didn't bother to keep their plot from the jester's ears. They thought no one would take the word of a fool seriously. But William the Conqueror did, and if he hadn't he may not have gone on to win the Battle of Hastings 19 years later.

The fool was important because his role was to remain separate from court intrigues. There was no reason for him to be involved because there was no benefit to be gained. From the jester's mouth often dropped satirical assessments of the court and its denizens— along with tidbits of information the king did not yet know.

Fools and jesters are no longer a common sight in workshops or conference rooms. What's the 21st Century equivalent? An outsider. A geek. The person with technical skills who doesn't interact so ably with others. There are plenty of people like *that* around.

You can use this concept of the Big Tent in your own life. Surround yourself with friends, but make certain that you are at least on speaking terms with your most bitter opponent. That opponent will serve you well. Of course he'll work hard to undercut your every move, but he has no cause to be shy about pointing out your shortcomings. If you make bad decisions, they'll fail, but the earlier you find this out, the better. The longer it takes to recognize that a bad idea has failed, the more costly it is.

The more and sooner you know about your weaknesses or the weaknesses of your administration, the better. Once you know you have a problem, you can fix it. Once that problem is fixed, you or your administration can move forward.

Leadership as a Historical Tool

A leader is a person who has commanding authority or influence over a group of people. More than anything else, a leader makes decisions. What's confusing and at times frustrating, though, is that the vast majority of people who are anointed as leaders want to do anything but lead. They like the job and its perks but when it comes to making a decision, they can't execute. This is precisely why so many companies, offices, organizations, projects, campaigns, businesses and associations fail. It's not for lack of a specific mission: it's for lack of quality leadership.

One of the noteworthy features of historical leaders is that they see the future and strive to meet its challenges. Roadblocks that would stall ordinary people are only nuisances to maneuver around. Since there is no single road to success, no single roadblock can bar progress.

When it comes to politics and public affairs, good leaders understand that governing is not merely a matter of having issues brought to their attention. The term *govern* means to control and direct the making and administration of policy. Thus, in order to remain in power—governing—a leader must move and make forceful decisions regarding those issues. History, politics, economics, and families are all dynamic. They are constantly changing.

In the 21st Century, being a leader is a bit more complicated because of the complexity of society and the corporate food chain. While the President of the United States or a General, like a Roman emperor, can bark out orders for immediate action, most of us have to use a wide variety persuasion. If you work in a state or federal office, for example, you can't fire someone for not carrying out your order—unless, of course, you're their employer. If you're the candidate in a race for Governor, you can't force the voters to choose you. But, you can develop an arsenal of persuasive weapons to aid you in getting what you want.

Of course, things won't always go your way, even with the best of planning. Great ideas can gradually turn to mush. Good men in key positions can fall to the wayside because of lust. Competent women can be lured to the dark side with cash. Department heads die, division managers don't live up to their promises, office managers find Christ, heads of the legal department join the Peace Corps, and your child may develop bone cancer forcing you to take a lower paying job closer to home.

Life, like democracy, is nothing more than an ongoing bar brawl and if you're able to make it out the door with a piece of furniture, you're doing pretty well.

The difference is that competent leaders realize this and know that they are not alone. They depend on hundreds, perhaps thousands, of people to maintain their position. It only takes one man to write a book but it takes an army to make a movie. Good leaders are like moviemakers. They understand that they must lead. Knowing this, what are the other characteristics that make a good leader? The following are a few shared by historical figures throughout history.

Perhaps the most important attribute is *internal desire*. Leaders are made, not born. People who have the internal desire to lead recognize that fact early in life and prepare. Rather than approaching education as something they have to "get through," their desire drives them to approach each academic subject with the attitude of "What can I learn here that I will be able to use later?" While it's easy to pooh-pooh your high school education, if you actually learned everything you were supposed to learn, you would be a highly educated person in today's society. The subject matter is designed to give you a general background of the basics. If, however, you waded through high school copying homework and dodging quality classes, you might end up a worker bee, earning only as much as the economy will allow or a union can negotiate. Leaders, on the other hand, use their education as a springboard, expanding the knowledge gained in the economics class by following the stock market or testing their political science concepts by reading about emerging countries in Africa in reputable news magazines. They understand that education does not stop when the dismissal bell rings. Their internal desire drives them to learn.

Leaders must also be *aggressive*. Leaders don't just see opportunity; they rush—albeit carefully—to meet it. Good generals, for example, don't run to battle, they advance carefully. They prepare for the confrontation long before a single flag is unfurled. Then, when the battle is nigh, they move. Perhaps this is best expressed by the old military axiom that "an army of sheep led by a lion can defeat an army of lions led by a sheep." In other words, the quality of an army is not to be found in its manpower but with its generals. The American Civil War illustrates this fact.

Looking back, it's hard to imagine how the South lasted as long as it did. The North had a larger army, more industrial capacity, more rail lines and better sources of food and supplies. But the South had the generals, men with cleverness and guile. Robert E. Lee was a military genius—but he was ably assisted by the stupidity and timidity of Union generals who replaced each other as fast as battle news was received by Congress. Lee was eventually defeated by a Union general Ulysses S. Grant who understood how to win a war. Grant, as President Lincoln said, was his favorite general because Grant "would fight." When the Union army finally replaced the sheep with a lion, the Civil War ended.

Leaders also have a great *sense of timing*. This, however, is another of those historical catchphrases that means very little on the surface. Looking back on an historical event, it often appears obvious that it would occur. Nothing is more powerful than an idea whose time has come, history teachers tell us. But, ideas are a long time coming and even though the pivotal event happened in a short enough time to be discussed in a history class, the true impact of the idea will take centuries to be felt.

Jesus brought forth a new theology during his 30 years on earth but it took 100 years for the New Testament to be written and *another* 200 years before Constantine made this new religion official. For a leader, a sense of timing *does not* mean that every possible factor has turned in favor of a move. It means that enough of the factors have turned to make success reasonable. Or, as a gambler would say, "the numbers look good."

Great leaders are successful because they move when they feel the moment is right. They are willing to take a chance. Poor leaders hesitate and the moment is lost, and with it, the opportunity is gone. History teachers often fail to mention that a large part of that critical timing is having the guts to move.

In early June of 1944, with tens of thousands of men on ships waiting to invade Adolph Hitler's *Fortress Europe*, General Dwight D. Eisenhower had to decide when to go. The weather the first few days of the month was miserable but his meteorologists reported that June 6th might be, could be, had the potential to be, appeared to be, clear. There was nothing certain about it—they were only guesstimates and hardly scientific.

By comparison, General Erwin Rommel's weathermen, looking at the same meteorological data, predicted that the weather would be miserable for the first part of the month. Rommel's weathermen also told him that the storm front would be in place for so long that he took the time off to visit his wife in Germany, far from the front. Eisenhower was bold. He took decisive action and ordered the invasion. As it turned out, Allied weathermen were right; the German weathermen were wrong. That tipped the scales slightly Eisenhower's way. Every mistake—Rommel being away from the front and trust that bad weather would stall an Allied invasion—gave the Allies an edge.

D-Day was successful because Eisenhower prepared well, acted aggressively and when the time came to take a calculated risk, he did. Had he waited for a day of guaranteed good weather, the German Army would have been there waiting for him. If that had been the case, the United States might be dealing with a Nazi empire instead of European commonwealth today. Good leaders realize that time is an ally and they seize the moment.

A good leader also *allows talent to rise*. One of the worst things a person in charge can do is known as "hiring down." This occurs when the boss wants to be the smartest man in the department. In other words, anyone who appears to be smarter or more talented is moved aside and promotions are only doled out to people who are less smart than the boss. Niccolo Machiavelli, the man believed to be the first great political philosopher of the Renaissance and author of *The Prince*, said it best when he noted that the best way to judge a prince is by the advisors with which he surrounds himself. A good leader has an eye for talent.

The best leaders don't care whether their workers are rednecks, got their job through affirmative action, are crippled and have to leave early to make it down the elevator before the 4:30 rush, are obese, worship Satan or are drag queens at the local gay bar on weekends. A good leader only cares about three things: 1) Does this person do quality work?; 2) Does this person finish on time?; and 3) Does this person have common sense? All other shortcomings can be accommodated if her advisors are worth their talent.

Perhaps the most important characteristic of the audacious leader is a belief in the *concept of solidarity*. Following the line of logic that he who travels fastest travels alone, a competent leader with an eye to completion of task, acts quickly and alone. The founding fathers were well aware of this principle and made certain to give the President of the United States as few Constitutional stumbling blocks as possible. While the United States Congress has a host of such obstacles—found in Article I of the Constitution—the President has very few—found in Article II. The result is that the powers of the President are very broad. For example, Article II, Section II, Paragraph 1 states, "The President shall be Commander in Chief of the Army and Navy of the United States, and of the militia of the several states, when called into actual service of the United States." In other words, if the President wants the 101ˢᵗ Airborne in Panama City tomorrow morning, they go. If the President wants the Alaska National Guard to patrol the Yukon River for walrus, they better start walking. This is all at the whim and will of one man, not a committee. In addition to carrying weapons, the United States military has been ordered by the President of the United States to deliver mail, track drug smugglers, patrol city streets, shoot looters, invade a foreign country with which the United States was not at war, fill sandbags, build shelters and run railroads. That's because the President can act alone. He has the power of solidarity as opposed to the United States Congress, a body that can't move until there are enough votes. The power of solidarity is *only* an asset if it is used.

Rewarding Stupidity

One of the toughest laws of movement to enforce is that of Rewarding Stupidity. While science has shown that there is an upward limit to human intelligence, common sense proves that there is no such downward boundary.

Stupidity and error are simply an essential part of human nature. In the words of English poet Alexander Pope, "To err is human; to forgive, divine." Sung by Sesame Street's Big Bird, "Everyone makes mistakes." We all make mistakes—some of us more than others—and no one wants to be quick to condemn someone else's error because everyone has a turn to play the fool. Further, we learn from our failures. Over the long run, you'll learn more from failures than success—it's just that the learning is more painful.

But the problem lies in the fact that the higher up the corporate food chain you are, the less chance you have of suffering from your own stupidity. Ask any United States Air Force aviation mechanic what happens when a plane goes down. Rarely is the loss attributed to pilot error. Usually it's mechanical failure and that means someone at the bottom of the enlisted ranks is disciplined.

When the president of a corporation makes a stupid move, it's the front line employees who have to explain the new policy—with all its glaring inadequacies—to the customer. Then, when business slows because of the new policy, the sales force is accused of not doing its job. And, should the company fall on hard times because of the new policy, top management always has a golden parachute.

If, however, you can reward those who made the mistake by living with the consequences of their actions, you will make certain that the mistake is not made again—by anyone. A recent example: forcing Swiss banks to repay the descendants of Holocaust victims $1.25 billion for bank accounts the Swiss "lost" after the second World War. As Hitler and Mussolini were consolidating their power, Jews across Europe began to fear for their assets—and for good reason. Thousands decided that a safe haven for their fortune was in Swiss banks. But these Jews did not appreciate how greedy Swiss bankers could be.

That wasn't discovered until half a century later, when it came time for descendants to collect their legacy. The Swiss grew testy, said they couldn't find the accounts in question, among a host of other excuses. Then there was the proof of death defense. Swiss bankers refused to open accounts to anyone who could not produce a death certificate proving that the original depositor was dead.

Considering that at least 6 million Jews died in the concentration camps, not even a partial list of victims exists. Even if such documents had existed, the Nazis probably would have destroyed them as the Third Reich was being hammered into submission by the Allies. Death certificates were superfluous considering that as many as 20 million people died during the war. So, with no death certificates, the Swiss banks would not release any assets. Those assets continued making profits for Swiss banks while Holocaust victims died, and with them the memory of how much money had been deposited by which relative in what bank. At the same time, the Swiss bankers and their families were awash in wealth they never believed they would ever have to repay. Then, half a century later, enough of an international squeeze was put on the Swiss banks to make a reasonable recompense to the descendants of their deceased depositors.

Capitalism and Stupidity

The great efficiency of a capitalist economy is that it allows all kinds of stupidity to form—but cuts support harshly from ideas that don't work.

Left alone, there is a natural culling effect in both the public and private sector. Just as most buggy whip makers were put out of business by the introduction of the automobile, so, too, will most typewriter and record player manufacturers due to the advent of the computer and CD player, respectively.

The trick to using history as your guide and keeping your occupation and life vibrant is *not* to stand in the way of the natural forces of selection, to paraphrase Charles Darwin. Failure is a great cleanser. Allow it to work. In terms of people, you must let the perpetrators of stupidity pay the penalty.

A good historical example of letting failure cull out the weak was the Great Depression. In the wild and crazy days of the Roaring Twenties, everyone who had money to burn was in the stock market. Buying on the margin was the rage. It was possible to buy stock for 10 or 15 cents on the dollar—so people did. By the thousands. And, when stocks bought on the margin returned more in dividends than had been initially invested, more sunny day investors were lured in. How could anyone turn down easy money? Millions couldn't. Then, came the crash in 1929. When the margin calls were made, few could pay and Easy Street became a very rocky road. Thousands of businesses went under. Wall Street was devastated.

The crash led to one of the worst economic slumps in U.S. history, and one that spread to virtually the entire industrialized world. Many factors played a role in bringing about the depression, which lasted for about a decade, but one of the main causes was the extensive stock market speculation that led up to the crash in 1929. The Depression brought the American economy to a virtual standstill; workers couldn't get jobs because employers wouldn't hire them; employers wouldn't hire them because there was no market for goods; and there was no market for goods because workers without jobs had no money to spend.

But capitalism survived and the American investment industry learned a valuable lesson. The stock market became more regulated. Poorly financed companies failed, leaving the playing field open to the more financially secure companies. The disaster made the companies that survived stronger.

In your life you've probably seen stupidity ignored, shrugged away or covered up rather than being allowed to reap its own reward. But there is a great deal of difference between ignoring one shortcoming and covering up mistake after mistake. We've all worked in offices where someone performs a string of mistakes and never has to pay for them. Or we've watched as department heads survive mistakes that would have killed lesser careers. But rarely does anyone pay a heavy price.

And, sometimes the very people who made the mistake are promoted to a higher position. Unfortunately, this happens so often that there is a term for it: *upward failure*. These are people who are unsuccessful at everything they do yet, time after time, they are promoted up the corporate food chain after each disaster. Perhaps it's because they are covering for someone higher up and the promotion is their reward. Or because it's cheaper for the company to promote the deadwood out of harm's way. Or any of a thousand other reasons.

But an office won't prosper if it doesn't apply some penalty for failure. There is a price for risk and you have to make certain that it is suffered. Bad products should not be encouraged to remain on the market. Subsidizing an industry only insulates it from market forces. Worse, it spreads the real cost of the product to consumers who may not even use it. Paying someone to let their land lie fallow to keep food prices high means that the only real winner is the farmer whose field is unproductive. To be progressive you have to adjust the system so that stupidity reaps its just reward. If you don't, the message you are clearly delivering is that failure is just as acceptable as success.

It takes a brave person or firm to allow stupidity to be rewarded. But it is also a smart move. Small headaches can grow disastrous and costly quickly. There is nothing wrong with taking a risk. At least, there is nothing wrong as long as it is calculated.

But allowing a stupid proposal to go unchallenged is dangerous. First, it encourages somebody else to try something else equally as lame brained. Second, it leaves the impression that calculated risk has no place in the workplace and that you are better off shooting from the hip than planning your moves carefully. Third, if the outcome is disastrous and no one pays for the devastation, the department ends up with the worst of all possible worlds: It's saddled with the cost of the bad idea and the cost to recover from the bad idea. It must fund the staff that pushed the concept in the first place, who aren't being fired. It must stretch its budget to promote the person who headed up the project to get him out of the department. And it must pay for the public relations effort to shore up the impression that the business is out of control.

Forcing stupidity to be its own reward, and allowing someone to take responsibility for his stupidity, is far less expensive.

Niche Development

Anyone can be a businessperson, all you have to do is drop thousands of dollars into equipment and product and then shuffle your product into the marketplace. It's all a crap shoot anyway, right? If you succeed, you guessed right. If you didn't, well, that's the way the cookie crumbles. But, if you don't try you can't win.

In reality, none of this is true. First, and most significant, the largest cause of business failure is not the ill advisedness of a product or the weakness of the marketplace; it's bad management. This is particularly true among small businesses and start-up operations. On the other hand, bad products can stay on the market for decades with good management.

Take cigarettes, for example. Very few smokers will say that smoking is not dangerous to their health. But they still smoke. If so many people who actually smoke know that they are taking a risk every time they take a puff, why are the cigarette companies still in business? The answer: good management. Tobacco companies get their name into the public's eye, are associated with popular things like professional sports, and have crafty advertisements.

Using history to manage the future, particularly when it comes to business, you will quickly discover that movement depends on finding niches and clawing your way forward. Suppose, for instance, you work for a bank. A lending institution can only increase its assets one of two ways: by having its existing customer base increase its average account; or by increasing the number of customers. The ideal scenario, of course, is to do both at the same time.

This is easier said than done. In most cities, the banks that already exist have split up the economic pie. The big customers usually get snapped up by bank presidents, leaving everyone else in the organization to scramble for the smaller, new clients. But if the best prospects are already taken, how are you, an employee lower on the totem pole, supposed to find new, paying clients?

Historically, the answer has been to develop niches. Unless a city is in the midst of a massive downturn, no good loan is going to get turned away. Does this mean you're left with just the bad loans? No, it just means you have to be creative in your approach. You specialize. Since the big customers are already taken, you look for the industry that the other banks are ignoring. If your bank has an iron clad rule about requiring some kind of real estate as equity, look to the companies that don't have any assets in real estate.

But, if the bank has an iron clad rule about only taking real estate as equity, why bother to go after anything else? The answer, quite simply, is that if everyone is looking for clients who have enough real estate to pledge for a loan, then everyone is only going to get a small piece of the pie. But, if you concentrate on companies with other asset bases, you have an open field.

Arrange for a loan to someone who owns a lawn mower repair operation or a bike store. Lend against their equipment or inventory. There are a lot of niche industries, and the larger the community you live in, the more niches there are. If you are the only banker in town setting up loans for that industry, you could get dozens of small loans. Lawn mower repair people talk amongst themselves. So do bike shop owners, plus-size clothing stores, video rental parlors, mechanics and at-home beauty salons. Sure, the economic pie is smaller, but if you are the only banker up to bat, you get the whole pie.

Everyone is different and each person has his own values. Even people within the same church have different values. While the churches, temples and synagogues of the world would have you believe that morality and ethics are, by and large, universal, they are not. The moral values of most humans are the same in the general sense that the most idealistic among us will treat others as we wish to be treated. But it's not universal enough to place bets. Besides, "actions speak louder than words." It's not what people think about doing that counts, it's what they actually do that's important.

Great leaders understand the values of the people around them and adjust for them. Herodotus, the Greek historian and father of history, illustrated this point well with a lesson from the Persian emperor Darius about 500 BCE. One day the emperor called into his presence a group of Greeks and asked, "What should I pay you to eat the bodies of your fathers when they die?" The Greeks told him that there was no sum that would tempt them to do such a thing and that the proper way to dispose of the earthly remains was cremation. Darius then sent for a group of Callatians from India, men who ate their fathers, and asked them, while the Greeks stood by, and knew by the help of an interpreter all that was said, "What should I give you to burn the bodies of your fathers when they die?" The Callatians were appalled. They stated that the proper way to honor the dead was to devour the corpse. In other words, if one were to offer men to choose, out of all the customs in the world, those that seemed the best, they would examine the whole lot and choose their own—convinced that their own customs far surpassed those of all others. Thus, Herodotus opined, the point of the encounter, was that a great ruler had to understand the values of all his subjects and make allowances for each nationality, tribe and individual.

Identicalness in real life is rare. Every oak tree is different from another. Just as every rat, sea anemone, blade of grass and snowflake differs from another. And, while every item under the sun may have similarities with its brethren, no two are identical. Identical twins aren't even identical; they walk, talk, think and speak differently, among other things.

Consider a Christmas tree lot. Take a stroll through the lot and you'll notice that all the trees may be the same species, and they may even be from the same tree farm, but no two trees are identical no matter how large the lot. Even manufactured items are minutely distinguishable from one another and grow more individualized as they age, due to such things as wear and tear, environmental conditions and how they get handled by their owners.

Use history to your advantage. Don't base any assumptions on a difference of values with your colleagues. Don't leap to any conclusions because your sales partner is black and goes to a Southern Baptist church on Wednesday nights and Sundays. And despite what the media shoves down our throats, all liberals are not pro-choice and many pro-lifers favor gay marriages, gun control and even decriminalizing marijuana. People can surprise you. Expect it.

However, in most offices, these issues aren't "on the table," so to speak. Even in state legislatures, moral issues are rare. The hot issues are usually those that have no ethical agenda—such as rent control, funding of a new school, approval of state employees' contracts, bonding provisions, establishment of a real estate commission, funding for the arts, the state budget, etc. Rent control doesn't have a social value. Neither do issues like computers in classrooms, gun control or prayer in public schools. While there are pockets of support and opposition, none of these issues has a universal appeal.

From an historical perspective, movement will only occur when humans rise above the whining over values. Good office policy, like good public policy, is a universal value. You either get along with everyone—no matter how different they are—or you move to a different office or an entirely different workplace altogether.

Cleopatra and Open Options

Without a doubt, one of the most important rules of history—and life—is that everything is changing all the time. Life is an ongoing state of flux, something like the middle of a chess game. There is no beginning and no end, just an endless middle game in which you maneuver yourself into better and better positions in the office, in politics and the community. Thus, it makes sense, that the best possible position to take is one that is flexible.

Great leaders in history are well aware that while having a plan is good, being flexible and allowing the circumstances to present opportunities is better. This is particularly true when generals fight in unfamiliar terrain. Often the difference between winning and losing is how well the natural environment is played. Cleopatra knew this.

Today, with the women's movement in full force, many of the great female figures in history are finally getting their due. While

Elizabeth I, Harriet Tubman, Catherine de Medici, Susan B. Anthony, Emma Goldman and Margaret Sanger have always stood out, Cleopatra has traditionally been relegated to the position of a second-rate ruler who relied more on male hormones than her own brains for success. But the Egyptian queen is an icon of determination. She fought hard for herself and her country until her last breath.

One of the greatest gifts technology has given us is the ability to retire. Retirement as we know it is a late 20th Century concept and a radically new one at that. Throughout the bulk of the history there were, economically speaking, only two classes: the working class and the leisure class. The working class worked because they had no choice. It was either work or starve. There were no such things as IRAs and 401(k)s. For centuries, money was in the form of metals that the strong carried on their persons and the weak buried in a secret place in the forest. Both men and women worked as long as they could and then counted on their children to care for them as they got older. Starvation of the old and infirm was common—if one made it to those years.

Then there was the leisure class, or what we call the "rich" today. The term *leisure* better describes the class because it implied that someone had an abundance of money. It also implied an abundance of time. The leisure class spent their days wasting time.

While being in the leisure class is a blessing in any era, in most ages there was an unexpected victim: women. In spite of the fact that history is replete with women of success, it was not until the latter half of the 19th Century that they came into their own. Prior to that, women were expected to be subservient spouses, good mothers and acquiescing partners.

But not all women were wall flowers. Cleopatra was born, quite literally, at the center of a vortex. In 69 BCE, the world was being swallowed by Rome. The golden days of Egypt were behind her and it appeared that nothing could stop her from becoming a Roman province. Egyptian military strength was on the wane while the Roman's was on the rise.

Cleopatra's father died when she was 18 and left her the reins of power—in spite of the fact that she had two older sisters. Her sisters were beheaded and, to consolidate her rule, she married her younger brother, Ptolemy XIII. But the marriage was rocky and Cleopatra soon dropped his name from official documents and had her portrait placed on Egyptian coins. Her brother, however, wasn't going to take things lying down. In 48 BCE he staged a coup that toppled Cleopatra from the throne. She fled to Alexandria and remained at large for the remainder of her brother's rule. But that didn't take long. Ptolemy made one huge mistake—he ordered the execution of his guardian, a Roman-appointed official. Four days later, Julius Caesar landed in Alexandria with 3,200 men and Ptolemy tried to make up for his bad judgment.

But Ptolemy was too late. Cleopatra already had her claws in Caesar. How it happened is the topic of much debate. It is unknown whether she seduced Caesar or he saw in her the makings of a puppet ruler.

Realizing that he had been outmaneuvered, Ptolemy raised an army of 20,000 Egyptians who were subsequently clobbered by the Romans. Ptolemy drowned in an attempt to cross the Nile after the disaster. After Ptolemy drowned, Cleopatra quickly married her 11-year-old brother and reestablished her hold on the throne, even though she was pregnant with Caesar's child.

Cleopatra returned to Rome with Caesar, in spite of the fact that her presence shocked Romans. And for good reason—Caesar was living openly with a mistress who was a foreign queen. Cleopatra proclaimed herself to be the New Isis, an affront to Romans, and wild rumors surfaced that she was to be the next First Lady of Rome—regardless of the Roman law against bigamy and the marriage of Roman rulers to foreigners.

Cleopatra slowly realized that Caesar's rule in Rome was tenuous. He had many political enemies. And her arrival only inflamed their animosity to Caesar.

⌒⌒⌒

When Caesar was killed on March 15, 44 BCE by a group that included various Roman senators and the politicians Brutus and Cassius, Cleopatra feared for her life and fled to Alexandria with her infant son. To solidify her rule in Egypt, she had her younger brother killed, establishing her son as co-regent. Then she waited. Caesar's death had left a power vacuum in Rome and no one knew who was going to fill the void. And, after Brutus and Cassius had been killed, the power shifted to the triumvirate of Marc Antony, Octavian and Lepidus. There was a lot of tension among these three. Although Octavian was nominally the most powerful of the three leaders he was sickly, which placed him in a weakened position in Cleopatra's eyes. Marc Antony—the famed general of the Roman army—came to Egypt to negotiate a tax deal. This made Marc Antony Cleopatra's most likely ally.

Caesar had been a worldly-wise politician. Marc Antony was a plain—even vulgar—soldier. Cleopatra had used guile and intelligence to wrap Caesar around her little finger; with Marc Antony she used sex. In many ways, it was an ideal relationship. Antony needed Egypt's gold; Cleopatra needed the Roman army. Cleopatra eventually bore Marc Antony three children, which did not endear him to Octavian—since Octavian's sister was Antony's wife. Octavian was even more concerned with Cleopatra as she had born Caesar's son—a potential rival to Octavian.

By 31 BCE, Marc Antony had divorced his second wife and married Cleopatra, effectively splitting the Roman Empire in two, at least administratively. Some of the Roman army stayed loyal to Marc Antony—but most of the legions allied with Octavian.

It was only a matter of time before the armies of Octavian and Marc Antony clashed. The confrontation was a quick one and Marc Antony's side lost—famously, at the naval battle of Actium. He committed suicide by falling on his own sword. Cleopatra tried to salvage what was left of her empire by attempting to seduce Octavian. But he wanted nothing to do with her and said he intended to display her as a slave to show the Egyptians who their true masters were. Cleopatra was not about to suffer this humiliation and had an asp (Egyptian cobra) smuggled into her apartment hidden in a basket of figs. She died in August of 30 BCE.

Cleopatra is remembered more as a *femme fatale* than the political genius she actually was. She was fluent in nine languages, was competent in mathematics and was a superb businesswoman and strategist. She understood economics and what makes an empire prosper; today she would have been called an expert on economic development. She was also a shrewd judge of men. Her relationship with Caesar was one of intellect; with Antony it was one of lust and excess. She bore four children from two of the most important men in the ancient world and was the last gasp of the Egyptian empire.

Cleopatra was the ultimate realist. She saw the world as it really was and maneuvered her way around the pitfalls and potholes that lay between her and her goal. She was a political chameleon with the ability to change to achieve her goal. It is amazing that she succeeded as long as she did. What is even more impressive is that she did it all before the age of 39.

One of the most significant lessons that Cleopatra offers is that being successful is based more on your state of mind than your surroundings. Cleopatra lived in a duplicitous, violent world where beheadings and palace murders were common. She seduced the most powerful men of her age and kept Roman legions from ravaging her nation for two decades. She succeeded because of *who* she was, not because of *what* she was.

And she almost succeeded. After being defeated at Actium, Cleopatra planned to save what was left of her fleet in the Mediterranean by transporting it *over* land to the Red Sea. Using hundreds of laborers she had her ships dragged out of the sea and rolled 20 miles over land. Once the fleet reached the Red Sea, she planned to flee to India where she expected to set up a new empire. But this effort failed and her ships were burned by local Arabs who were loyal to Octavian.

What Cleopatra should be remembered for is that she used her wiles, brains and ingenuity to achieve what she couldn't with force of arms. Her brains, beauty and body were her armies. She didn't allow the forces of history to decide her fate; she chose to alter the course of history. Cleopatra, like all creative thinkers, didn't merely adjust her thinking to fit her environment. She changed the environment to support her thinking. She was a cunning opportunist.

If you're wise, you'll keep your options open for as long as possible. This doesn't mean you should delay making a decision or make a decision at the last moment because you are indecisive. Rather, it means that you should make a decision based on the facts you have but that you shouldn't implement the decision until you know for certain that there are no new facts that would adjust your decision.

Read history and learn from the masters of mistakes. Keep your options open. Listen to all sides of the issue whether you believe them or not. Setting your mind on a course of action is fine as long as you are correct. But you will never know if you are correct if you ignore protests from the opposition.

Clever leaders listen to their opponents. If you want to know what you weaknesses are, listen closely to your enemies, as President Ronald Reagan advised, and "keep 'em guessing." As long as you keep your options open, they will believe you can be swayed.

Finishing requires movement; not motion. Cleopatra, like all the other successful people in world history, knew what she wanted to achieve and then harnessed every opportunity that presented itself. In a word, she was always moving. That, in a single word, was the key to her success. If you are not moving, you are not achieving. At the end of the day, all that really matters is what you have achieved. That's your legacy.

Law of Flux

The single most important law of movement in this book—and, in fact, the core thesis of this work—is the Law of Flux. There have been generations of historical philosophers who have tried to extract meaning from history but by and large they have all based their theories on the concept that history is a pathway leading somewhere. Most of them attributed movement along that twisted pathway as being part of some divine plan, implying that the further mankind progressed, the more perfect mankind became.

This is a very idealized view of history. In reality, history is an ongoing saga propelled by a mix of currencies, half-baked ideas, economic pressures, legend-based social practices, individuals of all social classes wheeling and dealing for a sliver of a percentage of advantage and being poisoned by illegal enterprises, cons, scams and deceptions while, at the same time, being cleansed by clerics and faith healers. There will be no Armageddon because every vice is born anew with each generation. But so is every virtue.

Jesus Christ made Biblical history by throwing the moneychangers out of the temple. But with the next generation the moneychangers were back. Thus, a new saint was needed. Every generation has its saints and villains; it's just that they are not all recognized for their handiwork.

History, and the world in which we live, is always in a state of flux. Worse for the religious person, that flux is directionless. God may work in mysterious ways but history is the product of human beings who are irrational and unpredictable. Religion and ethics will contain the ambitions of 90 percent of all humans, but it is the remaining 10 percent that shape the world. These people don't follow any rules; they make their own. They sculpt their own destinies. If they have no morals, they'll trample compassion and common sense in the rush to fame and fortune.

The lesson here is that no matter how well you understand the rat race in which you live and work, one invention can make you obsolete. One flick of a switch in a country you could not have found on a map yesterday can obliterate an entire city. Space aliens could land on the White House lawn tomorrow or a nuclear device the size of a U-Haul could be parked a block away from the federal building in your hometown. There are no guarantees in life; and the key to understanding history is realizing that people you will never meet have more to do with your destiny then all the forces of economics, politics or religion.

This concept frightens some people because it leaves no place for God or the divine place of humans in the cosmos. Religion, however, is a spiritual experience that transcends human existence. It doesn't depend on history. It depends on faith that is a reward in itself. Humans change the course of history with their actions and the fact that civilization still exists is proof that brains, innovation, sacrifice, humility and ethics are more powerful than greed, avarice, sloth and addiction to power and money.

Even more important, religion is the thread that gives every cultural tapestry strength. It is the hidden superstructure that provides anchorage for all the fibers and threads of society. It is the net that keeps our destinies from flying off into oblivion.

Conclusion

In order to finish something, you must be moving all the time. In order to move, you must make decisions. But, as history has shown, base that decision carefully on what you believe to be the ultimate good. Making political decisions based on your business interests is stupid and, in many states, illegal. Making a business decision based on politics is just as stupid, though not illegal. Trying to make economics moral is ridiculous.

Every day you have to make decisions based on guesswork, knowing full well that there is no ultimate arbitrator of your actions here on earth. Sometimes you're successful; sometimes you're not. Perhaps there is some force beyond this veil of tears that will weigh your life in a celestial balance, but don't count on Him, Her or It to become involved in the day-to-day decisions you make about your family, job or future.

That's your responsibility. The more open you keep your options, the more successful you will be.

The Laws of
Non-Movement

3

When it comes to unintentional comedy, nothing is more entertaining than a college graduation. Students, three-quarters of whom have no more intrinsic knowledge than the day they entered college, dress up in gowns from the 15ᵗʰ Century and listen to a key note address from a celebrity who gives them advice on how to advance their lives in the bold new frontier that lies before them. It's all very quaint. For 90 percent of the students in the crowd, the speech is useless. The last thing this 90 percent wants to do is leave the security of a college campus and venture into the real world. And, many of them don't. They go on to graduate schools.

This is not meant to belittle academics. The public and private sectors are not much better. Any office can be a hellhole, complete with its bullies, rumormongers, incompetent supervisors, corrupt legal beagles and other assorted dregs of humanity. Whether you work in the public or private sector, at a university or nonprofit, office politics are pretty much the same.

All of these organizations have something else in common. Every department, organization, office and workplace has its own internal speed.

One of the draws of the university environment to graduates is that they are familiar with its speed. They've already spent four years learning how to survive in the university system and leaving all this to go into the real world means learning a new internal speed the hard way: day by day.

Eventually, after the graduate enters the work force and learns the internal speed of the organization that pays his paycheck, the last thing he wants to do is change the pace of the rat race. He'll enjoy the "same old, same old" until he retires, 30 or 40 years down the road, and collects the pension dangled before him every day like a carrot before a mule.

When it comes to change in general, most people are virtually unanimous in their support of the gradational. If there has to be change, most people want it slow, methodical and highly predictable. This is key to understanding history. While 10 percent of any population— the talented tenth—are the people on the cutting edge of change, the remaining 90 percent will always be happy to see change only come in small doses and in such a predictable manner that it is easy to prepare for. This is like saying that you love to play baseball as long as the ball always travels v-e-r-y s-l-o-w-l-y.

Because the majority of the human population is only interested in gradational movement (if any at all), some rules of history are quite visible.

Since the only change the bulk of the population wants is gradational, they will make just about any sacrifice to slow down any kind progress. Stopping it altogether would be the best solution, but that's not entirely possible. It isn't that these people are opposed to progress, it's just that they are familiar with the speed of their surroundings. Change is painful and tosses chance into the mix. If you've put 18 years into a job, you don't want a major crisis to occur in the last 14 months that threatens your pension.

Worse, allowing the inertia of things as they are to draw you forward means that you are not in charge. It means you no longer have a grasp on things. Instead, you are just "going with the flow" as the '60s expression went. Going with the flow is not a disreputable action if all you want to do is survive until can you retire and collect a pension. This is known as *gradational thinking* and it is very dangerous.

The Dangers of Gradational Thinking

There are two problems with letting loose the reins of your destiny. First, you'll be unprepared for cataclysmic change. Consider, for example, a political party dominated by the extreme right wing of the party. Since the party is controled by the extreme right wing, everyone who is in a leadership position, right down to the local precinct level, will represent the extreme right wing. That's what controling the party is all about. So, the party is controled by the extreme right wing, the party does short and long-term planning as a unit, in this case, as an extreme right winger. That's the standard. Any proposal that is moderate will be met with derision.

Politely stated, if everyone in a group has a similar mindset, it is termed *group think*. Colloquially it is known as an *echo chamber*, among other terms. In more polite society it is now referred to as "a mutual admiration society." It's also called stroking. A good example of this effect is a group of Republicans talking about what a great job the party is doing. Since everyone in the conversation has a stake in the Republican Party at that moment, no one is going to call their bluff— even if someone should. The best way to find out how the Republicans are doing is to ask the Democrats and take that with a grain of salt.

Group think can chase out the diversity of opinion that makes a political party (or any institution) strong. If the extreme right-wingers dominate a political party to such an extent that no dissent were allowed, the number of disaffected party members would grow. If you are a liberal or moderate and you cannot find a voice in your party, you may not become a member of the opposition—but you may sit on the outside of your party and simmer. This will make the extreme right wingers happy because those pesky moderates and liberals won't be bothering anyone with issues like abortion, homosexual rights and elimination of the death penalty.

But, as more and more liberals and moderates leave the party, the party grows smaller in number and more radical in politics. As far as those on the inside are concerned, things are getting better and better and they can make long-term plans based on the apparent stability of the party. No one is complaining so those on the inside assume all is well. The only change party members on the inside can see is gradational, as in "what are we going to do in the next election."

But, all is not well. It is, actually, very wrong. Those liberals and moderates on the outside of the party structure are counting noses. They know that their party is in a transitional mode and that no political party in the United States can survive very long if it represents an extremely conservative or an extremely liberal point of view. Most voters don't like extremists of either ilk. Eventually, there will be enough liberals and moderates sitting outside of the party who are angry enough to do something—like flood the local party caucuses with votes. Those on the outside are just waiting until the party upsets enough people that a cataclysmic change occurs.

No person or group of people can control a political party forever. The only question is how the change will come: as a cataclysmic takeover, or a slow, methodical transfer of power until all interested parties have their corresponding say. The change will not stop until the Rule of the Big Tent is reaffirmed as the standard for the party.

Gradational thinking tends to corrupt any institution. This may seem counter-intuitive—but it makes sense. If you work in an office where everyone is just trying to make it through to retirement, very little of substance will get done. Since every decision has a 50 percent chance of being wrong, no one wants to make a decision. So, very few people are willing to take a chance that the decision they make will be correct.

But if it's the only game in town, so to speak, someone *has* to make a decision. Consider Japan, Inc., for example.

Japan, Inc.

Japan, Inc., for those born after 1980, is the generic term that was used to describe the 30 year-period (from the mid-1960s to the middle of the 1990s) during which Japan made money hand-over-fist, building up a big trade surplus, while the U.S. economy was mostly in the doldrums.

What was the Japanese secret? The country's political leaders believed they could defy market forces. The Japanese government invested heavily in Japanese industry, giving large loans at low rates and did everything possible to thwart foreign competition. As a result, Japanese companies did well. So well, in fact, that the growing corruption in the national government was overlooked in favor of keeping the money-making juggernaut rolling forward.

Whether you are operating a mom-and-pop bed-and-breakfast or managing a multinational multi-billion dollar corporation, there are two words that are guaranteed to cause more sleepless nights than an IRS audit. Those two words are "cash flow." You have to have it; there is no substitute. Cash is the lifeblood of any business and it has to be moving. And, usually it is; most often out of your ledger.

In spite of the fact that local, state and federal politicians tell you otherwise, governments are the same. Unless they have money to spend, they have economies that are dead in the water on a calm lake with no wind. If that was the sum of the difficulties, having a government that was broke would not be too bad. It would mean that the private sector would take up the slack and the economy might actually be better off because it was run by the real-world dictates of the Law of Supply and Demand. But governments are different because they can generate money using blue smoke and mirrors. They borrow it, billions of it, with little or no intention of ever paying it back.

The reason governments can borrow money—and borrow money so easily—is that they have a captive debt-paying guarantee: the electorate. Politicians today can borrow against the voters of tomorrow. It's easy because the voters of today have little understanding of how economics works and the voters of tomorrow have not been born yet.

A good example of how a government can borrow itself into and out of (and into again) trouble is the U.S. Presidency of Ronald Reagan.

Most Americans remember those eight years as ones of strong economic growth. But that economic growth was financed with government borrowing. And Japan, Inc. was doing a lot of the lending.

During his Presidential campaign, Reagan proposed to cut taxes, which would increase tax revenues. This was such a dubious notion that even the man who became his Vice President, George Bush, Sr., called the notion "voodoo economics." Once elected, Reagan went even farther. He began practicing what he called "supply side economics." Basically stated, *supply side economics* is the belief that if you have a lot of things to sell, the price of those things will go down, consumers will buy more things because they are inexpensive and that will generate economic prosperity. All of this is true. But the rub, as Shakespeare would have said, was in the initial generation of things. Somehow, you have to get that infusion of cash to start the chain of events.

Reagan's philosophy was to borrow the money and pour it into military spending. The logic was that as the military spent more money it would subcontract to private sector firms who would provide orders to smaller firms who would employ more people and subcontract down the economic food chain. This trickle down effect would then generate more tax revenue to pay off the initial investment.

While it is true that the supply side economics worked, it was at a staggering cost. The budget cuts plunged the United States into a massive budget deficit that took two tax increases and a "peace dividend" to correct. (The "peace dividend" was the money the United States did *not* have to spend to defend Europe after the USSR collapsed.)

The big winner of Reaganomics was the Japanese economy. To generate cash flow, Reagan went to the Japanese and borrowed billions. The Japanese were happy to lend the money because they knew they would be paid back and that the cash would be added to the billions they were already getting from the American consumers who were buying their cars, lawn mowers and electronics. Hard currency was flowing out of the United States and directly into Japanese bank accounts.

So much cash was flowing into Japanese bank accounts that they appeared more as a financial supernova than a trading partner. The value of the American dollar took a beating on the world market to the extent that there was serious talk in the financial community about replacing the American dollar as the international medium of exchange for the yen. The Japanese increased their economic dominance by investing in the United States and joint venturing with American companies. At the same time, the Japanese made it very hard for foreign goods to be sold in Japan.

Japan was a juggernaut that seemed unstoppable. Everyone was making money.

There were also a number of other reasons Japan was in a unique position to take advantage of America's economic weakness.

First, and probably most important, the Japanese government took an active role in participating in the private sector. The Japanese government provided business loans at well below market rate and thus was a partner in the blessings of the companies' balance sheets.

Second, Japan had a locked-in market. The Japanese consumer had to buy Japanese products because foreign products were kept off the market. And, because foreign products were kept off the Japanese market, this drove the price of local products up. Some Japanese products, like rice, were as much as ten times more expensive in Japan than on the world market.

Third, though the Japanese government was large in terms of people, it was small in terms of who made decisions. Loans were given quickly and with little regard to the consequences. In the United States, by comparison, so many power brokers have to be consulted that often it appears that Washington, D.C. is a swamp.

Another point: For an economic power, Japan spends very little on defense and its military. Its constitution, written after Japan's adventurism during World War II, strictly limits military spending. To some observers, Japan, Inc. was paying for military power by proxy in making all those loans to the U.S.

The predominant theme in Japanese politics during the good years was built on *no change*. Japan was making billions of dollars so any change would be bad. That meant keeping the same politicians in power. But that also opened the door to massive corruption. More and more money flowed into the pockets of businessmen and their political allies rather than their businesses.

All of that money had to go somewhere (other than loans to the U.S.). So, it went into real estate. Property values skyrocketed. The cost of living went up dramatically as did corporate salaries and benefits. Profits that should have been funneled back into plants and increased wages for the workers went to increasing senior level corporate benefits and perks. Corruption and cronyism flourished.

Inflation Makes More Trouble than Godzilla

By the end of the 1990s, Japan, Inc. had major financial problems. Then the economic rot erupted into full view. Japanese businesses suffered and, because the government was so closely tied to the economic fate of its businesses, it took a fiscal hit as well.

Inflation hit hard and as more Japanese businesses faced tough times, they laid off workers and unemployment in Japan was seen for the first time since the World War II. Land values were so high that it was not cost effective to build a plant in Japan so much of the work was sent overseas. Just as NAFTA drained jobs out of the United States, so did exporting Japanese plants overseas decrease the number of jobs at home for the Japanese. Thus, the downward spiral began. As more people lost their jobs, the demand for the government to "do something" led to investigations and the entire house of political corruption came tumbling down.

The mid-1990s saw a burst of the Japanese real estate bubble that was still crippling that country's economy 10 years later.

Of course, there were other factors in the downturn of the Japanese market as well. One of the largest was the rise of China as a competitor. China, through the use of very cheap (and sometimes slave) labor, has been able to flood the world market with cheap goods that had reasonable quality. The American consumer, always on the lookout for a bargain, has been able to find these goods through large discount stores like WalMart, Costco, RiteAid and others.

Technological advances during the 1990s—particularly related to communications and the Internet—allowed high cost labor markets to customize and improve products. Japanese firms were relatively slow to incorporate the Internet with the factory floor.

The array of products and the growth of the Internet has also increased, allowing small businesses a better shot at the national and world market. Even better, as far as the consumer is concerned, technology has created both a demand and supply for innovative products. Slicers, knives, exercise equipment and cooking appliances that were on infomercials last month are in WalMart and Costco today.

The most important lesson that Japan, Inc. has taught us is that there is no shortcut to fortune. Not even the best centrally-planned economy (which Japan was in the 1980s and early 1990s) can build in 10 years institutional wealth that lasts 100 years. Slow but solid economic growth based on classical economic principles means a better chance for long-term success. Consumers will always be fickle, there is always someone, somewhere who can produce a decent product faster and cheaper.

Japan, Inc. fell into a national malaise of gradational thinking. Political and governmental corruption was brushed aside as an unpleasant but necessary by-product of a booming economy that eventually lead to Japan's downfall.

〜🍃

The consistent problem with gradational thinking is that it is easy to fall into a mental rut. And, because every day appears to be the same, many people fail to understand that cataclysmic change is inevitable and one had best prepare for it. If you prepare for the future, you'll have a variety of options at your disposal.

How exactly can you prepare for change? If you work for the Georgia Department of Public Works, you can also sell real estate on the side—or build custom-made wood furniture, or create interactive Web pages. Survivors prepare for a disaster that may never come. Losers devote their entire working lives to the Georgia Department of Public Works and do nothing else. If they're laid off, retired or downsized, they have no back-up, no Plan B. Now disaster looms. They didn't expect to be unemployed; but now they are. They didn't learn any other skills; and now they need them. They didn't want to be on the street competing with younger men and women for the same low paying jobs; now they are. The mistake they made? Not planning for disaster—not preparing for change.

Never in the history of the world has it been more critical to have a back-up plan. Next year won't be the same as this year. The combined factors of the growth of the Internet, downsizing of businesses, collapsing of world currencies, fluctuation in oil prices, instability of national governments, shrinking of the global community, terrorism and the staggering influence of the computer are bringing about cataclysmic changes every second of the day. No one knows how a week, month, year or even decade of these combined factors will impact our lives.

Bringing it to the Office

That's a lot of heavy talking but what exactly does this have to do with using history to see into the future? If you want a real life example, look at the organization where you work. Does your office suffer from gradational thinking? If it does, you could be headed for disaster. While your office may look productive, there may be a lot of motion and not a lot of movement. If that's the case, you might want to start looking for a new job. Think ahead. See what lies before you. Organizations that worship gradational movement are dangerous to any career, particularly if you're competent, creative or interested in any form of advancement.

Of course, seeing your office this way isn't always that easy. On a day-to-day basis, every office appears to be doing its job. If it weren't, the office probably would not be there—and you probably wouldn't be there, either. On the surface, every office *appears* to be productive. But as we all know, *appearances* are not the same as actually *being* productive. Over the long-run, productive people make their offices responsive to the mission and get promoted. If you are not in a productive office, don't count on moving up the occupational food chain.

Further, as far as the gradational thinker is concerned, every opportunity to reduce movement of any kind should be taken. If a director only has two years left until she retires, she is going to want to finish her tenure with as few headaches as possible. Just as historical laws are telltale reasons for why a competent person should look for another job, a gradational thinker would view each as yet another opportunity to slow movement. Historical laws are like double-edged swords: they inform a competent person of the political games being played, but they also give the gradational player another means of slowing any movement in his domain.

For you to use history as a nuts-and-bolts tool, you have to understand the basic rules of the game and anticipate moves by your opponent.

Law of Mediocrity

In days of the U.S. military draft, the most common advice given to inductees by their parents was something along these lines: *Don't stand out from the group and don't volunteer for anything.* This was sage advice for anyone entering the military; the military was an organization that prided itself on uniformity. The downside: Individualism was not encouraged. The upside: the military did a commendable job at resolving cultural problems like racism. (As far as the military is concerned, everyone is green.)

But there is a problem with being nothing more than a face in the crowd. To fit into the group, you must become one of many. You have to do what everyone else is doing—whether you think it's a good idea or not. There is no reward for standing out as an individual. In the military, you're punished for being different. And, it's only worse if you stand out from the crowd because you become a threat to the entire group. After all, it only takes one poorly trained member of the platoon to get the entire group wiped out in a battle zone.

Any organization without dynamic leadership will find its own internal speed determined by the required output. In other words, in a leaderless office, productivity will be determined by how much is expected by the next department in line. If your office packages computer parts, you would assume that the number of shipments a day you package would depend on the number of orders coming in. This is not the case. In reality, the department's speed of packaging is going to be set by the lowest possible standard—a standard that "everyone" can meet. If the division head is a lackluster individual who has the personality of a log and makes no demands for speed, the packaging division will slow its output until the next department up the line—the shipping department—starts to complain.

Consider the reign of British Monarch King George III during the late 1700s, immediately preceding the American Revolution. Though he mended his ways later, George spent most of his reign as the epitome of a clumsy, inept king. He ruled for six decades, but inexperienced, self-centered, narrow-minded men dominated his first governments and their advice produced five different prime ministers in the first 10 years of his reign. Ministers and other high officials were shuffled so frequently that the government lacked even the appearance of stability.

To make matters worse, only males who owned a certain amount of property could vote, which meant that the middle classes and farmers (the bulk of the British population) were voiceless—not to mention the women and the poor. The only voices that spoke for the middle class and the farmers were the squires, small landowners who were subservient to the large landholders. But the squires were hardly likely to beat the drum for the poor and voteless. There was no advantage in standing against the lords. These were the days when positions, incomes and benefices were passed out through connections at court. It wasn't *what* you knew, it was *whom* you knew. And no one wanted to give handouts to troublemakers.

Since there was nothing to gain and everything to lose by siding with the middle class and against the landed aristocracy, few did. Parliament treated Americans, who were primarily middle class, the same way they treated the English middle class: they ignored them. The king was insulated from the middle class and had no conception of how or if his policies worked. The landowning aristocracy wasn't going to tell him the error of his ways, first because most of them could not see the error, and, second, even if they understood the roots of the uproar in the New World, it didn't serve their best interests— or pocket books—to let colonials vote when the middle class at home didn't have that luxury. And, the squires were not much help either; they were interested in their own 600 acres and not a gaggle of rabble-rousers overseas.

As there was no incentive to be bold and resolve the problem of the New World, few British policymakers stepped forward. Minister after minister bungled the diplomatic ballet with the 13 colonies until the colonies were lost forever. Even after the colonies had achieved independence, the governments of George III continued to blunder long enough to lose a *second* war in America in 1812.

Internal Pace

There is an internal pace in any office at which tasks are accomplished. In a dynamic, highly-efficient office, everyone is juggling staff, projects and budgets to meet deadlines. If, on the other hand, the office is dominated by someone who is not interested in fortune or promotion, the internal speed will wind down until just finishing a project—forget about the budget and deadline—is a major achievement. If you want to advance in your company, look for the dynamic office headed up by a competent commissioner or vice president because they won't shy away from change when it comes time to promotion and appointment.

However, you can't always assume that because you see a lot of motion and no movement in an office that nothing is happening. Sometimes this is the plan. Using history like a tool, many people know that a large part of their job—regardless of where they work— is to stop bad ideas. And what better way to stop a bad idea than to assign it to a department where nothing will become of it? These departments, known as "dumping grounds" or "ice boxes," are another way to dump a project being run by incompetents or to freeze a bad idea until all the kinks are worked out.

But how can you tell if your department is a *dumping ground* or an *ice box?* Simple, use your common sense. Ask yourself the following: *Is the project being assigned consistent with your office mission? Was the project assigned by someone outside of your usual chain of command? Was the project specifically assigned to someone whom you know to be incompetent? Or competent? Are the budget and time sufficient to complete the project?* And most important, *to whom is the project to be presented after it has been completed?* Being in an ice box is not necessarily a bad thing; working in a dumping ground means your promotion is in doubt.

England and Socialized Medicine

Pain. Disease. Suffering. They are all a part of life. Not a good part, but an inevitable consequence of living. Often, dying doesn't frighten people as much as the agony of a debilitating disease like cancer or Alzheimer's that brings pain with agonizing regularity.

Even worse than the deterioration of your body is the effect the disease has on your financial situation. Medical expenses are costly and with the advance of technology resulting in increased longevity, the problem has gotten worse. One catastrophic disease can leave a family bankrupt. For decades, presidents and congresses have tried to solve the problem of rising health care costs with little to no avail. If a program is not stalled by politics, it is stymied by a lack of efficiency or the rapidly increasing cost of drugs or medical procedures.

In the 20th Century, the most radical attempt at solving the health care crisis and an excellent historical example of "brain drain"—and from whence the term came—occurred in 1948 when England established its National Health Service. Ideally, a program designed to provide every person in England, old and young, rich and poor, healthy and crippled, with the same basic health care. You could buy better health care if you wanted to, but there was a floor beneath which no one could drop. The idea, steeped in British tradition, was that everyone would have a safety net. By establishing universal health care, everyone in England was entitled to medical care even if they could not afford to pay for it. It was a great social experiment but significantly limited doctors' incomes. And as a result, many English doctors left England for the United States where there was no restriction on how much they could earn.

Those doctors who left for the United States were the most competent because they had the reputation and ability to establish a practice in a foreign land. The less talented doctors remained in the United Kingdom. This subsequent "brain drain" was a blessing to the United States. It was also a corresponding nightmare for England as the country watched helplessly as its best doctors and its highest income-producing citizens left for greener pastures.

The results of England's socialized medicine experiment were disastrous. First, there was the expense. Socialized medical programs are often doomed to failure because they violate the economic reality that brought about insurance in the first place. Insurance has always been a personal hedge against adversity.

~~

During the Renaissance a shipping company—owned by a collection of individuals—bought insurance to cover losses in case a ship never came home. The insurance companies gambled that the ships *would* come home. The merchants wanted insurance for any losses accrued if a ship *didn't* come home. It was a marriage made at the bank because both merchants and insurers won. Enough ships went down that merchants needed insurance and enough ships made it home in good shape so the insurance companies made money.

Over the centuries this symbiotic relationship prospered because the insurance companies could only insure those ships for which the chance of return was good. And, in order to obtain insurance, merchants had to keep improving their ships to make them insurable. The health of the industry depended upon both parties and the relationship still stands today. Insurance works because insurance companies pick and choose who they will ensure. In order to obtain insurance, you have to meet the insurance company's minimum standards.

But the self-regulating economic system of insured/insurers collapses if the insurance companies are forced to cover bad risks. This tosses the bad risks in with the good. And then it's not so much a matter of gambling when an accident will occur; it's just a matter of waiting for the inevitable disaster. That is exactly what happened in England. There was a reason unhealthy Brits didn't have insurance— they didn't take care of themselves. By forcing the healthy Brits into the same pool as unhealthy Brits, the insurance companies were forced to take walloping losses. So they decided to raise premiums, which the British government paid. But the British government represents the people of Britain, so the costs were passed on to the taxpayer. When the taxpayers realized how expensive socialized medicine was going to be, they demanded a reduction in service to save money. This meant doctors had to be paid less.

What the British did not realize was that economics is a self-correcting system. Passing a law that makes something illegal, like gambling, doesn't necessarily stop gambling. And, forcing a doctor to take lower wages for the same services, doesn't mean that doctor will remain satisfied with less.

Health Care Is Hard to Manage Everywhere

Socialized medicine continues to be the bane of the First and Second World. President after president, prime minister after prime minister and nation after nation have wrestled with the problem and no one has come up with a reasonable, economically sound solution. Nevertheless, the issue of affordable health care remains a ticking time bomb. In the United States, for example, there are more than 40 million Americans who have no health insurance—nearly one-quarter of them being children.

Why is the issue pressing? If you don't have insurance then you don't get medical care, right? So, what's the problem? Actually, that's not correct. By law, a hospital can't turn away a patient. Patients without health insurance show up at hospital emergency rooms all the time—and are treated for their ailments. Then they walk out of the hospital and never pay their bills, leaving the expense to be absorbed by the hospital and ultimately the American taxpayers. This situation is particularly convoluted in large cities, such as Miami, where many of the indigents using the hospitals are not even American citizens. In Miami, women from Central and South America facing a difficult childbirth arrive at Miami International Airport, take a cab to the hospital, give birth with state-of-the-art doctors and equipment and then walk out of the hospital without paying a dime.

This would not be so bad if that was the end of the story. But it isn't. The hospital still has to show a profit so it is forced to raise its rates to cover its losses. That makes it more expensive for the insurance companies, so the insurance company raises its rates, which raises rates for insureds.

In the 2000s, a growing number of insured Americans are in their 50s or older. They signed into the health care system when they first started working and have excellent health benefits. But, they're not as healthy as their younger, paying counterparts, so they pass most of their costs on to the younger generations.

As the population of the United States expands and baby boomers get older, the problem of health care grows more onerous. The blessings of technology won't do any good if no one can afford them. What has made American health care the best in the world has been the amount of money that could be spent on the industry. But every time insurance rates go up and coverage declines, there are fewer dollars available in the industry, which affects quality of service. Doctors, nurses and other medical professionals are not immune from this rise in costs, either. Currently, there are some areas of the country where medical liability insurance rates are so high that doctors cannot afford to work, forcing them to move or commute to communities where insurance rates are more reasonable.

Uneconomic Plans Can't Be Forced into Success

The most important lesson socialized medicine has taught us is that it only works if it has an economic basis. Forcing an uneconomic solution onto a social problem will only breed disaster. Economics is far more powerful than politics and politicians would be well-advised to solve an economic problem with an economic solution no matter how distasteful they may find that resolution.

More importantly, no one can dictate economic realities. The best you can do is recognize this and ride the wave in the direction it is going. A business should only expect a longevity that makes its product or service to the market demand. R&D is a company's edge on expanding that longevity but not a guarantee for survival. The best advice for longevity is to understand the economic currents and ride them as long as they will carry you.

Suppose, for example, that you work for your state's Department of Community Affairs. Everyone who is politically active—and there is no substitute for rapid career advancement—knows that immediately following an election, it's a waiting game to see who will get what post. The election is a struggle for power and control of the reigns—and destiny—of the state and party. The careers of everyone below director level ultimately will depend on who is in charge of their division.

If the commissioner of your department is a dolt, then the message is clear: the new governor considers this department to be a throwaway. The governor gave the post to a political hack because she had no choice. It's also a very clear indication that the Department of Community Affairs is going to be a dumping ground. When the governor has to pay a political debt and considers the person incompetent, that person gets dumped into your department.

It won't take long for people working in the Department of Community Affairs to get the message. If they know anything about history, they'll see the writing on the wall and take their skills elsewhere. That's because they can see what's going to happen. An idiot commissioner will appoint other idiots to the critical directorship posts for all the divisions. Idiots attract idiots and any other political patronage there is will go to substandard employees, which means there'll be no advancement for competent people. Idiots, by and large, don't want intelligent people working for them—it'll make them look bad.

Thus begins the brain drain. Quality people leave on their own accord or get shifted sideways into jobs remote from the center of power. And, when more competent people are hired to replace the ones that left, it won't take them long to realize that the Department is in a downward spiral. They'll start looking for employment elsewhere, leaving the bulk of the work to the mediocre bureaucrats. Mediocre people means mediocre results.

❧

America is blessed because its political system allows for...practically calls for...constant upheaval. And, whether you are in the public or private sector, you can be assured that every crisis will bring new personnel. A new governor is elected and along with him or her come new commissioners, directors and special assistants. When a business is sold, personnel is shuffled. Over the long term, for a business to survive and move forward it must have new employees in mid-management, R&D, and upper management. When a company is sold, the new owners will bring in new people.

Innovation forces some companies to change. A small engineering firm that receives most of its work from a large oil company may be told that all future bids would have to be submitted electronically to the home office. This means the engineering firm will no longer deal with a "person" they know; they must now submit bids to a giant computer in Dallas that weighs their proposal on the basis of a mathematical formula. This means the engineering firm has to learn how to submit a proposal that will meet the standards of the home office—immediately.

America is a capitalist country and cataclysmic change is part of the business cycle. Thus, shuffling of personnel is a fact of life, and one of the reasons capitalism remains vibrant.

However, other countries are not so fortunate. In a small country, such as Iraq before the American invasion or Kuwait, where there is a ruling family, a crisis usually doesn't change any of the internal structures. If a cousin of the dictator of Smallgeria, for example, is in charge of building up the waterfront and a pier collapses because his cronies don't know what they are doing, no one is fired. Everyone keeps his job and the pier is rebuilt, which is fine with the cousin and his cronies. The more expensive the project, the greater their share of the booty. But, if you are mid-level management in the pier building department, you had better keep your mouth shut about why the dock collapsed—even if you see the same mistakes being made again and again. Why? Your job depends on doing it the way your boss wants it done—regardless of whether it's the right way or wrong. His job depends on doing the design and construction the way a crony of the dictator's cousin wants it done. Everyone takes his or her cue from the administrative layer immediately above them. Ultimately, the person in absolute control is the one who sets the tone for the entire organization.

Using a Brain Drain

To use the brain drain to your advantage, look at the corporate food chain at your office. If the head of your department is brain dead, don't expect to get promoted because of your competence. And don't expect your good ideas to go anywhere either. If you see people whom you consider intelligent leaving, you might want to think about leaving as well—you might be in a losing battle.

Perhaps most importantly, your ultimate success will depend on how well you can use history like a tool to manage your future. One of the easiest ways to get a glimpse of the future is to become politically active. Regardless of whether you choose to participate as a Democrat, Republican, Independent or whatever other party that interests you, what occurs in your state capitol will affect your job more than any other factor. State legislatures tweak the economy in ways that affect the private sector significantly and immediately.

State legislators confirm the thought and views of the people who respond to their point of view—men and women who can block your advancement in state service if you do not think the way they do. If you want to use history to manage your future, stay current on politics and realize that entrenched gradational thinkers use the brain drain to remove workers who threaten the internal speed of their organization. Creative thinkers and energetic employees need not apply. And if they're already there and reasonably bright, they'll leave. No one has to urge them to move on; they just do. If they don't get the message they'll lose their chance for promotion or be buried under a mountain of meaningless paperwork. People do not stay where they're not wanted; competent people move on to greener and more productive pastures.

Law of the Quick Fix

What if you work for the federal government where national political changes don't affect the food chain or you work in such a large department of a large company that you really don't feel political winds? First, that's not possible. You'll never work in an office that isn't affected by politics, local or national, or where you cannot feel the impact of office politics.

But suppose you are a recent transplant, not only to the job but to your state as well. How can you quickly piece together whether the department you are working for is destined for greatness or doom? One way: understand the Law of the Quick Fix. An example of the "quick fix" was the maritime rush for Klondike gold fields in 1898. If there is any one word that means "instant wealth" in every language on earth, that one word is "gold." Ever since man decided that gold—even with its multiplicity of uses—could be used as money, there has been an unending quest to find it rather than earn, steal or inherit it. After all, if you could find gold, it was free money. And to think of the things you could do or buy without having to work for your dollars, pesos, dinars, Liras, pounds, talents, Francs or Euros!

Gold rushes are nothing new; they just grow larger with each passing century. That's because the world's population goes up with each passing century and there are a certain percentage of people in every population that are addicted to the belief that there is a certain amount of "free money" just over the horizon.

Oddly enough, technology has very little to do with the generation of a gold rush. That will come later. First, there is a flood of humanity into the gold country. But as soon as 90 percent of the gold seekers discover that finding gold is not as easy as just picking it up off the ground, the tide reverses itself and there is a massive movement back to civilization. Only then does technology catch up with opportunity. The individuals who profit the most from gold rushes are those who form companies and use the technology of the era to reap the mineral harvest. This usually takes investment capital and, in the end, the big money in the gold fields will be made by corporations, not individuals.

❧

The infamous Klondike Strike began as did all other gold rushes. Some lucky sap made a large strike and then made the mistake of telling someone else who told someone else who told a newspaper, etc., and pretty soon everyone in the world knew. What made the Klondike Strike such a draw was that it occurred during a prolonged economic depression. And because thousands of Americans were jobless, the lure of the Yukon attracted many people who had nothing to lose by packing up and heading north.

While the original strike that made the Klondike a household name was made in midsummer of 1896, it took almost a year before news leaked to the rest of the United States. Then, in July of 1897, the news reached the lower 45 states in a most dramatic fashion: almost two tons of gold arrived in Seattle and a bonafide rush was ignited.

Seattle streets teemed with would-be millionaires seeking passage north on the first available vessel. Across the United States, thousands of men, and more than a few women, left their jobs without so much as a day's notice, grabbed a suitcase and headed for Seattle, the gateway to the Klondike.

From the four corners of the earth, the *argonauts*—the term coined from the legendary *argonauts* of Jason's quest for the golden fleece in the Greek epic—converged on Seattle, Portland, San Francisco and Vancouver with a single thought in mind: passage north. All that mattered was getting to the gold fields as fast as possible. Each day's delay was a fortune lost, a day in which someone else would claim *your* Eldorado. The gold went to those who got to the Klondike first while the latecomers were still sitting on a dock waiting for their ships to be loaded.

But getting to the Klondike was a bit more difficult than just getting to a port on the Pacific Northwest coast and catching a ship north. The fastest—and most expensive—route to the Klondike was by steamship across the North Pacific to Unalaska and then across the Bering Sea to St. Michael. From there, passengers boarded a river steamship and plowed their way against the current up the 1,600 miles of the Yukon River to Dawson.

But not everyone could afford the fastest route for this 3,000-mile trip, so they improvised. The most popular route was by steamship from Seattle or Portland to the twin cities at the top of the Lynn Canal in Alaska—Dyea and Skagway. From here, the argonauts would crest the Chilkoot or White passes into Canada's Yukon Territory and then move on foot up the watershed to Dawson. This route was cheaper in terms of sea fare but far more challenging to the human spirit, not to mention legs. But it was cheaper. While steamship to Dawson cost over a $1,000 (over $21,000 in 2003) the trip to Skagway was less than $200 (a mere $4,200 in 2003).

Those with even less money used whatever means they could afford. Some came by foot while others tried bicycles and canoes. At least one *argonaut* claimed he could use a balloon. On April 8, 1899, the *Seattle Times* ran a story of a woman who was intent on reaching Skagway in a catboat. According to the article, she intended to buy the fragile craft in Seattle and find another woman to row with her. The boat would carry 100 pounds of provisions. Upon arrival in Skagway, she and her co-rower would sell the boat and proceed on to Dawson on foot. The woman's name, ironically, was "Carrie R. Hope."

Other means of transportation were just as unusual. One of them, called an "Alaskan What-Is-It" was illustrated in the *Seattle Times* in April of 1898. Appearing as a cross between a "flying machine and a brick-clay mixer," it was 40 feet in length with a steering wheel in the bow and a paddle wheel astern. It was a "corker," the *Seattle Times* reported, and "worth the price of a photograph." Also considered for travel to or in Alaska were reindeer, camels and even 10,000 Mexican burros. Quite a few men walked and photographs of the Chilkoot Pass show the crush of humanity shoulder-to-shoulder, hiking up the ice staircase into Canada.

But the madness didn't last long. From start to finish, the Klondike Strike lasted about 16 months. Centered on the Klondike River near Dawson in Canada's Yukon Territory, the population drained as fast as it came. Most returned home empty-handed but many went on to participate in the Alaska Gold Rush with its major strikes in Nome and Fairbanks. While it is estimated that as many as 100,000 *argonauts* headed north, only about three or four percent of that number actually found any gold. For the rest, it was an adventure.

Why the Klondike Strike Struck

There are a number of reasons that the Klondike Strike drew so much attention. First, and probably most important, the strike was so short and so much gold was found that the term "Klondike" and "gold" became synonymous. Second, also because the strike was so short, most of the newspapers from the strike still exist—along with the memories of many of the *argonauts*. Third, the stories of author Jack London best known for his novel *Call of the Wild*—who participated in the rush—and the poems of Robert Service—who got to Dawson four years after the strike was over—have allowed the incandescence of the Klondike Strike to be renewed with each generation of readers. The Alaska Gold Rush, on the other hand, which started in 1880 and ended with the second World War, is largely forgotten.

"Klondike Fever" set the world ablaze and so many people got the gold bug that any ship in the Seattle or Portland harbors was a floating gold mine—excuse the pun. There was so much money to be made in such a short period that disreputable companies pulled derelict ships off beaches and out of salvage yards to be refitted for the Klondike rush. With a few new timbers, a fresh coat of paint and silver-tongued devil to sell tickets, these ships set to sea packed to the gunnels with stampeders and tons of their cargo. Many of them never made shore again, some turning turtle in the turbulent North Pacific and others being ground to splinters on the rugged shoal of Alaska's Inside Passage.

No one knows how many thousands of lives were lost by these fly-by-night steamship operators. Rather than take the time to outfit a good ship that would make many trips, many companies went for the "quick fix." Three years later, the only steamship companies still in operation were those who had provided a quality service from the beginning.

In every office there will come a time when a decision must be made. Usually the choice is between doing something the correct way—which will take time, energy and effort—or doing something the quick and easy way. The quickie may solve the problem immediately and cheaply, but in an inferior manner.

Suppose that you work for a large engineering firm and you have to get a proposal out to an architectural firm to design a $35 million elementary school. With less than a week to go, while putting the finishing touches on your proposal, you discover that it is unreadable.

First, it's so technical that only another engineer can read it. Second, the grammar is correct but disjointed. Third, many of the graphs are so complicated that they lose significance. And fourth, the glossary is worthless because of the complexity of the subject matter.

But you still have to turn your section of the proposal over to your architecture joint-venture partners in a week.

You have two choices. You could take the entire report to a technical writer and have him smooth it out, without losing any of the technical expertise, reconfigure the graphs and make the glossary usable. But that'll cost you—and good technical writers are not cheap. Or, your office can burn the midnight oil, clean up the report as best they can in the time available, insert a killer Executive Summary, and then turn the proposal over to the joint-venture partner.

In most cases, the company will do the latter. This is a quick fix. But now the problem is compounded. Engineering studies are not expected to be read by nonengineers so complexity is acceptable. The architectural joint-venture partner isn't going to be looking at the proposal that carefully anyway. He's only interested in the Executive Summary, and really, who uses a glossary anyway, right? So your section goes in with a perfunctory glance.

Slow Effect of the Quick Fix

Historically speaking, going for the quick fix is like taking a slow-acting poison pill. You can get away with it once or twice, but in the long-run it'll kill your firm dead. Why? Consider the above example. First, more and more nonengineers are reading those reports. In some states, proposals for schools are being read by a committee from the community, not engineers. Today, a proposal could be read by a teacher, member of the PTA, representatives from significant minority groups in the area, members of the school board, employees of the school district's facility and planning division, as well as some members at large from the community. It is quite possible that the entire committee many not have one engineer—yet they are going to read an engineering report. If the committee can't read the report, they can't understand the report. If they can't understand the report, they can't distinguish the merits of your proposal over that of another firm.

If you work for a firm, department or office that operates on the quick fix principle, you are at best living on borrowed time. The selection committees are not going to read reports they cannot understand and architectural firms will not joint venture with engineering firms who submit proposals that are destined to fail. No one is going to tell you that your company's work is inadequate. The architectural firm will put your firm on its only-if-we-really-need-them list. If you get on enough of those lists around town, your company will go out of business.

Seasoned gradational thinkers will use the Law of the Quick Fix to their advantage by deflecting the blame for any failure. Just as someone can be set up to fail, a far more insidious political tactic is to set someone else up to fail. For example, an office manager will give a subordinate an impossible task. Rather than admit that the task is impossible and fail immediately, the subordinate will do the best she can and save the day by getting the project out on time. But getting the project out on time is not the same as completing a quality project. Efficiency is not necessarily quality. When blame does come, it will be heaped on the woman who got the project out—not her boss. Thus, she will be punished for performing well under pressure. If she's competent, she'd be smart to look for a new place of employment.

The Klondike Strike carries one other important message. It implies that there will be many "golden" opportunities and the best way to take full advantage of those opportunities is to finish what you start. While not all of the people who rushed north found gold, those who actually got into the river had better luck than those who hung around the saloons and listened to the sourdoughs. Remember: If you aren't willing to take a chance and work hard for the opportunities that present themselves, you can't get anywhere.

Law of Bureaucratic Excellence

The flip side of the Law of the Quick Fix, is the Law of Bureaucratic Excellence. While a quick fix means getting something finished quickly and cheaply but with low quality, the Law of Bureaucratic Excellence means not finishing at all because the product is not perfect. As a result, an office is doomed to re-work a product or project to death because it does not meet some unspecified standard.

A good example of this paralysis of perfection would be the French military just before the second World War. At the end of World War I, the French decided it was time to create the ultimate weapon against the Germans. After all, the Germans had invaded France twice in the past 40 years and had taken Paris once. So, following the war the French built a huge cement wall along the 200 miles of her border with Germany. Named the Maginot Line after its creator, André Maginot—the French Minister of War at the time—the wall was meant to make a frontal invasion by Germany impossible. The key word here being "meant."

One of the murkiest questions facing historians is what brought about the great explosion of culture around the year 10,000 BCE. Prior to that, according to Darwinians, ape man was more ape than man. Then, quite literally overnight in geologic time, they were more man than ape. It was a miraculous conversion, setting a vertical walking biped on the pathway to the moon with Copernicus, Shakespeare, Adolph Hitler and Mahatma Gandhi in between.

The transition to humanoid was much more than simply biological or mental. It was also social. Apes and humans are both social beasts that require intra-species communication and bonding. No man is an island; neither is a caveman. As the groupings were formed, its members began to think as a unit. The "we" mentality led each group of humanoids to consider themselves unique. To maintain that uniqueness, certain rules had to be followed to ensure that the "we" did not become part of "them."

The best way to do this is to protect yourself, your extended family and their progeny. And whether this means living in a cave with a blazing fire to keep out the saber-toothed tigers or in a castle with its drawbridge raised, the goal is the same: keep harm away from the living unit.

The problem, however, is that being safe is as much a matter of being intelligent as frightened. Too much fright and humans develop what is known as "siege mentality," the state of mind where more protection is better and quality is secondary to quantity. *Siege mentality* is more than just inferior thinking; it's the refusal to consider the possibility that there is a more efficient path of choice. Worse, it is seductive because it lures someone into believing that old problems are not affected by the passage of time. As a result, someone with siege mentality attempts to solve a problem that no longer exists with a solution that never could have solved the problem in the first place.

André Maginot and the Maginot Line

By the end of the first World War, France and Germany had not been close allies since Charlemagne was crowned Holy Roman emperor in 800. And since then, the relationship had only deteriorated. In the 19th Century, France was defeated by the Germans in the War of 1870, which unified Germany. In that war, France lost the regions of Alsace and Lorraine. A generation later, in 1914, the Germans advanced close enough to Paris to send artillery into the city. Paris was saved by a mosquito fleet of taxis that drove the French army— four men at a time—from one side of the city to the other to stand off the Germans.

Convinced that Germany was a long-term threat, the French built a wall (the Maginot Line) between themselves and Germany. The wall, which sank 10 to 15 feet below the surface of the ground, rose to as high as 30 feet and was as thick as 15 feet in some places. There were about 50 underground strongholds with miles of railway tunnels, artesian wells and 75 mm guns that were cemented into the wall facing east, toward Germany. The wall was impregnable from an advancing attack—or so it seemed.

As far as the French high command was concerned, the wall was the perfect fortress. It could not be breached from the front, was completely defensible from the rear, had water and provisions within its bowels for an extended military campaign and had artillery large enough to destroy a tank with a single shell.

Secure in the belief that the wall would protect France from any German invasion, the French military concentrated on making the support of that wall perfect. The French military, suffering from the Law of Bureaucratic Excellence, failed to see the world as it really was. And, there was one other problem: the French hadn't brushed up on their own history. Specifically, at the start of World War I, the Germans had not invaded France directly across the border. Instead, German forces swept north through Belgium and then took France on her flank. The French were surprised by this move because Belgium had declared its neutrality—a move that the French had surmised would keep Germany from invading Belgium. That was a mistake. In the opening days of World War I German forces moved quickly through Belgium. When it was pointed out that Belgium was a neutral country, the Chancellor of Germany Theobald von Bethmann Hollweg dismissed Belgium neutrality as "a scrap of paper."

Believing that the Germans would honor Belgium neutrality better in the future than they had in the past, the Maginot Line was built with a political anchor at each end: Swiss neutrality on one end and Belgium neutrality on the other. And, when the invasion of France came in 1940, the Germans invaded using the same route they had in World War I: through Belgium. Effectively sweeping around the end of the Maginot Line, Germans divisions took France from behind the wall—without even firing a shot—making it worthless. The French had spent their time trying to make something excellent that never should have been constructed in the first place.

The importance of the Maginot Line disaster is not that it fell but that it was even built in the first place. Airplanes were making distance irrelevant by the end of the World War I and locomotives were transporting larger loads faster than half a century earlier. Invading German armies had come through Belgium on their last foray and there was no reason to believe that they would not do so again. But the French high command was wedded to the belief that a siege wall would defend France from Germany. History indicated that Germany would invade through Belgium, which it did, and thus the Maginot Line was a massive expenditure to solve a problem that didn't exit.

Dangers of Siege Mentality

Siege mentality is the brick wall we build between our ears. It is a mental condition that seduces us into a false sense of security. The danger of having siege mentality, particularly in the new millennium, is that time is no longer an asset. In the Middle Ages, an army holed up in a castle with enough rations could wait out the invader. Today, a technological lead can evaporate over lunch, a new product can have a competitor on the market in a matter of days and multimillion-dollar software can become obsolete in a matter of seconds. Siege mentality was once the key to survival; today it's the pathway to disaster.

Anyone can fall victim to the Law of Bureaucratic Excellence. This usually occurs when a department head feels that the pinnacle of perfection is his point of view and all work produced must meet his high standards. Since this is impossible, nothing is accomplished or it's accomplished so late that it's useless.

The good news is that the Law of Bureaucratic Excellence is easy to spot. If at your first interview for a job, an employer says something like, "We have very high standards here," or, "We strive for excellence," so far so good. These two expressions are meaningless because no one will admit they have low standards or that they don't strive for excellence. But, it's the next line that's the real killer. If that line includes the word "I," you should know you are in trouble. Usually it's a line like, "I take personal charge of every project to see that it meets my standards," or, "I take an active role in every project," or, "I maintain active control of the project from start to finish." If you hear any of these, you could very well be interviewing for a position in an office where perfection is more important than timeliness.

Law of Bureaucratic Excellence is a powerful ally for gradational thinkers. If your boss has a problem she cannot solve—or does not want to solve—she'll study it to death and she'll assign committee after committee, consultant after consultant and expert after expert to write report after report on it. Or, she'll just keep sending the report back to the authors for rewrites. The only limit will be how much money she wants to spend to kill the idea. If she hires enough consultants, simply by the law of averages she will find one who will write a report that supports her point of view. Your choice is simple: do it her way or find another job. If you do it her way, don't expect anything to change with the next assignment.

Institutional Stupidity

The Law of Institutional Stupidity is a more difficult law to recognize because you must be an insider and attuned with the mission of your office in order to recognize its presence. Consider, for example, the command of General Douglas MacArthur in Korea. Even though front line troops reported the capture of Chinese prisoners in early November of 1950, General MacArthur thought that China would never enter the Korean War against United Nations troops.

It was probably the riskiest naval operation in world history— with every possible factor working against the invaders. The approach to the harbor was a narrow channel, barely 30 yards wide, and so shallow that only small vessels could make the approach. The tides varied by 30 feet every 12 hours and the landing beach was mud—in addition to a sea wall and minefields. To avoid fighting the tides, the invasion had to take place during the afternoon with the small ships leaving the safety of the fleet at 15:30 and hitting the beaches at 17:30, two hours in the gun sights of the enemy.

It was such a risky operation that the Pentagon was against the operation. The only one man in favor of it: General Douglas MacArthur.

Though the invasion of Inchon during the Korean War was a spectacular victory in its day, today Inchon is largely forgotten. But on September 15, 1950, 70,000 United Nations soldiers in LST (land ship tank) from World War II hit the beaches at Inchon and took the North Koreans completely by surprise. In one bold move, General Douglas MacArthur divided the North Koreans in half.

In American history, there are two forgotten wars. One was the invasion of the Japanese into Alaska during World War II. In spite of the fact that one of the bloodiest battles of the Pacific Theater took place in Alaska, today the battle of Attu is merely a footnote in our history texts. The other: the Korean War, which lasted three years and one month and cost the United States 54,000 lives, about as many as the Vietnam War. (Korean and Chinese dead have been estimated at 550,000.)

Even more than the Vietnam War, the Korean War was a proxy for the real tension of the second half of the 20th Century—the Cold War between the United States and the Soviet Union

At the end of World War II, Korea was divided into two occupation zones. The dividing line was the 38th parallel with the USSR occupying the North and the United States maintaining control in the South. Two separate governments were established in 1948, the Republic of Korea (ROK) in the South and the People's Democratic Republic of Korea (PDRK) in the North.

But the division of Korea didn't last long. Relations between the two republics were not good and, on June 25, 1950, the North invaded the South and caught the United States and its NATO allies completely by surprise. North Koreans pushed south quickly, forcing a massive retreat of American and allied forces. Even as the United

Nations was condemning the invasion as an act of aggression, North Korean forces were moving so fast, many feared they couldn't be stopped. By September 10, 1950, the North Koreans had cornered all allied forces on the Pusan Peninsula at the southern most recess of South Korea. It looked as though there was nothing left for the NATO forces to do but withdraw.

But President Harry S. Truman had not been idle in those months. He was well aware that even though the troops in South Korea were technically United Nations troops, most of them were wearing American uniforms. If he did not act quickly and decisively, the entire war would be over before the United Nations stopped debating. Two days after the invasion began, he authorized the use of American land, air and sea forces and put MacArthur in charge of the theater of action.

There was no way to face the brunt of the North Korean advance. So MacArthur chose a risky tactic: to attack the enemy from behind. By landing at Inchon, MacArthur surmised that he would cut the North Korean army in two, sever the supply lines to the North Korean army in the South and open the floodgates for United Nations troops to enter central Korea. The idea was brilliant, daring and successful. As United Nations troops poured ashore, the North Korean army retreated, MacArthur's troops in hot pursuit.

As United Nations troops pressed the North Korean army backwards across the 38th parallel, they encountered a new enemy: the Red Chinese.

With American air power striking as far north as the Yalu River— the border between North Korea and China—the Chinese expressed concern about the approach of United Nations troops. These concerns were largely ignored by MacArthur who either did not believe the Chinese would enter the war or did not anticipate their entrance being a difficulty United Nations forces could not overcome. But, he erred on both accounts. On November 26, 1950, in a bitter winter, 100,000 Chinese suddenly hit United Nations front lines. There was a general rout and hundreds of men were taken prisoners as allied forces retreated backwards. Two months later, the North Koreans and Chinese forces had crossed the 38th parallel for the second time during the war. There the war stalled, neither side able to break resistance by the other.

$$\text{---}$$

A this point, MacArthur made his greatest blunder. Inchon had been so successful that he wanted to repeat the action. President Truman, however, wanted to negotiate a settlement with the North Koreans. And when it became clear that Truman's view was going to prevail, MacArthur began publicly criticizing the President's policy. This was a bad move on his part—eventually Truman fired him.

The fighting in Korea, called the "meat grinder" war, continued throughout the presidential election of 1952. Republican Dwight D. Eisenhower, a retired general, pledged an end to the war. And, shortly after his election, on July 27, 1953, an armistice was signed that simply stopped the fighting. Fifty years later, American troops remained in Korea—as did America's commitment to the South Koreans.

Why did Douglas MacArthur—in so many cases a brilliant tactical general—make such a critical mistake about the Chinese entry into the Korean War? He was tripped up by institutional stupidity, a kind of conventional wisdom that can snare even the sharpest individual mind.

You can expect a certain amount of stupidity to creep into your work as well as the work of your co-workers, your boss and your department or division at work. Institutional stupidity is not a crime even though it should be. All organizations contain a certain amount of stupidity. This is particularly true with state and local government. Suppose you work for a public utilities commission and the commissioners are considering a rate hike for a municipal-owned telephone utility. No matter how unjustified the rate increase may be, the utility is going to get a rate increase. It may not be all it wants—and probably won't be—but it should be a foregone conclusion that some rate increase is going to be given. That's politics.

If you work for a competent commission, the word will filter down the food chain to take a careful look at the numbers the municipal telephone utility provided and then turn your findings over to the director. Then it will be his or her job to deal with the commission. Staff will crunch the numbers and hand the results to the director—then come the political winds. But it isn't the staff's job to weather the squall. That's the director's job—and the commissioners'. They're paid to weather the storm.

You must be constantly aware of the political winds even though they do not fill your sails. Why? If you're working for a marginally competent director, she won't be able to "read the writing on the wall." No commissioner *tells* the director what to do. The director has to figure it out for herself. A good director catches on quickly and, somehow, magically, staff recommendations written by the director seem to support commissioner's positions.

An incompetent director, on the other hand, is clueless. If she's lost, she'll blunder badly, maybe by presenting staff recommendations that do not reflect what the commissioner requests. This can create major internal problems. Since the director doesn't know what is expected of her, the commissioners will go to the Assistant Director and make him the power behind the throne. If that doesn't work— and it rarely does—the commissioners will go directly to the specific staff members who crunched the numbers and, as legally as possible, demand that these staff members jigger the numbers. Once the commissioners have resorted to bypassing the top of the staff's food chain, institutional stupidity sets in. Suddenly there is no filtering mechanism to keep staff safe from political winds. Accounts are juggled for political purposes and dangerously close to the edge of the law. No one is in command and everyone is in a crossfire.

To avoid institutional stupidity and the snares it makes, keep a vigilant eye for the danger signs in your office. Gradational thinkers think there's nothing better than an office in turmoil. In fact, the more turmoil the better. As long as energy that would have been spent doing something productive is being expended in a vicious round of backbiting and office politics, nothing gets done. Like a seasoned streetfighter, the gradational thinker is a veteran of office politics. This is a field he knows well, a function at which he excels. Thus, in a choice between taking a chance on a new policy or engaging in a donnybrook to stop the new policy, the gradational thinker prefers to stay on familiar ground. Office politics never change; just the faces do.

You can use institutional stupidity to your advantage in this situation. First, examine the situation carefully. Forget office politics and look at the big picture. Office politics change from day to day; but the big picture remains unchanged for decades. If a municipal-owned utility wants to increase its rates, it's going to happen. Don't stand in the way of progress. Recognize that fact early. You don't have to adjust your numbers to support the rate increase, but leave yourself sufficient wiggle room. Like a good general, always leave yourself an avenue of retreat.

Law of Committees

The best known of the laws of non-movement is the Law of Committees. Simply stated, this law says that the best way to slow progress on any issue is to establish a committee to study the problem. If the boss doesn't like the recommendation of the committee, she'll set up another and another and so on. Given enough time, there will be no progress on the matter at all.

The Law of Committees is extremely important to the gradational thinker because it appears that the problem is being tackled. If you work for a municipal parking authority and there is a lack of parking downtown, the downtown merchants are going to be inside your shirt about finding more spaces. You can't create a parking garage overnight and probably don't have enough buses to run a shuttle service even if there is an underused parking garage halfway across town. But, while you wait for legislative funding to build the parking garage, you can assemble a committee to study the problem—and appear to take control of the problem. You can hold hearings to discuss closing off the downtown streets to foot traffic only, rapid transit grants and changing traffic patterns to speed shuttle service to the core area. The whole time you're holding hearings and making public comments on how the hearings are "giving everyone in the community a chance to have their say" and "these hearings are democracy in action," you are pushing as hard as you can for parking garage funding from the state legislature and federal government. No one can say you are not doing *something*, because you are. But what you're really doing is stalling for time.

Use this law of committees to your advantage. If the idea being studied is a bowser, make sure the committee hearings are long and complicated. As a public servant, as in the case above, your job is to stop bad ideas as much as it is to promote good ones. In the long-run, it's better to waste a lot of time and a little bit of money to let an idea suffer death by committee than sink a lot of money into a project that will never succeed.

Law of Co-Equal Adversaries

If you only need to stall for a little bit of time, say no longer than a year, the Law of Committees is the best way to go. But if you have a problem that is going to be an ongoing headache for years, then you can expect to see the Law of Co-Equal Adversaries applied. This is the use of two committees to counteract each other, each working to slow down the progress of the other.

Consider, for example, the destiny of forests on public land in the U.S. Since this timber belongs to everyone in the U.S.—lumber choppers as well as tree huggers—what policy should the federal government follow? Should every tree in the United States be logged? Should some be saved? If trees are cut, which ones should be cut and when will harvest occur? If not, which acres will be turned into national parks?

When the United States government wanted a balanced policy on timber harvest, two, co-equal agencies to oversee the fate of the forests were established. Keeping this complex matter as simple as possible, the government established the United States Forest Service, which is responsible for timber sales and the National Park Service, which is responsible for saving stands of timber for posterity. Acre by acre across the country these two agencies fight each other to increase the stands of timber within their jurisdiction. Sometimes the Forest Service wins and the trees are cut. Other times the Park Service wins and the trees are saved. Thus, to this day, these two bureaucracies fight each other tooth and nail, each one winning about equally. This ongoing conflict is designed to make certain that neither side wins every battle and, over the long-run, both the lumber industry and the environmental movement receive a share of a public resource.

It's important to distinguish between a momentary problem and one that will be around for decades. When you see a long-term problem looming in your future, carefully dissect the conflict. Then see if you can develop two reasonably functional reasons to divide responsibility to resolve the problem. Carefully suggest them and then keep your mouth shut. Nature will take care of the rest. Once an apparently reasonable solution has been suggested, everyone will tweak it to his or her own satisfaction. Turf warfare will set in. When the dust clears, you will find that the Law of Co-Equal Adversaries has established two competing responsibilities.

Why should you keep your mouth shut after you've made the initial suggestion? The shrewd office politician knows that the solution is important, not who claims credit for it. If you take a good idea and toss it onto the table, it becomes everyone's to twist and turn. You'll get credit for the initial concept but none of the blame if it fails. But the minute you become an advocate for any point of view *after* the initial concept has been placed on the table, you could very well become a casualty of the turf war.

Ongoing Options Retreat

If there is any governmental body that has made non-movement an art form, it's the legislative branch of government. Congress and the state legislatures, who are empowered to write laws, are masters at writing documents that leave loopholes large enough to stuff pork barrels through. When it comes to the law, nothing is as it seems and when you read the fine print, how the law is enforced depends on how the words are interpreted. Original intent has little to do with final product.

Legislators, however, should not be condemned for leaving those loopholes. Over the centuries their predecessors have learned that even the best ideas sometimes lead to a blizzard of bureaucratic red tape and quite a few unintended consequences. What starts out as a good idea can end as a three-alarm fire that consumes careers and reputations as it roars through the treasury. To save themselves embarrassment—and to ensure re-election—legislators give themselves as much wiggle room as possible when it comes to assigning responsibility. They do this, collectively and individually, by giving themselves an avenue of escape just in case it's needed. In other words, a law that seems like a good idea will be constructed in such a way that there are at least four safety valves. These four valves are as follows.

The first safety valve is intent. Legislators, like bureaucrats, are well aware that every decision they make has a 50 percent chance of inaccuracy. But unlike a bureaucrat, a legislator only has two choices on each bill: He can either vote yes or no. There is no "maybe." If there is even a shred of evidence that a good idea will go bad, legislative committees will water down the intent of the language.

Suppose a bill is being considered to fund sex education classes in junior high schools. On one hand, this is a necessary move because AIDS and teenage pregnancy are major health problems in America and sexual activity in American teens is starting at younger and younger ages every year. The bill could help prevent unwanted pregnancies before their hormones begin to dictate behavior.

If you happen to be a liberal, this is a reasonable expenditure of state funds. On the other hand, there is a large—and vocal—conservative element in America that is not interested in sex education at all. These individuals feel that sex education of any kind is the responsibility of the family unit or church and that teaching this subject in any guise is an intrusion of the state upon the rights of others. Further, there is the fear that once the door to sex education is open, other matters will be discussed that are not within the established scope of the class—such as homosexuality, deviate sexual practices, child pornography, interracial marriages and abortion.

But sexual problems are so pressing that something has to be done, so the legislature will do what is called the "all American weasel," and come up with legislation to solve the problem that satisfies no one.

Roe vs. Wade

Roe vs. Wade, the landmark 1973 Supreme Court ruling on abortion and privacy rights, is a good example of the "all American weasel."

Abortion is the most debated issue of the era. No argument is hotter, more divisive and more complicated in terms of both ethics and semantics. The issue breeds civil disobedience, as well as felonious violation of the law on both sides of the issue. It has been—and will continue to be—a litmus test issue for every candidate for any public office even if the office has nothing to do with abortion.

It would be easy to say that the root of the problem is the Bible but that would be inaccurate. Even if the Bible had condoned abortion there still would be a pro-life group because of the underlining philosophy that human life—born and unborn—is sacred. It would also be incorrect to state that the heartbeat of the pro-life movement, excuse the pun, is the Evangelical Christians and thus this is a right-wing Christian issue. The reality is that the pro-life movement and the pro-choice movement find converts across the political, religious and cultural spectrum.

The ethical pillar most used to support the pro-life point of view is the Biblical commandment "Thou shalt not kill," which is the Sixth Commandment if you are Protestant or Jewish and the Fifth if you are a Catholic. However, the actual word *kill* is a translation error. The actual word in the ancient scripture is ratzach, which means murder. This clearly opens a very large can of worms because the implications are that there are moral killings. Killing a combatant in a war, for instance, is not murder, clearly sanctioned by God because so many Biblical personalities were warriors. Killing civilians was also sanctioned by the Lord. When Samson brought down the temple of the Philistines, many of those inside were women and children. Other Biblical battles, like Jericho, have God's chosen people putting everyone to the sword—combatants and children alike.

Much of the argument over abortion is over semantics. While pro-lifers are against abortion, it is a gross mistake to assume that pro-choicers are on the proverbial "other side of the table." Pro-choicers are not in favor of abortion; they are in favor of a woman's right to choose whether she wants an abortion or not. Many pro-choicers are not in favor of abortion, they just want to preserve the right to make that critical decision for themselves. More accurately, the pro-choice position is summed up in the succinct phrase, "My body; my choice." Thus, calling all pro-choicers murderers is great theater but basically inaccurate.

No matter how the hairs are split and which words are used, abortion was and is an explosive issue. It has been a hot button issue since the early days of Christianity. It has been an explosive issue that was brought to the front of American cultural discussion in the early 1900s when Margaret Sanger and Emma Goldman publicly advocated a woman's right to reproductive choice. It exploded into national attention in the 1960s when Sheri Finkbine, a national television star on the popular children's program "Romper Room" discovered that her fetus was probably deformed because she had taken thalidomide during her pregnancy. So well known that she could not do what women who wanted abortions often did—find an illegal abortionist, Finkbine flew to Sweden for the operation. Her decision touched off the national debate that culminated with the Supreme Court ruling known as *Roe v. Wade* on January 22, 1973, when the Court ruled that the U.S. Constitution guarantees women the legal right to choose abortion, although subject to certain vaguely-defined restrictions.

But the Supreme Court ruling did nothing more than make what was being done illegally, legal. Setting the explosive moral/political issue of whether abortion should be legal in any form, *Roe v. Wade* created a watershed of issues. While abortion is legal in the first trimester, how accurately can any doctor predict on what second that trimester ends? Should public funds be used for abortion? Do females under the age of 18 need parental consent for an abortion? Do mentally retarded people have the right to an abortion? Is taking a birth control pill tantamount to abortion and, if so, should 14-year-olds take birth control pills? Is taking an abortion-inducing pill illegal if you don't know what trimester you're in?

There is no amiable resolution to the abortion question because none is possible. The best advice is to learn to recognize issues for which there is no resolution and avoid them. There can be no political solution to a moral issue, the primary reason a separation of church and state has been a standard in Western philosophy since Jesus advised his disciples to "Give to Caesar what is Caesar's and to God What is God's." Moral issues make no friends but generate enemies, the reason politicians stay away from controversial issues.

You should be quick to recognize arguments that hinge on semantic interpretation. The same words have different meaning for different people. Getting involved in a matter of dialectic hairsplitting is only advisable if you want to confuse the issue to stall for time. This is only a good idea if you want to stall for a short time because a definitive answer is coming. But, be advised, that in the long run, moral arguments have no resolution. When in doubt, be silent—once you're in the moral swamp you will never come out.

This federal mandate for abortion is a compromise that no one likes but with which everyone lives. Prochoicers feel it is too stringent; prolifers feel it is against God's will. But it is the law of the land, and like it or not, that's what the courts uphold. The legislature will water down the intent of the bill so it's not exactly what liberals wanted and doesn't upset too many conservatives.

Content

Once the intent of the bill has been established, the actual content or words have to be put to paper. In this case, the devil is certainly in the details. Legislative committees will work hard on the language to ensure that there are enough loopholes and weak paragraphs so that no one can come back pointing the finger, saying that the "legislature rammed this down our throat." For example, there may be a loophole limiting funding only to those schools where the local PTA and the school board agree to implement the sex ed class. Or, where there will be matching funds from the community. This wordplay gives the legislature—and the community—an honorable out, and a way of killing the intent of the bill without making anyone look bad. (An "honorable out" ensures that no one looks stupid. It's a time-honored tactic for people that know they'll see their opponent again. For centuries, wars in Europe inevitably led to other wars and with each war everyone's allies changed. A good diplomat ensures that every peace treaty is reasonable and fair because the next war might put the nation and the country on the other side of the table and on the same side of No Man's Land.)

Playing games with the wording of a bill gives the legislature another safety valve. If the sexual education concept is a complete bust, legislators can point to the wording and say, "we gave every community a chance to express its will. We didn't cause this disaster; the community did."

This kind of politics has led to semantic hairsplitting. Consider the following question: How many presidents of the United States have killed a man? This question is actually a lot more complicated than it seems. The question itself is a rat's nest of assumptions. First, there is the question of what we mean as "presidents." The traditional assumption is that the question involves only those presidents under the United States Constitution. But there were presidents beginning with the Articles of Confederation.

The first president of the United States was not George Washington—it was John Hanson. He was elected unanimously—including a vote cast by George Washington in 1781. Seven other presidents followed him, including: Elias Boudinot (1783); Thomas Mifflin (1784); Richard Henry Lee (1785); Nathan Gorman (1786); Arthur St. Clair (1787); and Cyrus Griffin (1788). There have also been three presidents who were not presidents of a united, United States—Abraham Lincoln, Andrew Johnson and Ulysses S. Grant—and one man who served as president for a day—David Rice Atchison who served on Sunday, March 4, 1849. That was the last day of the term of James K. Polk and the inaugural of the next president, Zachery Taylor. Taylor was a staunch Christian who refused to be sworn in on the Sabbath so the inaugural was set for Monday. But someone had to take on the role of president that Sunday as Polk and his Vice President were out of office. The Constitution stipulates that in the absence of a president or vice president, the president pro-tempore of the Senate is next in line of succession. Thus, Atchison was the main man for a day.

Teeth

To make absolutely certain that they have a grip on the outcome of the bill, the legislature dulls the bill's teeth. In other words, saying that you will support a bill is one thing; enforcing its contents is something else entirely. Just because the legislature passes a bill doesn't mean that anything will happen. Legislatures only make laws; they do not enforce them. Enforcement is the job of the executive branch of government. Your state legislature can pass a law that says anyone arrested with marijuana will be sentenced to 10 years in jail, but if your governor eliminates the funding for the measure or instructs the state troopers not to arrest anyone for marijuana possession, the law is worthless. This is why legislators work hand-in-hand with the governor. It's not that they like each other. They *need* each other. The governor *needs* the legal authority to act. The legislators *needs* the governor's assurance that the bills they pass will be enforced.

In a case like the sex education bill, clever legislators will ensure that enforcement is arbitrary. If the classes turn out to be a success, there is no problem. If the classes create controversy, the legislature wants to ensure there is a way to eliminate the problem without making themselves look bad. So, they cut a deal with the governor. If the classes fail, the governor will line item veto the funding for the classes in the next budget. No money; no classes. The legislature gets credit for being bold and passing the original bill; the governor gets credit for being bold and killing the program.

Backbone

The fourth safety valve is the backbone to continue the program. It's easy to get experimental funding to make an idea a reality. Legislators like new ideas and will trample over each other to be the one to proclaim that she has a better idea that *really was* a better idea. Getting the first $50,000 for an experimental fuel made from household garbage will be easy. Getting the next $50,000 a year later will be far more difficult. That's because the first year you don't have a record to run on. Funding for the second year will depend on how well you can sell the concept.

If the sex education class was a stunning success, there will be legislative money because everyone wants to support a winning project. But if there were any problems, no legislator will want his name associated with the disaster. The legislature may fund the "experiment" for a year to see what happens. But when it turns out that the good idea went bad, the legislators can neglect to re-fund the project. Thus, the fourth safety valve.

The biggest problem with the Law of Ongoing Options of Retreat is that too many people feel that the safety valves are more important than the content. Gradational thinkers leave themselves so many "outs"—and take them so frequently—that many ideas never have a chance to take hold. With many of America's problems long-term, a short-term swat will not even scratch the surface. Recycling the contents of our solid waste dumps is an admirable idea but it cannot be done with a one-year experimental program here and a two-year prototype there. Real problem solving takes time, effort and energy. Gradational thinkers lack the ability to give an innovative idea the time, effort and energy required to let it prove itself successful.

Legislators—like all politicians in office—are cautious. They want to keep their positions. But that doesn't mean they can't be motivated. Historically, the most powerful tool in dealing with a legislator is money. But this doesn't necessarily mean money in the legislator's pocket. Bribes, political contributions, donations, soft money assistance, etc., will only capture your legislator's attention for a moment— and a brief one at that. Money that will affect the legislature over the long-term, comes in the form of the long-term financial health of a community—and as close to the district of the legislator in question as possible.

To understand the true dynamics of the legislative process, keep in mind that the vast majority of voters have one overriding concern: employment. Support for all other issues pales by comparison. If the economy is good—and unemployment numbers are low—the current crop of legislators will most likely be re-elected. This is why economic issues are given so much more credence than moral ones. This is why almost every bill introduced has some financial angle. The limitation of the size of recreational cabins restricts the number of lodges. Weight restrictions on trucks mean more loads and thus higher wages for teamsters. Building a bridge allows more people to access local businesses faster and more conveniently.

When it comes to any bill, the paramount question in every legislator's mind is "What does this mean for my district?" All politics is local. It's easy to cut a budget if no one in the district is affected. It's a lot harder when 15 people in the district will lose their jobs.

Don't be mislead by the number 15. Those 15 people have spouses who will vote against the legislator in the next election. Now we're talking about 30 votes and if there are children in the household, the number could be up to 45. Toss in a handful of close friends and associates and the number rises to 100 or 150. That's a lot of votes in a district where only 3,000 votes are cast.

Negative factors are a far greater incentive to get votes than positive ones. That's why negative ads work so well. The voting public has the attitude that while there are good legislators, it's the 90 percent of bad politicians who give the other 10 percent a bad name. Pointing out something negative about a politician simply confirms what the voters assume to be true. With those 150 disgruntled voters going around and bad mouthing the incumbent, writing letters to the editor or buying small ads in the newspaper, that number could well blossom into defeat.

To use the forces of history in your favor, remember that politicians respond to local economic pressures. The closer you can tie an economic impact in your community to a bill in the legislature, the better the chance the bill will pass. Bills concerning morality don't get much attention because the same people keep pushing them. Once a politician upsets the Christian Right, she's not going to get their votes—ever. But that's only one-third of the voting population and it's a stable number. It won't change. She probably didn't have their votes in the last election anyway so it is no big loss.

What is important is the other two-thirds of the voters. As long as the economy is stable, she'll probably be re-elected. Staying in the good graces of these two-thirds means responding to their economic needs. She has to keep the money flowing. This means a healthy private sector.

Contrary to what you may have learned in your civics class, dealing effectively with a legislator does not mean pointing out the strong points of a bill. But it doesn't mean pointing out the weaknesses, either. It means linking the bill with economic conditions in the district. Sending a telegram to a legislator that says "I support HB 345 and I vote" is a waste of your time. A more effective telegram would be "HB 345 means 15 jobs and $500,000 in wages lost IN YOUR DISTRICT." (The $500,000 was derived from multiplying the 15 jobs by $35,000 apiece.)

Any politician worth his salt is going to immediately multiply that $500,000 by four. That's the number of times dollars turn over in a community. His district isn't going to just lose $500,000 in cash, it's going to lose $2 million in buying power. That's a lot of money to take out a house district. Maybe even enough to tip his vote.

If you can't use a dollar figure in your argument, use a number that the legislator understands. An example of what *not* to do is to tell a Republican legislator that your teacher's union has 30 Republicans in her district. A Republican legislator doesn't care how many Republicans are in her district, she cares how many of those Republicans *actually voted* and *how often* they voted. A better approach would be to say—and you had better be able to back this up—that there are 30 Republicans in the district of whom 60 percent voted in three of the last five elections. Now you have something. The legislator can now visualize 18 solid votes—and then double that to include spouses and increase it by another 25 for voting age children that still live in the district. Fifty-one votes may not sound like much, but in many smaller states that's enough to tip an election. National elections, too. Look what happened to Al Gore in Florida in 2000. Remember, in a Democracy all you need to win is one vote. (See Appendix E for an example of how this works.)

Conclusion

A word of caution on non-movement: When it comes to drawing conclusions on the laws of non-movement, a wise person understands that non-movement is both an ally and an enemy. When you want change to occur and your department seems to be sitting on its collective hands, non-movement is a sin. But when you see a bad idea being pushed hard, using the laws of non-movement can be to your advantage. Perhaps the best illustration is summed up in the words of an unknown legislator who said that 90 percent of his job was stopping bad ideas. Here was an astute politician. He might never have sponsored a bill that changed a single life but he stopped a host of bad ideas from becoming stupid laws.

There are times when you will have to use the laws of non-movement to slow down or kill a bad idea. While you may not feel that this was your destiny, it is most certainly your responsibility. Forward movement comes when good ideas outrun bad ones. Just as you must strive to introduce good ideas into the workplace, you must also sabotage the bad ones; movement for good ideas, motion for bad ones. Once you have learned the laws of non-movement, you can play the game like an expert. Remember, life is not a game because a game has an end. Life is an ongoing battle between those who want to change the world for their own personal gain and those who believe in good public policy and ethical corporate policy.

4   Signs of Ossification

Countries, political parties, committees and organizations that are unable to stop a downward spiral eventually reach a point where a reversal becomes impossible. At this point, gradational thinking will have such a tenacious grip on the people involved that they no longer have long-term vision. All that matters is the short-term—what they *can* control. Quality people have left the fold and now there's no movement at all—they're just going through the motions.

An excellent example of this scenario is the Soviet Union after Soviet Premier Mikhail S. Gorbachev stepped down.

One of the most difficult things for a human to do—any human, alone or in a group—is to admit error. While making mistakes is human, there are not a lot of people who are willing to own up to those mistakes and admit that they have erred. Even when an error has been made, someone will always try to make it look as though it was not really a mistake at all.

Consider, the Preamble to the United States Constitution. It begins: "We the people of the United States, in order to form a more perfect union . . ." But there is no such thing as being "more perfect." Perfection is what it is—the best. It cannot be improved. If it could, it wouldn't be perfect. It's like getting an A⁺ on a report card—it's meaningless expression.

It was clear that the Founding Fathers—and just about everyone else in the 13 colonies—knew that the Articles of Confederation were an abysmal failure. But the new nation couldn't afford to admit that so the colonial spin doctors developed a clever way of saying that the United States Constitution was simply an "improvement" on the *perfection* of the Articles of Confederation. Double-talk it may have been but every day students are required to memorize the Preamble and all of the glittering generalities it contains.

If nothing else, the Founding Fathers should be honored for having the courage to admit that the Articles of Confederation didn't work. That's the first step to solving a problem. Just as an alcoholic must admit his addiction before he can be cured, a nation has to admit its shortcoming to set itself on the road to recovery. A good example of this is the Soviet Union before Gorbachev.

Socialism, as practiced by the Soviet Union, didn't work. In fact, it hadn't worked for a long time. The economic and social rot began in the 1950s and finally collapsed the structure in the 1990s. It is not surprising that the Soviet Union imploded; what is surprising is that it lasted as long as it did.

Then again, the slow reckoning probably shouldn't have been such a surprise. While Soviet leaders were lousy socialists, they were very good totalitarians. They simply ordered their people not to recognize their failures.

Gorbachev was the last man who could have saved the Soviet Union. His plan was very simple—and very capitalistic. He wanted to accomplish two things at the same time. First, he tried to attract Western capital into Russia under his policy of *Glasnost*, the loosening of governmental regulations regarding investments. Then, at the same time, he tried to jumpstart local economies by giving Russian entrepreneurs the green light to try business Western-style, *Perestroika*. Both were necessary for the survival of the Union of Soviet Socialist Republics. It was a very clever scheme.

Under *Glasnost*, Gorbachev would have attracted hard currency into the Soviet Union. Once this hard currency made it into the Soviet economy, it would, like money in the West, circulate. With more and more rubles circulating, more and more Russians would have been able to sell goods and services and make a profit "Western-style." *Perestroika* allowed Russians to take entrepreneurial risks, the basic building block of capitalism, with the blessing of the Soviet government.

Gorbachev realized that he was in the last days of his empire and tried to breathe life into socialism with the combined impact of *Glasnost* and *Perestroika*. But the reforms were too radical for the old guard socialist and communists at the highest levels of the Soviet government. Sensing that their end was near, many of these bureaucrats let fear make them more rigid and extreme. Gorbachev was removed from power and the world will never know if he would have been successful.

Instead of embracing reform, the Soviet Empire collapsed messily. Many republics reclaimed their independence and the urbane, professional Gorbachev was replaced with the charismatic but erratic Russian nationalist Boris Yeltsin. Yeltsin had little interest in a Soviet Empire saddled with bankrupt republics or experiments in socialism.

In the 21st Century, Russia is trying to rebuild itself out of the rubble of the collapsed Soviet Empire. Its success will depend on how well the Russian people understand the basics of what went wrong half a century earlier. It's the same lesson that every city, county, state and company must learn. The problem, however, is not that people don't know what to do; it's that they don't know how to go about dealing with the forces of chaos and the "old guard" that doesn't want to see its slice of the pie grow any smaller.

The bottom line for any government is, quite simply, the bottom line. If you don't have a healthy economy, you won't have a healthy political system. With a healthy economy, anything is possible. It also provides for political stability, the single most important attribute for investment.

Companies, large and small, foreign and domestic, are reluctant to invest time, money and credibility in a country that is politically unstable. The larger the company, the longer it needs to recoup its investment capital if it fails. A large mining or petroleum company, for example, will think of its investment in terms of decades.

In many cases, large companies act like the Soviet bureaucrats under Gorbachev when they're faced with radical change. They withdraw. They become rigid. They beat their dead horses.

In this chapter, we'll consider the tools people use that get in the way of movement. These are the tools the bad guys use to get in the way of change.

One of the better e-mail chain letters that circulated on the Internet in the early 2000s included a list of 21 ways to ride a dead horse. In the interest of passing along valuable insight from dead horse trainers...

What to Do When Your Horse Is Dead

1) Buy a stronger whip.

2) Change riders.

3) Say things like, "This is the way we have always ridden this horse."

4) Appoint a committee to study the horse.

5) Arrange to visit other sites to see how they ride dead horses.

6) Increase the standards to ride dead horses.

7) Appoint a team of tigers to revive the dead horse.

8) Create a training session to increase our riding ability.

9) Study the state of dead horses in today's environment.

10) Change the requirements declaring that, "This horse is not dead."

11) Hire contractors to ride the dead horse.

12) Harness several dead horses together for increased speed.

13) Declare that, "No horse is too dead to beat."

14) Provide additional funding to increase the horse's performance.

15) Do a Cost Analysis study to see if outside contractors can ride it more effectively.

16) Purchase a product to make dead horses run faster.

17) Declare the horse is "better, faster and cheaper" dead.

18) Form a quality circle to find uses for dead horses.

19) Revisit the performance requirements for horses.

20) Say this horse was procured with cost as an independent variable.

21) Promote the dead horse to a supervisory position.

While common sense would dictate that the best thing to do when you find yourself riding a dead horse is to get off, not many people are willing to do that. But then again, to paraphrase Abraham Lincoln, common sense isn't all that common.

Economics Are Built from the Bottom Up

A healthy economy is built from the bottom up, not the top down; with small businesses thriving and growing larger and larger, not large businesses supporting a host of dependant providers. Having a large company move into a depressed area increases the number of jobs in the area and creates a plethora of small and medium sized business to support that large company. But the economy is unstable.

It creates cities like Detroit, Seattle and Las Vegas that are overly-dependent on one industry. And if that one industry goes, the entire region suffers.

The derogatory term for this kind of an economic reality is "Banana Republic" and carries with it all the negative attributes of a one-source economy.

The term *Banana Republic* was coined in the early years of the last century and was meant to define the small Central American countries whose sole resource was bananas. Its economy was based on bananas. If the banana crop was good, everyone would eat that year. If bananas were not selling well on the American market, then everyone would suffer. Today the banana republic means an area that is overly depending on a single resource for economic survival.

The strength of the American economy is that the small business frontier continues to expand. Most innovation comes from small business with the larger corporations handling the nuts-and-bolts of nationwide and worldwide marketing, service, advertising, sales and collections. It's a symbiotic relationship that leads to economic stability.

Perhaps the greatest myth is that this model is somehow a unique American invention. It is not. Business is a system of ensuring the flow of goods and services in one direction and compensation in the other. But it only works if every seller has faith that he or she will be paid and that every sale will be honored with a valid check or that the product sold is the same quality as advertised. It's the government's job to encourage faith in the marketplace by enforcing basic standards of fairness.

But you cannot force economics to obey political whims. Economics is a force unto itself; to be a successful businessperson you have to ride the back of economic opportunity. To have a stable political system, you have to ride economic opportunity wherever it takes you.

The Soviet Union had every attribute necessary to become a major economic player on the world stage. What it didn't have was the basic understanding of how to fit the pieces into a cohesive, functional unit.

Gorbachev understood what the Soviet Union was lacking. He knew that money didn't need central planning to flow efficiently. If anything, the central planning for which Russian bureaucrats were so proud *interfered* with the free flow of money. Consider a working mother who spends $60 on groceries. The grocer uses the $60 to pay the janitor who, in turn, uses the money to pay his rent. The landlord then uses the same $60 to pay his electric bill and the original $60 is returned to the mother's employer (she works for the utility). Thousands of people working and paying bills means that hundreds of thousands of dollars are cycling through the economic system.

Then the economic news gets better. Once the cycle starts, it doesn't make any difference where the money enters the cycle. Suppose the grocer was Russian and suddenly got a large contract to provide food and hard goods to an American construction working nearby. The grocer would then take the contract and get credit at a bank. He would buy food and hard goods. This means that more food and hard goods would have to be trucked into the area. The grocer would then have to buy trucks to transport the supplies and he would have to hire drivers and mechanics. He might have to build a garage, too. This means buying timber, planks and steel beams along with hiring carpenters, electricians and welders. With more warehouse space, he would need more janitors and security personnel. He will also require more heating and more lighting, increasing the cost of his electric bill and providing that working mother with more money to spend in the local economy. The grocer is now making more money but he is paying more bills. He is also hiring more people so the entire community is benefiting from that single large contract. With more investment, even more monetary cycles would be started.

Gorbachev was an astute observer of Western economics. He understood that the Soviet Union would never pull out of its negative spiral unless it could solve its basic economic woes. Logically, those woes could be resolved by drawing large Western contracts into the Soviet Union through *Glasnost* and then stimulating local monetary cycles by encouraging businesses to start up (*Perestroika*).

What he didn't have was enough time.

Slavery, Ossification and the U.S. Civil War

When movement within the entire system has slowed to the point that it is frozen, the system is said to be ossified, or changed to bone-like hardness. There is no flexibility and change does not occur. Motion may continue because motion is required for a paycheck but there is no *movement*.

An ossified workplace is one in which nothing is done correctly or on time and no one is fired for incompetence. Everyone remains there because they are connected. Work that is completed disappears into a black hole somewhere and no one ever comments on it. Further, there is no accountability and the office is never called upon to justify its existence.

These are danger signs. If you work in an office where this occurs, nothing is going to change until the department has no funds.

Often the easiest decision is indecision. In other words, when faced with a problem, if you do nothing, the natural course of events will generate a solution. Of course, you may not like the solution, but the solution is inevitable if nothing is done to take advantage of other options.

The history of slavery in the American South demonstrates this. Slavery was one of the negative consequences of the Second American Revolution. It was also the primary cause of the Civil War. From an historical perspective, it was inevitable that slavery would fail for many reasons, including the following:

- It was morally repugnant to many people.

- It was only economically feasible in the early days when the land had to be made ready to grow cotton. This involved dropping trees, building fences, making roads, constructing docks, etc. There was no machinery to do this kind of work so human labor had to be used. And human labor meant slave labor.

- Even if slavery had been economically feasible, mechanization would have eventually made it obsolete.

- The only reason it lasted so long was because of the South's influence on political power in Washington, D.C.

- The only reason the South's influence on political power was so strong was because America was not yet an international player and thus pressure from the world community opposing slavery could be ignored with impunity.

Slavery was a hot topic with the Founding Fathers and they did exactly what politicians do with every hot issue they can't resolve: they foist it on to the next generation. Under the United States Constitution, the original delegates agreed to dodge the issue by counting a black person as only three-fifths of a real person and then made it unconstitutional to prohibit the importation of slaves until 1808—nearly 20 years after the United States Constitution was ratified (See Appendix C for an excerpt of the Constitution's Article I, Section 9, Paragraph 1.) This was the first compromise.

The next major blow to slavery came when Missouri petitioned to become a state in 1850. Again, Congress tried to pass on the issue of abolishing slavery to the next generation. This time, it didn't work. The problem was so great that it had to be dealt with. It couldn't wait until the next generation. As a result, the Missouri Compromise—also known as the Compromise of 1850—was enacted. In short, the

Missouri Compromise said that the Mason-Dixon Line would be the demarcation of slavery in the U.S. States to the north of the Line would not have slavery; states to the south would.

But the Missouri Compromise only lasted seven years before the Kansas-Nebraska Act was enacted, which came with a list of agreements to make it palatable to everyone in Congress. This act lasted 12 years before the American Civil War broke out.

The point here is cold-blooded and simple. Rather than resolve a matter that was clearly a problem in the 1780s, Americans kicked around for several generations until a bloody war brought a solution. And the repercussions of that failure to reach a resolution are still with us today. Nearly 150 years after the Civil War, race relations are still a front burner issue in America. Affirmative action, reverse discrimination, and a broadening of the concept of the term "minority" means that this problem is still with us nearly 150 years after the war to end slavery.

Not to Decide Is to Decide

For gradational thinkers, indecision may seem like a good policy. If you've ever worked in an office where no problem was ever solved on time—or at all—you've seen an office operating by "crisis management." Others call it "going with the flow." Whatever it's called, this mindset involves being forced to live with a solution that circumstances have dictated rather than a decision that was well thought through. And it's the logical end of ossification.

If you work in an office where management leapfrogs from crisis to crisis, one of three things is happening. First, someone in the company may be trying to get rid of your department by slamming crisis after crisis down the pipeline, which turns your work schedule into a mad rush to the finish only to have to start on the next project—late.

Second, your department may be legitimately understaffed and overworked. If this is the case, the solution may involve *not* doing some of the assignments. In other words, when an assignment falls into your lap, you have to explain that you don't have the manpower to do it, period.

Third, the boss may be a complete idiot. In this sense, idiocy doesn't necessarily relate to intelligence. A smart person can be a bad manager.

While an occasional crisis a year here and there is acceptable, if you have four in a row, you have serious problems. In most cases, a crisis is the result of someone's bad planning. A competent individual learns to anticipate disaster. Competency is a sign of maturity and shows that you know your history.

If you know your history, you can accurately predict the future by looking for clues in the present. If a project is due in six weeks and your boss is about to leave on a two-week vacation without assigning anyone to the task, you can be assured that two weeks after she returns, there will be a crisis. If you can see six weeks into the future and your boss can't, you can exercise your prescient powers in another way, too: Look for a new job now while you have the time or ride the wave and wait until your department disbands because it can never seem to get anything done on time.

Law of Attendance

Another sign of ossification, the Law of Attendance, is the belief that being present is more important than producing anything.

It is often true that the longer someone works at a job or in a department, the better that person understands his job as well as the unique office mentality that keeps the place operating. Even more important—and particularly important to using history as a guide to the future—the longer you work for a company, the more mistakes you'll see made. Over the long-run, the more mature workers stop making the same mistakes over and over again. This is the positive side to seniority.

But just because an employee has worked for the company for 15 years doesn't mean he or she is any more valuable than a person who punched his first time card six months ago. You can attend a math class for a semester but that doesn't mean you understand calculus.

Attendance is an appealing standard because it's easy. You can rank people on the basis of the number of days they've worked for the organization. It's an automatic criterion. There's nothing wrong with advancing people because of seniority, but it is dangerous when it is the *only* standard for advancement. When that happens, the boss is basically telling the employees, "the longer you can stand me, the more I will reward you." In the end, the only people who will make it into the administrative positions will be cronies.

Time in grade is important, but when it becomes the only consideration for promotion, the law of attendance is a sure sign of ossification.

Consider the Roman Senate under Julius Caesar. As a group, the senators didn't like Caesar, didn't trust Caesar and were furious that he had usurped so much of their power. After all, he had taken Rome by force and, with his soldiers in the city, demanded and received a wide array of unprecedented powers. Finally, moved to action in 44 BCE, a large contingent of senators stabbed Caesar to death in the Forum.

While that murder ended Caesar's reign, it did absolutely nothing for the Roman Republic. Most of the senators had been sitting around for years doing nothing constructive. They no longer knew how to rule. They had ceased being active participants in government. With Caesar gone, there was no one to step into the power vacuum. And, when the Senate did not take the initiative, the Second Triumvirate of Anthony, Lepidus and Octavian did. Thus, the Roman Republic was killed and the Roman Empire was born.

Suppose you work in a state office. In most cases, the director and assistant director are political animals that have been placed in charge because of political patronage. As long as the governor is a Republican, these two Republicans will have their jobs. However, their function is probably not to perform a specific duty. Rather, they may be there to ensure that the governor's ideological program is carried out.

Suppose, more specifically, that you work for a rural energy development department. If the rural areas went predominantly for the Republicans and the governor is a Republican, your director will be a competent individual blessed with a directive from the governor to make his people happy—with low interest loans, grants, jobs and other things that make rural areas livable. That's the advantage of being governor: you can make people very happy.

If, on the other hand, the rural areas went strongly Democrat and the governor is a Republican, the director will be a strange duck. She might be someone who had to be placed somewhere and made it to your department because the Republican governor doesn't care what the rural Democrat voters want. Worse, you could get someone at the head of your department that will use state dollars to try to turn the vote count around. There will be underhanded deals, strange grants and "consultants" in and out of your office regularly.

If you're not in politics and still want to see where your department sits in the pecking order, watch for the first promotion after the new director arrives. Every director will bring "her people" with her. But it's how she handles the department that is more important. If she talks about a "new approach" and "innovative thinking" and the first promotion is George who's been working in the office for 10 years but hasn't had a creative thought since Nixon was President, you're working for the wrong department. Ossification has arrived with the new director.

Law of Editing

Yet another sign of ossification is the Law of Editing. This occurs when someone in charge rewrites the rules to conform to his wishes. This is also known as changing the rules in the middle of the game. The Law of Editing is one of the more powerful weapons used to stop change because it gives the individual the power to alter the course of history.

An excellent example of the law of editing was Pius IX's declaration of papal infallibility in July of 1870.

In any collection of human beings, from multinational corporations right down to the husband and wife doing their weekly shopping, the biggest question is, "Who's in charge?" While a husband and wife fighting over which brand of anchovies to buy may be humorous, any decision made by a large corporation is going to affect millions of people. So, too, will be any decision made by a religious or political leader.

Prior to 1870, and particularly with regard to the Christian religion, there had been a great diversity of opinion as to who was in charge. In 1517, Martin Luther challenged the authority of Rome and generated the formation of a new Christian religion: Lutheranism. The splintering of the old Christian Church continued when Henry VIII established the Church of England of which he was the supreme authority, and the spread of Protestantism that continues to this day. Those individuals who remained with the original Church were called "Catholic," a term that also continues to this day. (The term *catholic*, from Latin, means "universal.")

But prior to 1870, there was no designated supreme authority in Christian religious matters. There had been a few centuries where the Roman emperors claimed that right as *Pontifex Maximus* (i.e., the head of the Church), but some emperors went even further, declaring themselves living gods and thus to be against the emperor was to be against God with punishment that would extend beyond the grave. As far as the Catholics, specifically, were concerned, the closest that anyone had come to declaring that the pope and only the pope was in charge of all aspects of life were the writings of St. Augustine in the Fourth Century that stated, with regard to a controversy, that "Rome has spoken [so] the matter is settled."

The question of who was in charge of the Catholic Church came to a head in 1870 when Giovanni Maria Mastai-Ferretti, also known as Pius IX, convened the First Vatican Council.

Elected in 1846, Pius IX had been forced to face ferocious infighting within the Vatican and an increasing secular world around the Church. During his reign, the longest on record at 30 years, he would see Italy and Germany unified as nations, the War of 1870, the growing strength of socialism, the publication of both Charles Darwin's *Origin of Species* and Karl Marx's *Das Kapital*, the American Civil War and the Year of Revolution (1848).

There was also growing unrest in the Papal States, or the Italian provinces held by the Vatican. The population there, as throughout Italy, was intent on increased political freedom. The previous pope had been against any loosening of restrictions so when Pius IX granted a general amnesty, he was immediately hailed as a reformer. But that didn't last long. Many of the people he released were radicals who used their newly acquired freedom to continue their quest for revolutionary reforms. Far from being appreciative of this new-found freedom, the radicals began to foment civil distress and urged the population to be satisfied with nothing less than a constitutional government for all of Italy, a dream that was achieved in 1861. Eventually, riots broke out and Pius was forced to flee Italy in November of 1848. When he returned to Rome in April of 1850, it was with the support of the French Army. Understandably, when he returned he was no longer a pope with liberal leanings.

For the next two decades, the secular power of the pope was in decline. Italy became a unified nation and on September 20, 1870

Victor Emmanuel seized Rome and made it the capital of the new Italian state. The pope was allowed to retain what are now the Vatican City and a few papal palaces in Rome. From then until his death in 1878, Pius IX sequestered himself within the confines of the Vatican.

Beyond the confines of the Vatican, Pius IX will be remembered as the pope who lost the Papal properties to the Italian state. Within the confines, however, he is revered as the pope who established the infallibility of the Papacy. During the fourth session of the First Vatican Council, on July 18, 1870, he established the supremacy of the pope in spiritual matters.

Prior to 1870, when it came to a dispute within the Church, the pope's point of view was given a great deal of weight—but his point of view was not considered the final word. To resolve the ongoing internal disputes within Catholicism, Pius IX declared that whenever the pope spoke *ex cathedra*, he was presenting the unedited word of God. As the pope proclaimed, such was the voice of God. When the pope spoke *ex cathedra*, it is not his voice but that of God and that word was indisputable and undebatable. This effectively put an end to any discussion of any topic Pope Pius IX did not want to discuss. Or future popes for that matter.

Infallibility is an important religious concept because it separates what God *says* from what God *reveals* or *inspires*. An excellent example of the law of editing was Pius IX's declaration of papal infallibility in July of 1870. That which God reveals or inspires is subject to interpretation by the ministry; what God *says* is not subject to dispute. The infallibility of the pope binds the entire Catholic Church to his wishes. It also solves religious disputes. As a specific example, once granted infallibility, Pius IX declared *ex cathedra* that the Immaculate Conception was a fact, solving a long debate on the subject.

Infallibility remains a powerful tool even today. Catholics have grown in number and their influence can be felt around the world. Within the United States they are a substantial voting block and many of the issues they support are of concern to non-Catholics as well, issues such as abortion, euthanasia, organ harvesting and the patient's right-to-die or physician-assisted suicide. These are all moral issues that have political consequences. When the pope speaks *ex cathedra*, Catholics listen.

A more recent example of this law of editing is how the Bible has changed over the past few decades. In addition to the linguistic difficulties of translating any document from and through myriad foreign languages, some of them dead, there are also a number of English versions that take liberties in editing passages that are difficult to explain.

Bible Changes...and Ossifications

When it comes to discussing the Bible, everyone has his own opinion and every opinion is in error. Liberals will fault the orthodox for their interpretation of scripture—and vice versa. Many secular humanists consider biblical stories to be allegorical while Evangelicals consider every word to be that of God. Cynics plumb passages for inconsistencies as conspiracy buffs decipher codes that may or may not be within the textual structure of the books of the Bible. There are even some who contend the New Testament is an elaborate fabrication of Roman aristocrats.

The actual construction of the Bible has added to this complexity. Far from being a composite work, the Bible is a collection of passages, chapters, letters, prognostications and history that are not necessarily sequential. Some are apocryphal, that is, without known authors, while others tell the same story from different perspectives (i.e., Matthew, Mark, Luke and John). Then there is the question of translation. The Bible is at least a mix of oral tradition along with Greek, Hebrew and Aramaic that was translated to Latin. Later, courtesy of the reform demanded by Martin Luther, the Latin was translated into German. Thereafter, the Bible was translated into all known languages.

Since there were few literary standards in the early days of Christianity, each community had a different collection of books that made up its Bible. That lasted until the year 325, when the Roman Emperor Constantine convened the Council of Nicea to decide definitively what would be included in the universal Bible. Constantine himself decreed that the Trinitarian view—The Father, the Son and the Holy Spirit—was to be accepted as dogma, thus ending the debate as to whether Jesus was human or divine.

The standardization established by the Council of Nicea worked well until the Bible was translated from Latin. As an example of the complexity that evolved, leaping forward to the 20th Century generally and the John T. Scopes Trial (See page 218 for more on the Scopes Trial) specifically, the plethora of Bibles and the slight differences between them even made the term "Bible" difficult to interpret.

In 1925, the Butler Law, which outlawed teaching the theory of evolution and mandated the biblical interpretation of creationism, under which Scopes was being tried, simply referred to the "Bible" but not which one. When Attorney General of Tennessee and chief prosecutor A. Thomas Stewart tried to introduce the King James version as the standard, the defense objected by stating that there were at least three versions of the Bible in print and usage at that time: King James version of 1611, Catholic version of 1609 and a New Testament published by the English College at Rheims in 1582. Further, the Hebrew Bible had 39 books while the Protestant version had 60, and the Catholic publication had 80. And, the latest *King James Bible* differed from its original publication in 30,000 instances.[1]

By the end of the 20th Century, the proliferation of Christian churches and sects along with the need to make the Scripture more readable produced a spread of Bibles with varying degrees of uniformity. While the publishers were careful to keep their versions realistically close, there were a number of revisions. For a specific example, consider the following four versions from Ezekiel 23:20.

---

[1] Ginger, Ray, *Six Days Forever*, Beacon Press, 1958, page 122.

- *New International Bible:* "There she lusted after her lovers, whose genitals were like those of donkeys and whose emission was like that of horses."

- *New Revised Standard Bible:* "She lusted after her paramours there, whose members were like those of donkeys and whose emission was like that of stallions."

- *King James Version:* "She dotes upon their paramours, whose flesh is as the flesh of asses, and whose issue is like the issue of horses."

- The American Bible Society's *Good News Bible:* "She was filled with lust for oversexed men who had all the lustfulness of donkeys and stallions."

All four examples slightly differ from each other, but differ enough to be considered revisionary.[2]

Another example of hedging on the vocabulary can be found in the definition of the word "day." Since the term is critical to some religious conservatives—as in God made the earth is six "days"—developing an adequate definition became quite convoluted. A sample follows from *Unger's Bible Dictionary*, 1957:

Day (Heb. *Yom*; GR. *hemera*), one of the commonest and most ancient of the divisions of time. As used in Gen. 1:5, etc., day marks an entire revolution of time, as of natural day and night—not day as distinguished from night, but day and night together.

. . . .

Figurative. Day is often used by sacred writers, in a general sense, for a definite period of time—an era or season, when something remarkable has taken place, or is destined to do so.

---

[2] This example is from *Ken's Guide to the Bible*, Blast Books, 1995, pages 14-15.

The greatest revisionism of the Bible comes not from what is printed but what is spoken. Many children have been raised believing that Moses came down from the mount with only Ten Commandments, that Noah only took two animals of each species aboard the Ark and that Jesus carried his own cross to Golgotha and said as his final words "Forgive them Father for they know not what they do." None of these statements is accurate. God gave Moses hundreds of laws, Noah took as many as seven of each animal, and Jesus did not carry his own cross. Simon carried the cross and he was forced to do it. As far as the last words of Jesus, Matthew (27:46) and Mark (15:34) agree that those words were "My God, my God, why have you forsaken me?" Luke (23:46) records the last words as "Father, into Your hands I commend my spirit," and John (19:30), "It is finished."

So, the Bible itself is not consistent; not that it should be. After all, it was not written by one person and then run through an editing process where all the nuances were smoothed over to make marketing easier. It has been around for a long time—since the first day or 4004 BCE depending on your point of view—and Bible-bashing is easy because there are so many passages that can be nitpicked. But the important point is that all documents from the United States Constitution to the parking codes for your city, can be and have been interpreted, adjusted and twisted to fit circumstances.

Lawyers are famous for reading intent into language that the law never intended. They are the ultimate editors.

How Ossification Sets In

For most people, the greatest danger is chaos. If no one is in charge, nothing will get done. So a manager will establish stability in a way that is comfortable to her. It is only natural that she will want to put her own fingerprints on the destiny of the office—her office actually because if her head is on the block she gets to call the shots. While there is nothing wrong with running the department to suit your own personal standards, there is great danger in tweaking the rules here and there for personal political reasons. Once it starts, it never stops. Reducing time in grade to promote a friend lowers the standard for promotion. If it happens once, it'll happen again. Thus begins the erosion of quality. First it's giving Joe a job and then it's giving Mary a promotion and then the favor is for Mary's friend. Once the floodgates have opened, politics become more important than quality.

Ossification occurs when rules are meaningless. There may be office procedures and policies, but if they're ignored or twisted in one circumstance but not the next, they cease to be important. In its most dangerous form, the rules are brought out selectively to punish those who advocate a return to quality. Suppose George asks for a promotion, but doesn't get the boost in status and pay because, he is told, he has to have three years time in grade. But if Julia got a similar promotion and has only been in the office for two years, George gets the sneaking suspicion that he's the victim of discrimination. He's right. But if he complains, he's also on the fast track to losing his job.

But the law of editing is not all bad. Sometimes being vague with the words you use is an asset. Perhaps the best example of using the law of editing to tap dance through a minefield was Abraham Lincoln's Gettysburg Address. The address was delivered on November 19, 1863 at the Soldier's National Cemetery at Gettysburg, Pennsylvania, overlooking the battlefield where more than 7,000 soldiers, Union *and* Confederate, had fallen during the three days of fighting that summer.

Gettysburg was a great Union victory and it was becoming clear that the South was in retreat. Thus, Lincoln was considering ways to ease the South's return to the fold of the United States.

With this in mind, the last thing that Abraham Lincoln wanted to do at Gettysburg was to appear to gloat over the Confederate dead. But, at the same time, he could not appear to be "soft" on the Confederates, either. To heal the nation and alienate no one, Lincoln composed the Gettysburg Address, a masterpiece of obfuscation that dodged the real reason the 15,000 Northerners were gathered at the cemetery.

In the Gettysburg Address (See Appendix D for a reproduction in its entirety) Lincoln talks much in generalities of the "unfinished work" that the dead have left for the living but never actually states what that "unfinished work" is. He speaks of being "dedicated to the great task remaining before us" and "the cause for which [the dead] gave their last full measure of devotion." But he never outlines the "great task" or the "cause." Remembering that there were both Union and Confederate dead in the battlefield, Lincoln's used "glittering generalities," or phrases that sound grandiose but are hard to define. The only specific item he mentions is that "all men are created equal" a verbal concept included in the Declaration of Independence but he cleverly did not apply that to the Civil War. Note that he uses the term when talking about the Founding Fathers, not about the "great civil war."

The beauty of the Gettysburg Address was that it was so well written that the South could get as much from it as the Union. It was pleasing to both sides, offensive to neither. It was the perfect speech to honor the Union dead and not offend the Confederate living. Edward Everett, who was considered America's foremost orator at that time, spoke for two hours that afternoon but it was Lincoln's brief dedication that history remembers. Everett later wrote to Lincoln "I should be glad if I could flatter myself that I came as near to the central idea of the occasion in two hours as you did in two minutes."

Loyalty as a Performance Standard

In many offices and positions, loyalty is the *only* standard for measuring job performance. But this isn't the same as the loyalty one refers to when talking about God, their country or being true to their school. This is the nebulous worship of a company or office that has nothing whatsoever to do with honorable sacrifice.

Sadly, this kind of loyalty is like a weather vane that changes with every gust of a political wind—a fair weather friend. For the gradational thinker, loyalty is a requirement for employment. Why? Because loyalty is the easiest way to get people to do things your way. For underlings, it's a Malayan tiger pit. Humorist Warren Sitka says that, "whenever I hear someone talk about loyalty I know I'm about to be fired."

Historical examples of the pros and cons of loyalty run amuck are so numerous—many recent—that there is no standout illustration. On the positive side, in August of 480 BCE, Leonidas and 300 Spartans fought to the death at Thermopylea to cover the retreat of the Greek Army. Rather than renounce their faith, early Christians were fed to the lions and Jews were scattered over the known world during the Roman Empire because they refused to forsake their religion. On the negative side, a 20th Century example of loyalty at its worst was President Richard M. Nixon who willingly tossed staff, aides and secretaries to the ravages of the press and congressional investigators.

The primary problem with loyalty is that it is inconsistent. Those who praise it are usually those who demand it. This, of course, makes sense. They are the ones with the most to gain from loyalty. The ones with the most to lose are those who owe it. Loyalty, when all is said and done, is demanded from the bottom up. Rarely will you find it from the top down. When someone at the bottom gets the boot, rarely does someone at the top come rushing in to get him a new job. This is true even if the person gets the boot for being loyal.

That's the good news. Loyalty to a leader who deserves it is one thing. But loyalty to a scoundrel is yet another. In some cases, loyalty is not a value, it's a cover-up for a scoundrel. Unfortunately, scoundrels do not walk around with a sign on their lapel or blouse. You have to discover them by yourself. Alas, in most cases when you've finally discovered the scoundrel you're in so deep that it's difficult to reverse directions.

For the seasoned gradational thinker, loyalty is a powerful tool. Many people are persuaded to do it the boss's way. It may be wrong, stupid, unproductive or downright dumb, but employers know how to appeal to workers' sense of loyalty. Of course, this is a very low thing to do but it doesn't stop people from doing something stupid when the boss demands it. Stupid ideas lead to stupid results and when blame is placed, don't expect the boss to accept responsibility for any mistakes. To paraphrase John F. Kennedy, "Victory has many fathers but defeat is an orphan."

The best way to save yourself from being sacrificed on the altar of loyalty is to avoid the field of play. Use guile. As Chinese general and philosopher Sun Tzu noted, "even though you are competent, appear to be incompetent. Though effective, appear to be ineffective." Allow the swirl of battle to pass by without taking part. Loyalty is only asked of those who are considered players, insiders, the "movers and shakers." No one expects a secretary, mailroom clerk or other low-level functionary to be privy to what is happening at the seat of power. They are out of the loop of power and are therefore not required to pledge oaths of loyalty. Neither are people who are generally believed to be incompetent or ineffective. They are simply tolerated. But, they never go to prison for lying to keep their boss out of jail.

The Moral Hammer

In many situations, ossified bureaucrats will dress up their fear of change in the clothes of morality and immorality. They will use the moral hammer—the assumption that most people make that morality trumps all other concerns

When someone is an ossified troublemaker who has the moral hammer, just about any issue becomes an immoral nail.

To understand the law of the moral hammer, suppose you work in a bank as a loan officer. As you look over the applications sitting on your desk, you notice that one is from a recently-released felon who had embezzled thousands of dollars from United Way. On top of the form is a sticky note, unsigned, basically saying to ignore roll the applicant. In other words, the bank doesn't want this person's business. No one else wants to take the heat for discriminating against this particular individual so they turned the problem over to you. You can wield the moral hammer and ignore the application on the grounds that you don't think the bank should loan money to felons.

The moral hammer suggests that there is a moral reason for doing something—or doing nothing, as the case may be. But the moral hammer isn't moral at all, it's just another way of making a political move.

The biggest problem with this concept is that morality has no place in business, politics or life outside of the home. Anything illegal is handled by the appropriate authorities. Morality is a personal commitment to a set of values. It's not universal. Your morals aren't the same as your neighbors', nor should they be. Allowing your personal moral beliefs to alter business or government practices will bring you grief.

The real question here is not whether the loan is good or bad or if the person is dependable enough to pay the money back. The underlying issue is that someone has a moral objection to giving this loan. This is a very dangerous road to travel because it means that business decisions are being made for moral reasons. This isn't a smart way to run a business. The next person to be denied a loan on moral grounds might be a Cohen, Mohammed or Garcia—and three denied Cohens in a row could mean a federal lawsuit for your bank.

The greatest danger posed by the moral hammer is that it often hurts the person trying to use it. The person making a business decision is the one with the most at risk, even though he or she may not realize this. If you are the loan officer who has to say "no" to the felon, you had better have a very good, identifiable, fiscal reason for denying the loan. You should also have a good back-up position. Anyone can get a lawyer. If the denied felon sues, it's going to cost your bank a lot of money—not to mention a lot of bad publicity.

The ossified decision-maker usually doesn't see the risk of inaction. He may focus on the fact that he's a good moral person trying to do the right thing. Or he may think he's loyal to the company first—and loan applicants second. Whatever the rationalization, this person thinks there's safety in inaction. But history—and business—don't work that way. They reward smart action.

Conservative Versus Conservative

This is a logical point to discuss conservatism and Conservatism. Ossified decision-makers often believe that they are being conservative or prudent (if not moral) in their inaction or slow action.

In some cases, they will confuse their conservative sensibility with Conservative political beliefs—which they think are essential in business. This is all nonsense. Ossification is one of the things that gives Conservatism a bad name.

In fact, political Conservatism is often marked by decisive movement—even radical vision. Current political pundits often forget the sensibility that U.S. President Ronald Reagan brought to the office when he took over in 1981. Despite a number of political faults, Reagan did articulate a vision of small government, low tax resolutions of the "stagflation" and "malaise" that had characterized the mid— and late—1970s. Reagan's Conservatism was anything but conservative. Be wary of trusting conservatism. It can be a sign of ossification.

If you work for a large company, you might be told that "the higher ups" are particularly concerned about the project that you're working on so you should be extra careful. Or that there is a hot-shot consultant on her way to town to work out all the bugs in the proposal. Or that there is something special about this particular proposal that you won't know until "the proper time."

Most of the time these statements aren't true. If the higher-ups were so concerned about the project, why aren't they doing it themselves? The same goes for that hot-shot consultant. If she's needed so badly, why isn't she here now? If there were something special about this project, wouldn't it be good for you to know now rather than later?

Unless you are in a religious order, miracle has nothing to do with working in an office, meeting deadlines or presenting a good sales package. Even in the military you know the authority of the person giving orders. You had best not be mysterious when you make presentations and if you don't have the authority to make certain promises, don't.

Bread and Circuses

Another sign of ossification is the transformation from a productive organization to one of bread and circuses.

The term *bread and circuses* is from Roman history. After the Roman republic gave way to the authoritarian empire, the Caesars supplemented their political power by cynically controlling the mobs in the street. Rather than have city residents run amok, the emperors used public dollars to give the mobs something to eat and something to do with their time. The solution: coliseums. While the coliseums throughout the empire were not specifically built to satisfy the need to give mobs something to do, the structures certainly kept mobs occupied. The upside was that the mobs were kept off the street—for a while; the bad part of this arrangement is that once you start giving bread and circuses, you cannot stop.

The rule of Bread and Circuses runs rampant in many work places. An excellent example is referenced in the old joke that there were so many vice presidents at a large automobile company that there were two for door armrests: one for the driver's side armrest and one for the passenger's side armrest. Banks are also infamous for giving people the title of "vice president." If a friend of a member of the board of directors is appointed as a vice president somewhere down the food chain in any company, there's a good chance that it had something to do with the law of bread and circuses. In the old days, these jobs were called *sinecures*, positions that had a lot prestige, paid a fair amount of money but came with little or no responsibility. Once a company starts handing out these positions, it's hard to stop.

If a "new" vice president who appears to know diddly squat about what your department does is assigned to your department, you can bet that one of two things is happening: 1) the company has a hidden agenda and this person has been assigned to carry it out; or 2) when the company needs to hide someone or pay someone off with a job, your department is the dumping ground. In either case, tread carefully around this person.

As a rule, incompetence expands to fill the available job slots. If the board of directors can stick your department with one dolt and the workload does not seem to suffer, then two or three—or even five—can't do it any more harm.

Offices that have a buildup of nonproductive people slow down, (see the Law of the Brain Drain on pages 119 and 125). Productivity goes out the window in favor of...favor from above. Appearance becomes more important than product sales. Workers are more concerned with having a clean desk than getting work done on time. Or going to the "right" social event may take precedence over working late to make a sale. The moment that productivity takes a back seat, your department has become ossified. If you're still working there when this happens, it won't be long before you and everyone else you work with are out of job.

If you're stuck in a department that operates under the bread and circuses philosophy, your best bet is to gracefully suggest a budget cut to someone up the corporate food chain. Think like a politician. Popularity and money go hand in hand. Popular presidents preside over booming economies. VPs without budgets lose their popularity. The quickest way to get rid of someone is to cut his or her budget.

What's in it for Me?

The rule of WIIFM or What's in it for Me? is the basis for all wheeling and dealing. A popular concept in economics, politics and business, the WIIFM philosophy is the bottom line for any negotiation.

However, it is important that you don't mistake the negotiating concept of WIIFM for the historical concept of the law. The negotiating term is tied to the idea that both sides of the table have specific needs and requirements and when a critical threshold of wants and needs on both sides have been met, an agreement is possible. Consider, for example, a teachers union requesting a raise in pay. After the teachers are offered a pay raise and an improved advancement policy, their negotiating team will claim success. But to get to that point, they may have to renegotiate their requests for more vacation time, smaller class sizes and fewer after-hour duties. Both sides have to compromise to reach an agreement.

An excellent example of WIIFM is the Teapot Dome Scandal that took place during President Warren G. Harding's administration. In the early days of the 20th Century when the American Navy was changing from wind to diesel power, far-sighted strategists "withdrew from the public domain" three petroleum reserves. "Withdrawal from the public domain," means that the public land would be established for a specific purpose—like a military base—and therefore off limits to the general public.

This meant that Congress took three oil-rich areas and gave them to the Navy as underground oil storage. This insured that the United States Navy would never be faced with an oil shortage—particularly in a time of war.

Because these three areas were so rich in oil, oil companies were interested in the fields. Why? They wanted to drill on public land for free and sell the government's oil on the open market. And, it could have worked. If they had stayed out of the reserves, everything would have been legal. But two oil companies—Mammoth Oil Company and Pan-American and Petroleum Company—thought it would be a lot cheaper to bribe someone to let them drill *in* a petroleum reserve.

They were the ossified players in the drama that became the Teapot Dome scandal.

Teapot Dome

There is an old saying that with every blessing there comes a curse. One of the greatest historical blessings of the United States is its geographical isolation from both Europe and Asia. Combined, the Atlantic and Pacific gave America a significant buffer against invasion. With the exception of the War of 1812, American territory has only been violated a few times by Canada and Mexico and only once did enemy troops actually seize and hold land for an extended period of time (during World War II when Japanese troops seized the last two islands of the Aleutian Chain—Attu and Kiska—in Alaska.

But the buffers quickly became a curse when it came to the American military's might. Before American troops could arrive "over there" in Europe during the WWI or invade the Solomon Islands in the South Pacific during the WWII, thousands of miles of ocean had to be crossed. This meant that American supply lines necessarily had to be long and air support from American-based fighter planes limited.

Just before the turn of the 20th century, a visionary in the Navy postulated that there might be a way to turn the thousands of miles of Pacific Ocean between the United States and Asia into an asset. In his book *Influence of Sea Power on History*, Rear Admiral Alfred Thayer Mahan suggested reaching out into the Pacific and acquiring critical islands that could act as fuel depots—among other uses—for the American Navy. Mahan, who had spent his early years in the Navy serving with the Union during the Civil War blockading Southern ports, was well aware of the importance of being able to move supplies unhindered.

One Washington D.C. politician who immediately realized the significance of Mahan's postulations was the Undersecretary of the Navy, Theodore Roosevelt. A geopolitical thinker, Roosevelt was convinced that America's greatness lay in extending both its military and commercial reach into the Pacific Ocean. He suggested that a canal be built to link the Atlantic with the Pacific. This became known as the Panama Canal. He also suggested, "acquiring," at the very least, Hawaii and Midway.

Roosevelt, both as Undersecretary of the Navy and later President, was involved with the United States Navy's transformation from a fleet of wind-driven wooden vessels to steam-driven steel ships. He was—in this context as well as others—a force of change. The new navy would depend on coal or oil, instead of the wind. There was only one problem: While the United States had plenty of coal and oil, the resources were not readily available in the geographical areas where they could be easily extracted and transported to naval vessels. But Roosevelt was not to be deterred. Anticipating that coal and oil would be around long after he had retired, he planned for the future. To assure that the Navy had all of the coal and oil it would need, he selected certain acreages of coal-and oil-rich land and "withdrew them from the public domain."

Roosevelt made a number of withdrawals of oil and coal lands in Alaska and California. The best-known withdrawal was in Wyoming where the name of the withdrawal became synonymous with the scandal it generated during President Warren G. Harding's administration: Teapot Dome.

In the parlance of the oil industry, a "dome" is the geologic structure that houses an oil find, like an umbrella. Once the roof of the dome is punctured, oil can be extracted. Teapot Dome is located near Casper, Wyoming and was so-named for a teapot-appearing structure in the area.

The Teapot Dome scandal broke in 1924 when it was revealed to the public that private companies were drilling for oil on the Teapot Dome Naval Oil Reserve. Private oil companies had long contended that the concept of a Naval oil reserve was an admirable concept during the time of President Theodore Roosevelt but, by 1920, was outdated. The private sector could now provide the Navy with all the oil it could pay for and deliver it anywhere the Navy wanted. But, if this was the case, why was a Naval oil reserve needed? This may have been true but the oil companies did more than talk about changing the concept of the Naval oil reserve. Two oil company executives made overtures to the Secretary of the Interior, former-Senator from New Mexico Albert B. Fall, about opening the Naval oil reserves for drilling.

Fall had been an outspoken opponent against conservation and, once appointed, used his clout as the Secretary of the Interior to convince Secretary of the Navy Edwin Denby and others in the administration to turn control of the Naval oil reserves over to the Department of the Interior. When they complied, Fall leased the Teapot Dome lands to the Mammoth Oil Company. (In California, the Elk Hills reserve was leased to Pan-American Petroleum and Transport Company.) In exchange, Fall received "gifts" and "loans" from the owners of the two companies amounting to about $400,000.

When the news of the lease broke, Fall made headlines and was able to hold his own against the scandal-hungry media hounds. The leases, after all, were quite complicated and as Secretary of the Interior, he was authorized to lease public lands. Strong support from United States Attorney General Harry M. Daugherty didn't hurt Fall's cause, either. But eventually the money was his downfall because it linked Fall and the presidents of the two oil companies.

Things were going well until August of 1922 when the United States Congress started investigating. The Teapot Dome uproar lasted through the 1920s. Even the death of President Warren G. Harding didn't stop the demand for an impartial investigation. President Coolidge appointed special prosecutors to look into the matter and the case made it all the way to the Supreme Court.

Fall denied that he had done anything wrong. The high court found that the oil leases had been corruptly obtained and they were declared invalid; Elk Hills in February 1927 and Teapot Dome the proceeding October. Fall was found guilty of bribery in 1929 and spent a year in jail. He also paid a $100,000 fine. And the presidents of the oil companies? Harry F. Sinclair was found guilty of contempt—but not bribery—paid a $500 fine and spent 7 ½ years in jail. Edward L. Doheny of Pan-American never spent a day in jail or paid a dollar in fines.

The most important lesson from the Teapot Dome Scandal is as colloquial as it is true: evil never sleeps. Every hour of every day, there is someone, some group, some company, that is willing steal from the public. And, there's only one way to stop this from happening: exposure. That exposure comes from a free press, an inquisitive Congress and a concerned public. There is no substitute for an informed public.

For the honest, the rule of WIIFM is a powerful motivator to do nothing. But it's not at the street level that corruption is dangerous. A crooked cop will be discovered because there are too many people watching all the time. But the higher up the food chain you go, the more difficult it is to distinguish between politics and corruption. Most people have worked in an office where the majority of decisions are made "higher up" the ladder. But not all these decisions are based on corruption and the rule of WIIFM. And unless you have rock-solid proof—in writing—that corruption is taking place, you should be very careful about making such accusations.

Further, if history is a guide, often it's the whistleblower who is spurned for confrontation. In the real world, honesty and integrity are rare commodities because the penalties are so high. The woman who turns in her company for cheating on a government contract is going to have a hard time finding another job. The man who points out military cost overruns is going to have to change careers. But the United States is blessed with enough people with integrity that competence outruns corruption. There are enough whistleblowers that every reasonably intelligent corporate administrator knows there are watchdogs on duty. But greed will out the corrupt and, if there are no watchdogs awake, the rule of WIIFM can stop progress dead in its tracks.

Solving the Wrong Problem

One of the most reliable ways to ossify and stop progress is to channel all of an organization's energy into solving the wrong problem. This doesn't mean solving a problem with the wrong solution. It's when you substitute a problem that you *can* solve for one you *cannot*.

A good example is how America has dealt with racism. The primary problem, which comes as a surprise to no one, is that racial minorities are not statistically equal in all economic strata of society. More specifically, while black people represent about 12 percent of the U.S. population in general, they do not represent 12 percent of the top layer of decision-makers in business, politics, entertainment and other equally lucrative fields. The same could be said for other minorities—though the percentages vary.

What caused this disparity? Slavery? Perhaps...though a more direct cause was the era of so-called Jim Crow laws that dominated the southern U.S. from the late 1800s to the mid-1900s. These laws—a more subtle kind of racism than slavery—put legal limits on the things free black people could do, and even the places they could go.

The Great Migration

One of the most understudied but significant American events of the 1920s and 1930s was the so-called *Great Migration*, the movement of blacks out of the South. American history classes often overlook this event, instead offering the time-and-place snapshots as opposed to a progressive chronology of the period. During a session on the 1920s, you probably learned about flappers, the rise of the automobile, illegal booze, the "Lost Generation" and Black Tuesday. In the next session about the 1930s, you heard about Al Capone, speakeasies, the end of Prohibition, Hoovervilles and the prelude to World War II. But throughout these decades a mass movement of peoples was occurring, which dramatically changed the social and racial face of America.

Prior to the end of the Civil War, the black population of the United States was concentrated in the deep South. While the Emancipation Proclamation may have liberated the blacks from ownership, it did nothing to enhance their economic conditions. Neither did a host of federal agencies, charitable causes or political activists. By the mid 1870s, it was clear that it would take more than a few generations to put the South back on its economic feet. For many blacks who were eking out a living as sharecroppers, migrating seemed a better prospect than staying.

By the mid-1920s there was a mass exodus underway, and by the 1940s, blacks were migrating out of the South in staggering numbers. Lynching, poor economic conditions and no hope of a future drove them out of the South while the faint promise of a better life drew them north and west. Blacks flooded into large cities and small towns. Chicago, Detroit, Cleveland and New York saw its black populations increase by 20 percent over a decade.

The Great Migration changed America from a racially divided nation to a melting pot. At the time of the Civil War, less than 10 percent of the population in the North was black. By World War II about 10 percent of America's population was black but that population was scattered across all 48 states and Alaska.

Another element to the emerging melting pot was a document signed by then-President Harry S. Truman on July 26, 1948 titled Executive Order 9981. This document called for the integration of the United States military; it capped the long struggle of blacks in the military to be treated fairly and attracted many blacks into the service. This enhanced the migration of blacks across America further. The document also made integration the policy of the United States government. And, anyone who wanted to do business with the military had to follow these same guidelines. The result was a universal integration in the public and private sector.

In retrospect, the Great Migration made race relations a national issue, not just a Southern one. Once blacks began moving into large cities and small communities across America, race became a national issue that culminated in the civil rights movement of the 1960s.

The Great Migration is an excellent example of what could be called "pressure cooker economics." You cannot expect negative economic conditions to continue forever. Living in squalor is only acceptable if there is a reasonable chance you can work your way up a food chain to a better life. If economic conditions get worse, there will be a growing sense of anger that will result in dramatic action like riots or a revolution.

Economics is self-correcting. Putting pressure on any commodity—including human labor—will have an effect. Blacks that found a better life out of the South did not return and gained more civil rights throughout the decades. If enough pressure is put on any commodity, it will move. The longer the pressure continues, the greater will be the movement to change.

So, how do you make things equal? The real answer, unfortunately, is that you don't. Life is unfair and you cannot legislate it to be fair. The best you can do is install mechanisms that will keep the playing field level. In the case of racial discrimination, you keep the playing field level by making cases of proven discrimination very expensive to the racist. To date, the penalty for racism is slight and the people who ultimately pay the price (in most cases, employers) usually aren't the people who did the discriminating in the first place.

When a large company is found guilty of discriminating against female employees, the women involved are promoted and paid for lost wages and opportunities. But those promotions are often at the expense of men didn't do the discriminating. The company then claims the cost as a business expense and the American taxpayer picks up the tab. The person who actually discriminated against the women probably got a golden parachute; so much for equality in America.

When Congress had the chance, it solved the race problem the wrong way. Since it was too difficult to punish discrimination with a heavy hand, Congress decided to force integration with quotas. If a police force was 90 percent white and the city was 30 percent black, many thought that at least 30 percent of the police force should be black—or at least minority. This is known as *affirmative action*[3] and, in the rush to be politically correct, qualified whites were passed over for hiring and promotion in favor of less qualified blacks. This, in turn, created even more problems.

Hand-in-hand with the rule of solving the wrong problem is the rule of expanding incompetence. In the case of affirmative action, every step down the wrong road creates more problems. And, the longer it takes to recognize that a mistake has been made—the worse the problem gets.

Affirmative action is a classic case. As more and more blacks were being promoted, whites began to complain of reverse discrimination.

[3] Strictly speaking, affirmative action applies to racial quota programs used by the U.S. government and its contractors. However, it has come to mean any quota program or similar system designed to remedy past discrimination.

And as the number of blacks being promoted continued to grow, Mexican-Americans, Filipinos, Hawaiians, Alaska Natives and American Indians followed suit, excuse the pun, and the official list of minorities expanded.

Today, those claiming to have minority status represent about 70 percent of the population. These groups are hardly cohesive. Minority groups are suing each other because in this city or that county there are more blacks than Hispanics and therefore the blacks should have a larger slice of the economic pie than the Hispanics. There are women suing companies because they were not promoted over another woman or a minority.

The courts in the U.S. have done little to discourage these lawsuits—or remedy the problems caused by affirmative action. Two high-profile lawsuits involving admissions practices at the University of Michigan and its law school were heard by the U.S. Supreme Court in 2003. The high court's decisions on the University of Michigan's practices were inconclusive—and even somewhat inconsistent. They forbade explicit quotas (x number of each class to be blacks, y to be Hispanic, etc.). But they allowed race to be a "factor" in the University's admissions decisions.

Overall, affirmative action is a mess. Worse yet, it has not eliminated the problem it was meant to solve. There is still a disproportionate percentage of minorities in the upper economic strata and rather than making progress on racial harmony in the United States, affirmative action pits Americans against each other. Sooner or later the entire program will be junked and U.S. Congress may solve the problem the way it should have been solved in the first place: incredibly stiff penalties for those who discriminate.

Both the rule of solving the wrong problem and the law of expanding incompetence are indications of an office, business or career in deep trouble. They are career terminators. If you find yourself in an office where you're solving the wrong problem, it's time to find another job. Immediately. Incompetent thinking will only resolve problems by accident and it is more likely that your original problem is going to grow in complexity and intensity. It will take some time for the corporate office to realize that they're trying to solve the wrong problem but when it does happen, they're going to clean house. And that means getting rid of everyone in the department. If you're still there when the axe falls, you'll get tossed whether you were responsible for the blunder or not.

The toughest yet smartest tactic is to stop making a mistake when you realize you are making the mistake. As the adage goes, when you find yourself in a hole, stop digging. While the price for failure is always high, it's much higher if everyone knows that you are aware of your mistake. When great leaders knew they made a mistake, they corrected immediately. They did not wait for the problem to get larger. As always, it's best to "cut your losses and run."

Conclusion

Every office is a bureaucracy of sorts, whether you work for the federal, state or local government or in a business where you are faceless. Unless you are in a brand new business, on your first day of work you'll be introduced to the "way we do things around here."

But how did "the way we do things around here" ever get started? In most cases, when a problem initially arose, someone solved it. If the problem didn't return, then this became part of the body of the institutional memory of the office, company or organization. Thus begins a progression by which an idea becomes a rule and thereafter, in progression, a regulation, law and—finally—an institution.

Institutional paralysis occurs when no one is making any decisions without checking with everyone else to make sure no one is upset. The competent people are gone and the deadwood remain. Memos are used to cover your ass rather than pass along information. The position of your desk means more than whether you are doing anything of importance. Bad decisions are enforced unchecked and everyone is afraid to go higher up because every indication is that the incompetence extends all the way to the top. Productivity falls. Animosity builds. Trust is extinguished. The office becomes a battle zone with everyone expecting the plug to be pulled any day.

A humorous example of institutional paralysis is the old farmer who was watching two men in a state truck working on a roadway. The first man would dig a hole while the second one sat in the shade of the truck and drank water. When the first man finished, he sat in the shade of the truck while the second man filled in the hole the first one had just dug. Then the truck would move forward 15 feet, stop and the digging would begin again. After a dozen holes, the farmer went over and asked the men what they were doing.

"Well," replied the first man, "my job is dig holes for trees."

"Mine," said the second man, "is to fill in the holes after the trees have been planted."

"But where are the trees?" the farmer asked looking back down the row of filled holes that lined the roadway.

"Oh, that's George's job," said the second man, "but he's sick today."

Countries, political parties, committees and businesses that are unable to prevent people from getting in the way of movement eventually reach a point where they are operating under the mindset *of* ossification. At this point, gradational thinking gets in the way of long-term vision...and movement. For the bad guys, all that matters is the short-term—what they *can* control—the tools they use to beat their dead horse. Quality people have left the fold and now there's no movement or change at all—they're just going through the motions.

The point of this chapter is to give you the tips and tools you need for *recognizing ossification* before it leads to a bad end.

5 Myths and History

It would be easy if all you had to concern yourself with was movement or non-movement of history. But history is not that simple. • History and the people who make history are complex and unpredictable. You can know with *some* certainty what a person might do in a given circumstance, but you wouldn't want to bet your life on it.

History is complex because people are a poor conductor of information. No one ever has all the facts they need to make a truly informed decision. This is why people leap to conclusions. Of course, some of us leap to conclusions more quickly than others. Some make assumptions that are incorrect.

In most cases, though, our assumptions are based on some information. Most of the decisions we make are based on our own experiences. Beyond that, we rely on information we've received from others. Sometimes this information is reliable truth from legitimate sources; other times it's sketchy myth from no particular place. The myths can be dangerous.

Historically speaking, every neighborhood and nation leaps to conclusions every day on everything from handling an unruly child to balancing the national budget. And each neighborhood and nation leaps in its own way. What works for the Johnson child may not work for the Jefferson twins and how Italy handles inflation may not work in Botswana.

One of the ways that the differences are described is by myths handed down among people in neighborhoods and nations. These myths are a kind of short-hand way of conveying the specific ways that different people do things. Myths are rooted in reality—but they're usually not literally real. They often combine several (or many) points; they often compress long periods of time into short bursts.

Just because a myth isn't literally true doesn't mean it's false. Myths can convey important things—so-called "greater truths."

Greek myths told of the exploits of the gods but the tales shed a little insight into human behavior. Homer's epic poem, *The Odyssey*, for example, is much more than simply a story of a soldier on his way home after a long war.

All myths are rooted in fact; many do a good job of convincing greater truths. Why, then, can myths be dangerous? Because the conclusions that are drawn from them are not always accurate.

Historical myths—both good and bad—happen everywhere, all the time. The weak ones—like all blacks being ignorant, women only being worthy of raising children and Jews draining the blood of Christian children for *matza*—go away. But others are very hard to dispel in spite of the fact they are in error. At the same time, however, myths never die. They are constantly reborn and tailored to suit the times.

Over three and a half centuries, the United States has been the primary beneficiary of every myth gone wild anywhere in the world. When hatred drove minorities out of Europe and Asia, for example, the United States absorbed them. The U.S. is a mecca for the dispossessed. But that doesn't mean it has always embraced them with open arms. The United States has gone through periods of intolerance focused on a wide variety of targets including "witches," British, French, Canadians, Indians, Southern European immigrants, blacks, Mexicans, Arabs, communists, anarchists, Japanese, Jews, Baptists, liberals, abolitionists and gays. Fear of some thing or someone you know nothing about and have no contact with is as human as worrying about how long a recession or harsh winter will last.

From the perspective of understanding historical movements, myths can poison the stew. They make the unpredictable nature of history more entropic, that is, more random and less orderly. In this chapter, we'll consider a few of the most common historical myths.

The Myth of Stability

One of the most prevalent myths throughout history is that of stability. The myth of stability is the belief that change occurs dramatically over the long-run, but not in the short-run. This is in error. Society is constantly changing and it is important to understand that every day is different even if you cannot see that change taking place.

Further, shrewd individuals understand that they must plan for a future they cannot see. They will take a real estate class while working part-time so they have something to fall back on after they retire—all while continuing to work at the paper mill. Musicians often plan their future but keep their day job. Every writer has a best seller in her but she continues to work from 9-to-5 to make those pesky house and car payments.

Wherever you work, you'll find that, unfortunately, things do not change that much. Year after year, the rat race seems to be the same. The faces may change and the technology may advance, but the politics remain the same. History doesn't change the rat race much, either. Every culture has to deal with economic downturns, murderers, electing tax commissioners, repairing bridges and distributing water to myriad areas.

Usually change comes so slowly, that it's hard to detect any change at all. It's like the old saying goes, the more things change, the more they remain the same. If you talk to someone who's worked at the same office for several decades, he'll tell you this particular statement is true. Yes, human behavior doesn't change and human problems are never solved. But things don't remain the same even as technology advances. There's always a new wrinkle being added—even if you don't recognize it—yet. The only blessing—in most cases—is that you'll get plenty of warning.

As you read this book, there are problems brewing even if you don't choose to think about them: pollution of the environment, threat of nuclear terrorism, drug addiction, starvation in the Third World, global warming. Most of us don't worry about these issues because they are beyond our control to solve and, because we've got our own worries—a mortgage payment, child support, college tuition, etc.

The key to using history to understand the myths of your era is to see the future as it develops. Life moves at a rapid pace. Cyberspace is moving into our lives at a phenomenal speed. There are more businesses on the New York Stock Exchange and NASDAQ than ever before. Smaller businesses are gnawing at the foundation of larger ones. Scientists are penetrating the secrets of the cell and exploring the outer reaches of the universe. To survive in the future, you must plan for the future.

The myth of stability can be summed up in a phrase coined by humorist Warren Sitka, "salmon mentality." This is the belief that there were salmon last year and the previous five years and, presumably, the salmon will be back this year—and next year as well. In most cases, this is true. But the price of salmon is on a roller coaster because of the fickle nature of the human palate, the deterioration of the environmental quality of the ocean meadows, *El niño*, governmental red tape, mariculture and a host of other problems. The smart fisherman knows that he must diversify his income. He does the same thing that any wise businessperson does: he anticipates change. The future holds no promises and the only hope you have of long-term survival is using history as your guide. Things will change and that change will be abrupt. The people who are most damaged are those who cling to the belief that life is stable and that things tomorrow will remain the same as they are today.

Any business, culture, neighborhood or nation is only as stable as its population. Many people view stability as lack of movement. If the economy is doing well, this in itself, is enough of a reason not to change anything. But, there is no such thing as stability. Stability is a myth. There will always be ethnic, political and regional unrest.

Technology is constantly tweaking economics that, in turn, affects wages, benefits, opportunities and investments. The Middle Ages were riddled with instability though the rudimentary technology made it slow and regional in nature and impact. But those slow, regional impacts gave birth to the Reformation, Renaissance and modern Europe. Stability is, at best, a fleeting commodity. All things change and history has proven that nothing is permanent. What most people don't understand is how fast the world is moving.

The Myth of Organizations

Another historical myth: the existence of an organization. In fact, there is no such thing as a nation, state, business, club or association. There is no such a thing as a corporation or a congress or an assembly or a parish council, either. All of these terms are simply delineations of people who gather in groups and follow rules they prescribe for themselves. Once the groups form, they take on a life of their own and run themselves.

Consider your neighborhood grocery store. An organization of people started that business, even if it was only Mom and Pop Jones, and from there it grew to what it is today, a supermarket. It now has $30 million in inventory sitting on its shelves at any one time and an army of workers who restock shelves, log inventory in and out, make salads, fill the fruit and vegetable trays, sweep the floors, slice sandwich meats, make sushi, straighten out the health food bins and run the cash registers. Then there are the vendors, ranging from Coke and Pepsi to the local meat stick distributor who sends their stock people in to maintain their displays. Managers and assistant mangers cruise the aisles rechecking floor department work. Security personnel prowl the floor on the lookout for shoplifters, teens trying to buy cigarettes, employees filching food in the back room, quick change artists, hijackers, scam artists and pickpockets.

At this size, the grocery store has a life of its own. It is a machine that needs constant feeding. Millions of dollars have to pour in to the business in order to return a few percentage points of profit after taxes. A 6 percent net return after taxes is good—if you can get it.

But this grocery store can't create itself and can't run itself. It's simply a machine run by humans. But while humans created it, once it existed it took on a life of its own. When Mom and Pop Jones opened their doors for the first time, they didn't know that in 10 years they'd be selling reindeer and musk ox teriyaki jerky, nonfat yogurt, pig skin snack foods or serve-yourself salads. That happened over time as circumstances dictated. No one can know the impact of his decisions but, on the average, collectively, more good decisions than bad ones allow a business to grow and prosper.

But even before the grocery store was in place, thousands of other businesses had to have existed. When Mom and Pop opened that original corner store, they had to buy glass for the windows and counters for the cash registers. They needed electricity, gas, water and a security system. They needed bread, butter, meat, cheese, canned beans and toothpaste for their shelves. Each of these products, in turn, required an army to make, process, ship, inspect, mix, package, label and store the product. A taxation system had to be in place to pay some of these people. Banks had to be operating to loan the money to get these businesses started. Stock markets had to be . . .etc., etc.

But, this is the chapter on myths, not economics—which brings up the next critical point. All organizations are based on economics. People may organize for many reasons but all organizations must have an economic base. All organizations have expenses. Even a monk living in a cave in medieval times had expenses. All organizations—nations, glee clubs and the campfire girls—exist because they are funded. Someone, and usually many someones, are paying for that organization to stay alive. You can call that economic base dues, taxes, membership fees, tithes or offerings. No group can exist without economic support and that's the point of an organization.

Lost? Don't be. Every group needs some form of economic support. And, as soon as they find it, they are loathe to change their behavior. Consider a small nonprofit organization formed to help the poor make their homes more energy efficient. First, they establish their office in someone's spare bedroom and solicit contributions from local building supply brokers and stores. They enlist volunteers from local unions, retirement homes, high schools, churches and temples of all denominations to help their cause. If their efforts prove to be successful, they will establish a network of people and businesses that can be counted upon to supply and refurbish homes.

Once they have established this network, the organization will grow as large as the environment allows it to expand. In a small town, it might never have more than a dozen steady volunteers and that office in someone's bedroom. In Los Angeles, it could have a full-time staff, 15 satellite offices and a fleet of donated pick-ups while the members of its board are made up of executives from Fortune 500 companies.

But once the organization has been established and finds a means of surviving, it is loathe to change. Why should it? If your toy store allows you to bring home $100,000 a year, why change? Sure you could make more. But you could also make less and it's a lot easier than it is to up your take home pay to $120,000. This would be an easy decision if you were a sole proprietor, but there aren't many of them around. The larger your organization, the more people you have to consult before making a decision and while the number of your organization increases incrementally, the number of relationships between people goes up exponentially. Personalities then become as much of a deciding factor as economics. Decisions about multi-million dollar issues will be made on the flimsiest of pretexts. If you don't believe me, then try to explain a pork barrel project.

Quite obviously no organization can allow all its members to participate in all decisions. This is why executive boards—councils, assemblies, state legislatures and even a Congress—are established. These positions are held by people who were appointed, elected or selected for a seat. And they make decisions for the people they represent.

We haven't wandered far from the grocery story and the economics lesson, though.

All organizations need an economic base and some means of doing their own business. Over time, man has learned how to develop the most efficient means of ruling an organization. One of the most important historical lessons we've learned is that no one person, party, family or dynasty can effectively rule for very long. Further, each culture has a unique view that makes it difficult for Germans to rule Hotentots or the French to run Vietnam or America to rule Iraq.

Success is difficult to achieve—a mystery to many people. Once you have built a niche in the market, you usually don't want to change. Mom and pop opened their store because they saw a need for a grocery store in town. The nonprofit that set up shop to increase energy efficiency of the homes of the poor saw a need for the service. But, after both of these organizations got established in their niche, they didn't want any sudden changes. They didn't want anything to rock the boat. They plan for changes they could plainly anticipate, like an increase in population when a new military base is built nearby, but any sudden or dramatic alterations are viewed as too much change.

As a result, organizations grow more and more conservative. They understand how "the game is played" and what their niche in the market is. So, the more they profit from their position, the more unlikely they are to change. This is particularly true of bureaucratic organizations, such as political organizations. In political organization, the people in charge have used the system as it exists to rise to the top. They know how the system works and how to stay on top. The last thing they are going to want to do is change the system and give someone else a chance to take their place.

An important key to using history as a tool: the belief that organizations do not exist. They are a myth. Not all Republicans were in favor of the war in Iraq. But the press lumped them all together.

Organizations are simply people banding together, often following rules that worked once and have now become sacrosanct. People exist and, collectively, form the organization. Every person in that organization is responsible for maintaining the status quo. At the right moment, any one person can change an organization. If they do nothing, organizations fail. Unions become ineffective when their membership abandons the right to have a voice in the collective decisions. Companies fail when the front line people who *know* why the company is failing *don't* tell management what they know. Organizations are collective and are only as effective as the competent people in the ranks.

Myth of Attendance

The myth of attendance, closely related to the Law of Attendance, is based on the assumption that simply being in the right place at the right time is more important than being productive. For example: a junior high student who fails to turn in homework but shows up every day will be passed on to high school. That's because he was present. But, another junior high student who cuts class all the time will be held back even if the work he turns in sporadically is superior. Why? Because attendance often is more important than productivity.

Consider an office where there is a secretary who is inefficient but who shows up every day and works hard. Chances are her employer won't replace her. Instead, her workload may be lightened, she won't be assigned complicated tasks and when the office plans a party, she'll be sent to the supermarket for the napkins and plastic forks. Compare this secretary with the single mother who is a highly efficient typist, has exemplary computer skills and is attending night school to get her college degree. If she is very good, her employer won't want to lose her—but that college degree guarantees that she'll move on to bigger and better things. Her qualities may even leave the boss with second thoughts about hiring her. After all, if she knows how to run the office on her own *and* she has a college degree, they might not need him anymore, particularly if they can hire her at half his salary.

The first woman will always find a job because offices need worker bees. Worker bees arrive on time, meet minimum standards, threaten no one, aren't discipline problems and usually aren't ambitious. Under these circumstances, a worker bee will never be fired.

Historically, the safest place to be is in the bureaucracy. Once you're there, you can stay forever. Few bureaucrats die and even fewer retire. And, the larger the bureaucracy, the easier it is to get lost in the masses. As long as you don't make a scene, you'll blend in.

But problems arise when too many of those merely in attendance make up the backbone of the bureaucracy. When this occurs, the public sector acts as a brake rather than a service provider to the community and private sector. The bureaucracy was designed to perform those services that the private sector could not or would not provide. If the bureaucracy is packed with individuals who are only concerned about being in the office from 9 to 5, the cross-fertilization of public and private sectors is impeded. The public sector ultimately draws its paycheck from the private sector. The private sector keeps costs down by using the services of the public sector. The Public Utilities Commission, for example, regulates the electric company to ensure that it doesn't gouge its customers. When the electric company raises its rates then there is more tax revenue for the city or state. Customers see the cost of living go up and receive raises to cover the increase, which also means more revenue for the city and state. Part of that increased revenue is used to fund the Public Utilities Commission. Everything is more expensive but everyone gets a raise so no one notices the change.

But if the electric utility has a crisis on Friday at 4:15 P.M. and staff at the Public Utilities Commission won't discuss it until Monday morning, both entities are headed for disaster. The electric utility manager may be forced to make a decision that the public utilities commissioners may not like, which, in turn, means lots of hearings and courtroom antics. This will cost the utility money and, in turn, mean that these business expenses get rolled into consumers' bills with no corresponding increase in service. The Public Utilities Commission then has to take time off from other business to hold hearings and go to court. The taxpayers get that bill, too (again with no increase in electrical service).

Using history as a guide, alas, there is no way to cut back on the weight attendance has in the workplace. Once deadwood is in place, it's hard to remove it. The key is to keep deadwood out of the system. This may mean refraining from hiring someone for a needed position. Think twice about whom you hire, even if it's for a janitorial position. Once that person's in the office, they may be there forever. Good people are hard to find—and impossible to keep.

Myth of Prophets

Every period and nation has its prophets. These are the people, usually long dead, who form the central spirit of the culture. Newer nations have newer George Washingtons, while more established nations and societies can chart their ancestry back to the beginning of time. Some prophets are mythical; others are flesh and blood. In the United States, the prophets worshiped most are Jesus, Karl Marx, Charles Darwin and Albert Einstein. Western culture is a product of their theories.

But the problem with prophets like these is that while much of what they said is critical to our collective reality, there are gaps in their philosophy that create great havoc in our society. While the message of Jesus is commendable and clear, the blind acceptance of all aspects of the man and his work leads to fanaticism. Were Jesus alive today, he would disavow many of the sermons, actions and orders that are prepared in his name. His message was one of peace and acceptance, yet many feel that violence in his name is a perfectly acceptable path of action. Were he alive today, Jesus would disavow the shooting of a doctor who performs abortions or blowing up and abortion clinic.

Karl Marx, the German social philosopher and revolutionary, has also left an indelible mark on our culture and many of his predictions and assumptions have proven to be true. But many of them are false.

Economics is clearly one of the great building blocks of every society, but it's not the only stone in the foundation. It's also not the only driving force. Millions of Americans prefer a lower salary and a richer lifestyle rather than the other way around. Communism isn't very healthy. The former Soviet Union is paying a dear price for marching down the wrong road. In the end, it'll cost millions of lives, a large portion of them from starvation, an affliction that should have been eliminated from the face of the earth by this time.

Charles Darwin certainly has his supporters and there is no question that the theory of evolution has ample evidence to convince even the fiercest critics that there is more than a grain of truth to his theory. Those with fundamental religious backgrounds remain unconvinced, however. But they're concentrating on the wrong part of the theory. The problem with Darwin's theory is that it only tells us accurately how species evolved *after* they became species. It doesn't tell us anything about how the species became animated in the first place.

Albert Einstein also has flaws in his philosophy. While his theories of time, light and energy are considered accurate, too firm a belief in his theories limits our theoretical options. For example, if a scientist applied for a grant to develop a time machine, he would be laughed out of his department. That's because the scientific establishment believes that Einstein's theories of time, light and energy preclude time travel in the science fiction sense. Teletransporting might be a bit closer to the scientific mainstream—maybe—but in either case, the defense of the project would depend on linking Einstein's theories to the grant request. This dependence on one theory to the detriment of others is bad for the quest of knowledge. But, if Einstein's theory is the myth of the day, it'll be hard to develop alternative scenarios with money from the scientific establishment. It is unlikely you could get research funding to develop a time machine because traveling "through time" violates Einstein's principles.

Good ideas that solve problems can also have bad side effects. There's nothing wrong with keeping a good idea, but it's a bad idea to keep doing something wrong just because it's attached to a credible source. For centuries, it was believed that a five-pound weight fell five times faster than a one-pound weight. Why? Because the Greek philosopher and mathematician Aristotle said it about 350 BCE and Aristotle was the source of all knowledge at that time. Galileo, however, disproved this theory in about 1600 CE but it wasn't sanctioned by the Vatican until 1993. It took nearly 2,000 years for someone to have the courage to correct what any school child could figure out by dropping two weights out of a tree. Then it took almost 400 years for the authorities to admit that it was true.

Once you understand the myths that penetrate your neighborhood, office and nation you'll view the world from an entirely different perspective. Your job is to learn from the success and failure of others. No genius is always right and no fool is always wrong. Chart your way through the labyrinth of daily life with common sense as your guide.

Myth of Profit

This myth, which is hardly new, is the belief that the ultimate morality of any action is acceptable if it is profitable. For some, child pornography is acceptable not because it falls within freedom of the press, but because it's a profitable business. Slavery, on the other hand, was legal in the United States for 250 years. It was legal, cynics will quickly point out, because it was profitable.

This is one of the sad facts of life. If something turns a profit, there is no shame in engaging in the enterprise. When the Roman Empire was short of funds during the reign of Vespasian, (CE 69-79), the emperor established pay toilets to generate income. When his son, the next emperor, Titus (CE 79-81), complained of the indignity of the enterprise, Vespasian allegedly passed a coin beneath his son's nose and asked, "Does this smell?" Perhaps the coin didn't smell but Vespasian is remembered today in a somewhat odiferous manner. Public urinals in Italy are called *vespasiani*. And, you don't have to venture too far to find a version of the pay toilet today. Chicago's O'hare, for example, has adopted the pay for a seat idea in its restrooms.

If there is any one thing that Karl Marx should be remembered for it is the dominant place of economics in our thought process. Economists hold almost god-like positions in our culture. A casual statement by the Chairman of the Federal Reserve Board can send the stock market into a steep tailspin. Some American presidents have survived impeachment because the national economy was good. Others have been dumped from office because inflation was running at 15 percent. We've suffered meatless Tuesday to adjust the price of beef, wage-and-price freezes to hold down inflation and dumped milk to increase prices at the counter. We pay farmers not to plant crops and subsidize tobacco farmers in spite of the fact that the more crops they raise the higher the national cost of respiratory disease. The list of economic insanities is endless and each congressional session adds to the list.

Overall, the concept of profit is given far too much credence. And, while there is no question that economics has always been a major pillar of civilization, it's not the only pillar. Economic arguments, which are sound in theory, do not work in fact. For example, according to the Law of Supply and Demand, as the cost of a commodity goes up, the use of that commodity goes down. Following this line of logic, if the price of gasoline goes down to 20 cents a gallon, people will drive more than if it's $1.20 a gallon. This, of course, is ridiculous. Americans drive pretty much the same mileage regardless of the price of gasoline. They don't shop around much either, thus negating the belief that the best deal will get the most customers.

The greatest flaw in the presentation of economics is the belief that if it can be quantified it must be significant. This is a significant part of the profit myth. Take the hamburger business, for example. Suppose a family of four walks into a hamburger joint and buys $20 worth of burgers and fries. That $20 then becomes part of the income stream of the franchise and its parent company. This is called gross revenue and that's what the economists focus on.

But, this is only half the economic story. That $20 worth of burgers and fries comes with a lot of paper and cardboard that is thrown away. This increases the cost of garbage disposal—or street clean up if patrons are irresponsible. There's a lot of fat in those burgers that adds weight to the family and increases their individual chances of heart disease and other health problems. The family also has to drive to the franchise and this causes some pollution—another cost that is not calculated into the equation. Nor are parking fees and tickets, upholstery cleaning expenses when the children dump ketchup on the car seats, and the fender bender that was caused when hot coffee was spilled in the driver's lap. Collectively, economists call these "social costs." These costs don't end up on any spreadsheet because, legally, the hamburger joint is not responsible for those costs.

But someone has to pay for those so-called "social costs." Every time an abandoned vehicle is dragged off the streets of Tallahassee, local taxpayers have to pick up the tab. Everyone who pays auto insurance has to absorb the cost of uninsured motorists in accidents. The business loss estimates of shoplifting do not include court, police, social worker or probation/parole officers' hours.

This is where the concept of profit breaks down. Economists, politicians and businesspeople concentrate on numerical proof that doesn't take into account social costs. By the definitions we use, profit means money left over after all the bills are paid. Or in a bureaucracy, it's the service that was delivered for the dollars spent. But in either case, the myth of profit has us focusing on the "bottom line." We tend to ask ourselves what we get for our dollars spent. But this is an artificial number, even if all of Wall Street finds it significant.

From an historical perspective, profit is fleeting. Companies come and go. So do empires. Businesses are notorious for making a profit today and leaving the consequences for tomorrow. The myth of profit is the belief that profit is more important than good policy. This is about as logical as slitting your throat to fill your pocket. Historically speaking, those people, companies and nations that exchange short-term gain for long-term prosperity usually end up losing both.

Myth of the Private Sector

Another business myth that has gained wide acceptance is the existence of the private sector. Traditional economic thinking divides the world of occupations into two general categories: 1) the public sector where people work for a governmental body; and 2) the private sector where people work for businesses. At one time there was a significant difference between the two; today the line has blurred substantially. While at one time there was a legitimate reason to divide the economic world into these two spheres, today the concept is virtually meaningless.

Very few people in what we call "the private sector" actually make their living with their wits. The vast majority are actually business bureaucrats. They have a set salary as well as a contract that gives them such benefits as sick leave, vacation pay, health insurance, retirement, etc. In larger companies, there are unions that enforce these benefits. A better definition of someone in the private sector is a person whose income is tied directly to productivity.

It's important that we recognize the myth of the private sector because far too many companies press for special legal and tax consideration using the excuse that they are "in the private sector" and what is good for their company is good for the nation. Thus, the United States Congress, state legislatures and city councils end up giving so-called businesses special deals that end up costing the consumer millions: an airport here, a bridge there, a pollution waiver overhead, zoning change for a subway, etc. The guise of being in the "private sector" has clearly proven to be a profitable ploy. The private sector has traditionally been the "risk taking" sector. But there's not a lot of risk in owning a bank, newspaper or large automobile sales company. Banks rarely go out of business, newspapers are usually bought out and cars are going to be part of the world for the rest of our lifetime. Even if one of these companies failed, the bankruptcy laws are written so the rich can stay rich. So, even if these businesses are called members of the private sector, there's not a lot of risk involved. Because of this economic stability, the concept of the "private sector" has changed.

Myth of Harmonics

Probably the most important myth in history is that of harmonics. Simply stated, the myth of harmonics is the belief that there is some external purpose to all of history. Sometimes this is called meliorism, other times, orthogenesis. Harmonics is closely tied to the concept of God or a Supreme Being, the belief being that there is some higher power that dwarfs human affairs. This God or high power is the ultimate judge of all things and, when the Day of Judgement comes, gives each person what he or she individually deserves.

At the beginning of recorded history, there was no distinction between religion and secular life. In ancient societies, all of nature was part of religion. All of society was part of religion, too. Consider the pyramids, for example. They were designed and built as extensions of the Egyptians' religious psyche. The pyramids reflected the cosmos. The pharaoh ruled on earth and when he died—*she* in the cases of Nephertiti, Hatshep and Cleopatra—he took his place among the stars. Ancient Greeks reflected on the unique position of man and the gods and postulated that earth was the central point of the cosmos. Celestial charts from the Middle Ages in Europe perpetuated the myth and depicted the heavens circling the earth.

Through the Renaissance and into the modern age, the concept of God being the central feature in the universe has been consistent and around this precept all scientific facts were supposed to converge. Where science differed from the scriptures, it was presumed that the facts were in error. The best-known confrontation between science and faith in the Old World came when Galileo boldly and publicly backed the Copernican theory that the Earth rotated about the sun rather than the other way around. Of course, he was forced to retract his belief before the dreaded Inquisition and was sentenced to an indefinite imprisonment—though the sentence was later reduced to house arrest for the rest of his life.

Copernicus and Galileo

One of the saddest characteristics of mankind is that we waste our own genius. As a composite culture, we are far more likely to honor something we can see and touch rather than a concept that is difficult to transform into something useable, like a pair of gloves. This is why celebrities are so popular. It isn't that we all believe we *could be* a Tom Cruise or a Julia Roberts. It's that we can see their good looks, perfect bodies and income stream and attach all three in a logical continuum and believe that the easiest route to personal happiness is through good looks, perfect bodies and a substantial amount of money in the bank. Unfortunately, there is a sad truth to this assumption. Sex sells and people with good looks and perfect bodies have a tendency to do better in all walks of life—for a while.

The problem is that good looks, perfect bodies and cash do not last. All are victims to the march of time. Brainpower, however, lasts longer. But there is a downside to brainpower: brainpower, as opposed to IQ, will only be as successful as the period in which the individual lives. In other words, simply having a high IQ doesn't mean you're smart. It just means you can learn faster than someone with a lower IQ. Having a high IQ will not make you successful or have any more common sense than a person 10 points down the IQ ladder.

Brainpower, however, will start you on the road to fame and fortune—or notoriety. In the vernacular, brainpower is the ability to "make a pair of gloves." It's using the knowledge you have to create something that was not there before. Brainpower is the ability to use the IQ you have to synthesize knowledge to create new frontiers, products and services.

But making that pair of gloves will only work if your new frontier, product or service is in sync with the culture. If you're before your time, your invention may sit on a shelf for generations before someone recognizes its true worth. If you, personally, are *persona non grata*, your discovery may be ignored because of *who* you are or if your observation is not consistent with the politics of the moment.

Two excellent examples of genius coming in conflict with the politics of the moment are Copernicus and Galileo. Both expanded the intellectual envelope of the day and gave mankind a new horizon to contemplate. Copernicus, born in Poland in 1473, came to the attention of the intellectual world in 1514 when he distributed a small, handwritten book titled *Little Commentary*. Because it was handwritten, and not printed, a few copies were sent around to a select number of friends of Copernicus. The work contained seven axioms that, today, are self-evident. These included the postulations that there was no "center" of the universe, least of all Earth. The rotation of the earth accounted for both the change of seasons as well as the apparent movement of the stars in the sky. Finally, that the distance between Earth and the sun was "imperceptible compared with the distance to the stars."

In spite of the fact that these are all logical, rational, scientific facts that can be proven easily, they were so revolutionary that *Little Commentary* was written anonymously. This was because all of the axioms were diametrically opposed to the stand of the Christian Church.

Furthermore, and even more important, the concept that Earth was not the center of the universe opened a proverbial can of worms. If this was true, was mankind not God's chosen creation? Did this mean that there was lack of harmony in the universe? Were there other worlds with other people out in the ether?

Fortunately for Copernicus, he never had to weather the ecclesiastic criticism. Galileo was not so lucky. Galileo, however, was a different case because he had such a high profile in his community and the church was much stronger in Venice than Poland.

Galileo was born in 1564, two decades after Copernicus died. He had a solid background in geometry and astronomy, ironically, because he taught medical students in Padua who would need an understanding of astronomy to use astrology in their medical practices. In 1609, he was advised of a new invention that might assist him in his astronomy studies, a spyglass that had been perfected by a Dutchman. Galileo seized the concept and proceeded to grind his own lenses.

The power of the lenses was phenomenal, increasing his vision by a factor of nine or 10. Galileo, never a man to bypass a profit, immediately began using his spyglass—which he called a *perspicillum*—for commercial purposes. He arranged to have Venetian merchants pay him to inform them when their competitors' ships were on the horizon. A rice merchant, for instance, would want to know if his competitor was coming into Venice. Galileo would be the first to know because he would be in a high location looking at the commercial flags of the ships as they popped over the horizon. If Galileo spotted a rice ship coming in, he would inform the rice merchant in the marketplace. The rice merchant would then cut his price so people would buy as much rice as they could. The rice merchant thus got rid of his entire stock and when his competitor landed, he would discover that no one wanted to buy rice.

Galileo's use of the spyglass was so profitable that other Venetians wanted to get into the business. To limit the competition, Galileo then sold the rights to manufacture the telescope to the Venetian Senate—for an increase in his university salary. That didn't last long because as soon as the Venetian Senate realized that Galileo didn't have the rights to sell to them, they froze his salary.

Galileo's troubles with the Church originated with his support of the Copernican concept of the universe. At first, he kept his opinions to himself but as his stature—and pay—increased, particularly as the Chief Mathematician at the University of Pisa and the "Mathematician and Philosopher" to the Grand Duke of Tuscany, he could not stay silent long. When he finally publicly affirmed support for Copernicus and refuted Ptolemy and Aristotle's statements that the world was the center of the universe, he drew the ire of the Church.

Pope Paul V ordered the Sacred Congregation of the Index to decide on the validity of the Copernican theory. There was very little doubt as to the outcome of the tribunal. The much-feared cardinals of the inquisition met on February 24, 1616 and took evidence from theological experts who, naturally, did not support the Copernican theory. Galileo was ordered not to hold Copernican views. This lasted until the election of the next pope, Urban VIII, who met with Galileo six times and led Galileo to believe that the Church under this pope might not be so steadfast in its opposition to Copernican theory. Galileo spent the next six years completing his next work, which supported Copernicus.

Even if Urban VIII had been soft on the Copernican theory, the Inquisition was not. Galileo's book was banned and Galileo was taken to trial. Threatened with torture, he recanted his belief in the Copernican theory. Nevertheless, he was found guilty of believing in the Copernican theory and sentenced to house arrest for the rest of his life. He died in 1642.

It is said that as Galileo rose off his knees after hearing his sentence he muttered, *"Eppur si muove,"* Latin for "It still moves." Long believed a legend, a portrait of Galileo, circa 1640, includes those words.[1] On October 31, 1992, Galileo was finally pardoned.

John T. Scopes and the Monkey Trial

Even into the 20th Century, science and religion battled. In 1925, the question of Darwin's theory of evolution was the centerpiece for the famous Scopes Trial in Dayton, Tennessee. This time, however, science triumphed.

One of the most persistent problems facing all civilizations—primitive, ancient and modern—is the tendency for religion to mix with matters of state. While the reverse is also true, for the most part governments have tried to stay out of religion. This was particularly true in the ancient world where the larger empires included a spectrum of races, cultures and religions. Alexander the Great's empire, for example, stretched from present day Yugoslavia to India and from Egypt to Southern Russia. Within that empire were people who worshiped Alexander as a living god, Greeks who had a pantheon of deities living on Mt. Olympus, Jews whose God had no defined form and Egyptians whose idols and representations were local and a mix of human and animal forms. Alexander, like Darius and Xerxes before him, were careful to let his subjects worship the gods of their choice. This was pragmatic political science. Three centuries later, Jesus made it clear that there should be a distinct separation of church and state: "Render therefore unto Caesar the things which be Caesar's, and unto God the things which be God's." In the United States, the Founding Fathers did the same with the United States Constitution.

But the reverse is not true. Religions have constantly infiltrated their morality into political life. While it's certainly true that a basic

---

[1] Fadiman, Clifton, *The Little Brown Book of Anecdotes*, Little Brown, 1985.

moral code is necessary to live in civilized society and that compassion is hard-wired into almost every individual at an early age, pressuring for political change along religious grounds usually ends badly for religion. That's because politics will corrupt religion far faster than religion will purify politics. In fact, a cynic might be wont to say, politics will *always* corrupt religion and religion will never purify politics.

An excellent example of this process at work was the so-called Monkey Trial of John T. Scopes in July of 1925. Famous for the furor that it created and immortal by the movie *Inherit the Wind*, the trial had actually begun as a publicity stunt. Dayton, Tennessee was facing hard times in 1925. Its Coal and Iron Company had gone bankrupt a decade earlier and the subsequent migration had reduced the city from 3,000 to nearly 1,800. Now a farming community, a group of local businessmen were desperate to revitalize the economic base of the city. They focused on what Dayton had that other communities did not: a new high school while many similar-sized communities only had elementary schools.

Meeting around a table at Robinson's Drugstore, the businessmen decided to fake a teaching incident that would violate the recently passed Butler Act, which made it against the law to "teach any theory that denies the story of the Divine Creation of man as taught in the Bible, and to teach instead that man has descended from a lower order of animals." They thought the trial would give the city the statewide publicity it needed and draw huge crowds to town—at the very least for the duration of the trial. It seemed to be a perfect opportunity because the recently formed ACLU (American Civil Liberties Union) had been actively advertising for some teacher to challenge the law hoping to generate some attention to its cause. Everything seemed to be in place to give all parties publicity. Little did they know, they had underestimated the impact of their decision.

But first they needed a martyr. The man who would carry the mantle for everyone was John Thomas Scopes, one year out of college.

Scopes had finished his first year teaching in Dayton and was planning to return to Kentucky that summer when he met, in his words, "a beautiful blonde," and decided to stay another week in Dayton in the hopes of getting a date. Midway through that week he was approached by a group of businessmen who persuaded him to allow himself to be arrested for teaching Darwin's theory of evolution—even though he had never taught the subject before.

From that moment forward, the so-called "Monkey Trial," turned into a farce. It was a pivotal trial in American history as much as for who showed up as for the issue being discussed. Clarence Darrow, the greatest human rights lawyer in American history, was retained for the Defense of Scopes. A special assistant for the prosecution was William Jennings Bryan, three-time candidate for President of the United States on the Democratic ticket and Secretary of State under Woodrow Wilson. The most acerbic, cynical newspaper columnist of the day, H. L. Mencken, covered the trial. And WGN Chicago sent a radio announcer to Dayton for what was the first live coverage of a trial in American history.

In "the atmosphere of a blast furnace," wrote Mencken, the trial was a three-ring circus pitting evolutionists against creationists. Dayton's population increased dramatically for the trial, as Scopes recalled later, with many "men and women who considered the case a duel to the death."

The trial reached a crescendo on the eighth day when Clarence Darrow called Bible expert William Jennings Bryan to the stand. It was an historic standoff that was more puff and bluster than persuasive. Both sides of the issue were staunch in their beliefs. The trial ended with a fine of $100 for Scopes. At his sentencing Scopes spoke for the first time during the entire hoopla: "Your honor," he said, "I feel that I have been convicted of violating an unjust statute. I will continue in the future, as I have in the past, to oppose this law in any way I can." The Tennessee Supreme Court later released Scopes from the $100 on a technicality but left the Butler law in place. William Jennings Bryan died in Dayton five days after the trial.

The traditional view of the trial is that it was a confrontation between Darwin's theory of evolution and Biblical scripture. While this may have been true when the indictment was filed, it was not how the trial ended. In the end what was on trial was the actual wording in the Bible, not Darwin's theory. This may have made "good press" for the new ACLU, but it did nothing to advance the acceptance of Darwin's theory of evolution or undercut Biblical scripture. Both sides went away feeling vindicated.

The primary lesson to be learned from the Scopes Trial was actually nothing more than a reaffirmation of what Jesus and the Founding Fathers had made so clear: there must be a significant separation of church and state. When the two clash, there are no winners. Today, the Scopes Trial is viewed as a victory for Darwin inasmuch as the leading creationist of the day—Bryan—could not intellectually defend the wording of the Bible.

The grip of Christianity on Western philosophy has been vice-like. So powerful was this influence that even the giants of historical philosophy have been swayed. English historian & historical philosopher Arnold Toynbee, German philosophers Georg Wilhelm Friedrich Hegel and Oswald Spengler viewed God as being both a unifying feature of the past as well as the pathway to the future. Hegel went so far as to credit God with providing an end to this pathway that was identifiable by the supposed direction the path was leading. Only Karl Marx was able to avoid the grip of religion when it came to interpreting historical movement. He also dodged the question of the concept of God when he stated that "for man, man is the Supreme Being" and that religion was an "opium for the people." However, even though he denied that God was the prime mover of society, he came up with a substitute. All of human history, Marx concluded, was a pathway to the highest form of government: communism.

While it is very calming to the soul to believe that there is a divine plan for the human race, few historical events would lead one to believe that God can be credited with hands-on influence. Every person may be the vessel of God but humans are not getting any morally better with each generation. That's why we still have the rapists, serial killers, Osama bin Ladens and Sadam Husseins of the world. But we're not getting any worse, either. It seems that seeds of the seven vices and seven virtues are born into each generation and the ultimate outcome is more dependent on individuals than morals or divine wisdom.

Harmonics involves the belief that there is a divine plan that is inalterable. Given enough time, humans as a race will probably not become spiritually pure. In fact, the entirely opposite is true. Science has shown us that rule of the universe is entropic, that is, it is evolving toward a more random state. Thus, in the long-run, rather than having the human race draw closer as a species, we'll be doing exactly the opposite. The melting pot theory only works as far as skin color is concerned.

Even if there is a divine plan, you are not privy to it. With rare exception, throughout your life you'll be on your own, making your own decisions and living with the consequences of those decisions. If there is a divine plan for you, it probably won't be revealed on this earth. As a consequence, we must all live with the realization that the best statement of God's influence on earthly matters comes from President John F. Kennedy who noted, "God's work on earth must surely be our own."

Conclusion

Myths are short-hand manner of conveying cultural information and standards. Myths are neither good or bad on their own—they're often an effective way of communicating complex information. The problems come from how the myths are understood and applied.

Many myths can't be proven. We must take them on faith. In many cases, this faith is justified. Love is more powerful than hate. Power corrupts and absolute power corrupts absolutely. But we must be careful not to believe myths which, upon close examination, are flawed. No matter how popular a theory is, that doesn't make it—or it's interpretation—correct or reasonable. One million people can believe in a foolish idea. That doesn't make it right.

6 The Power of the Individual

The most powerful factor in the movement of history is the individual. This fact has been somewhat obscured by the belief that events move forward only when the "right person is in the right place at the right time." This, however, is inaccurate. More accurate is the reverse: The right person determines the time and place, in which significant events occur.

Even more important, however, is the lesson that whenever the right person is present, change occurs, even if it's not recorded in our history books.

This lesson is important, and should be examined carefully. People often learn history as though it evolves only when significant events occur that push human culture forward. Martin Luther's posting of his 95 theses on a church door or launching a Soviet satellite would be such events. These dramatic events coupled with a changing social climate at the time, open doors for more change. The Christian Church had been unified for 1,200 years, yet, within three decades, a handful of competing religions emerged throughout But this all started with Martin Luther.

One of the challenges of using history as a tool is that historical records are so selective—and so incomplete. Most people and events are never recorded as history. And, despite academia's best efforts, the selection process of what gets recorded as history is wildly subjective. This is why it' so important to look past myths to the greater truths behind them.

Use History Like a Tool

This *looking past* can be tough.

Current philosophy of history generates its own myths. Scholars looking at original documents discover a logical progression to an event. Studying *Sputnik*, they would chronicle the rise of the Soviet space program, discuss the various scientists who were involved over the years, the elimination of space craft designs that proved to be inferior, the fight to get financing from the government, the mechanical problems of the prototype, and, finally, the last minute problems with the launch.

If a book were being written, the last chapter would be a prognostication of "what it all meant" and the long-term impact of the event today and into the future. Once written, it would be a fairly definitive study of *Sputnik*.

What's wrong with this? Nothing, if all you want is conventional history. It's a great story; but it's not the whole story. Because of the way history is written and presented, the launch of the successful project is viewed as the pinnacle of that technology. *Sputnik* was praised because it went up first and all other prototypes were not worthy of further study. After all, the American scientists used the technology of *Sputnik* as their first stepping stone on the way to the moon. So, *Sputnik* had to be the superior technology.

Once again, there's a problem. The problem is that *Sputnik* was not necessarily the best prototype. It was just the one that went up first. Experimentation is not a process through which the perfect prototype is produced; it is a process through which the best possible prototype at that moment is created.

The original *Sputnik* had characteristics that were out-of-date before the satellite even went aloft. It was too small to carry a human, didn't stay in space very long, and brought back little new information. But what it did do was generate a publicity boom for the study of science generally and the American space industry specifically. For the Soviets, it may have been science; to the Americans, it was grist for our propaganda mill. Then hysteria emerged that we were "behind" the Soviets in the space race. Actually, we were ahead. We just hadn't sent anything up yet.

Clever American rocket scientists who understood history applauded *Sputnik* while, at the same time, they were scouring the record of Soviet failures. Far more important to them than the success of *Sputnik's* launch were the reasons the Soviet's launch had failed. In many cases, those failures were political, not technological.

Some of the prototypes were rejected by the Soviets for political reasons. Others were rejected for budgetary reasons. Maybe one had instrumentation that was too complex, another too heavy. Maybe a serviceable unit was designed by Igor whose mother was a peasant while another was designed by Ivan whose mother was married to a Politburo member. Gregor's superior electronic design might have been too intricate to complete on time—even after the launch date was moved back so the event would coincide with a Communist Party event to make the news more dramatic.

The key point here being that the *Sputnik* that went up was the one that went up. That's all. It may not have been the best one, but it was the one that successfully went up. It was the one that went up based on a sequence of events that involved humans. The technology was not so advanced that the Americans were light years behind. Our national priorities were different. We weren't looking forward into space; we were concentrating on domestic products like cars, washing machines, second homes and the like. As far as technology is concerned, we were not behind. In 1957, American scientists were designing lasers, developing a polio vaccine, launching programs to use nuclear power for peaceful projects, creating artificial intelligence and experimenting with the superconductivity of metals.

The space race was one of many concerns until the right person made it the focus of the U.S. government. That right person was John F. Kennedy, who promised in his address at Rice University on the space effort that before the end of the 1960s, an American would walk on the moon and return safely to Earth. Kennedy's promise crystallized all of the culture and technology into historical movement. Historians later looked for a starting point to the space race and found *Sputnik*.

Smart People Use History

Clever scientists use history. So do clever stockbrokers, business executives, high school teachers and shoe salespeople. And, they all use history as an ally. Succeed is important but failure is just as critical to understanding and overcoming the problem. That's because the key to the future is in the past.

If you want to leap into the future, you have to do two things simultaneously. First, of course, you have to build on the success you already have. In the case of *Sputnik*, it means taking what you know that worked and incorporating that tidbit into the new design. Then you have to reexamine the failure and ensure that you don't make the same mistake again—and that you don't discard a good idea whose "time was not right" the first time around.

Because history is about chains of movement, it is the key to the future. The past is a good indicator of what will happen in the future. When you have a problem, look to the past. You may not like the answer you get, but you will find an answer that works.

In the late 1990s, the United States military was lamenting that it could not find enough qualified personnel to fill its lower ranks. This was hardly a surprise to historians. In the early 1970s, at the height of anti-Vietnam War protests, the United States Congress made a tragic error. It got rid of the draft.

The basic problem with the draft was that it was unfair. It forced men into the Army who would rather have been in the Peace Corps. The rich and the clever had options not available to the poor and the presence of minorities was statistically higher on the front lines than in general population. Women were exempt, deferments were granted or denied on arbitrary and/or capricious manner, and objectors were treated as malingerers.

Rather than fixing the problems in the draft, the United States Congress established an all-volunteer army. This change made for good politics—but bad policy. It set in motion developments still being felt 30 years later.

The military draft was more than just a way to fill army units; it was a common public service that many Americans shared.

One reason the American army was effective during World War II was that it contained a cross-section of America. More importantly, since there were so few deferments, a substantial chunk of the most talented people were drafted or volunteered. Translation: Competent people in the service made for a quality service.

During World War II, the most reasonable and popular idea for making military service equitable was to draft everyone. Male and female. Crippled and healthy. Catholic and Quaker. There were no exemptions but everyone could choose how and where they served. Those who had an objection to carrying a rifle were allowed to teach in inner city schools, work as medics, join the Peace Corps or fight forest fires. But everyone was required to put in two years of service to the country some time between their 18th and 35th birthday and receive the same pay wherever they served.

But with the all-volunteer army, huge chunks of the American public could legally avoid military service.

The flow river of the most talented people into the military slowed to a trickle. The Army, a leg of the armed forces never high on the list of social prestige, had to be content with who showed up at the recruiting office. It couldn't reach into the population and take a statistical handful of recruits. So, the quality of recruits diminished. And, as the quality of recruits went down, more and more competent personnel left. The United States military thus began a long, agonizing decline.

Three decades later, the Army found itself in a negative spiral. Not enough high quality people were coming into the service—in the enlisted ranks or as officers. This is hardly surprising if you look at history, see the Law of the Brain Drain on pages 118 and 124. The problem is not the quality of the American who *could* be in the United States military; it is the method that is used to get Americans into the military.

The War on Terrorism which followed the al Qaeda terrorist attacks on September 11, 2001 may end up being the jolt needed to reform the ways that the U.S. military recruits soldiers. It gives the armed forces a compelling mission—something they had lacked for decades. Ironically, a restored morale in the U.S. Armed Forces may be one of al Qaeda mastermind Osama bin Laden's most significant achievements.

Vietnam and the Selective Service Act

No one is perfect. Everyone makes mistakes, including businesses, agencies, associations—and nations. There's nothing wrong with making a mistake. But, when you refuse to admit that you made a mistake, that's another story. That's embarrassing.

Often, rather than admit a mistake, people devise clever ways of avoiding the obvious—they lie, claim they were misquoted or that their words were taken out of context; hint about a dark conspiracy out to get them; insinuate that "it's just politics" or that "this would not be happening if I were Republican/Democrat/Mormon/Catholic/Jewish/liberal/conservative, etc." Or, they can simply lie and say that they never said what they said in spite of the fact that the statement is on record—because they know how *reliable* the press is these days. Or they pretend that the mistake they made was not a mistake at all.

When it comes to the Vietnam War, there are very few Americans who will not admit that it was a mistake. It began as a brush fire war in Southeast Asia and ended as a street-to-street battle in the United

States. In the end, even the primary architect of the Vietnam Policy—Robert McNamara—admitted that the Vietnam Arm could not have been won.

By the end of the ordeal, America had lost about 60,000 men and women in combat. More than 150,000 Americans were injured, which was a drop compared to the estimated 3 million Vietnamese casualties in both North and South Vietnam—not counting the dead and injured in Cambodia and Laos. The war decimated wildlife in the jungles, coated civilians with Agent Orange, which has led to genetic defects in children two generations removed from hostilities, left landmines and pongee sticks hidden and scattered in the recovering jungle and dealt a savage blow to the credibility of America and its military worldwide.

But the Vietnam War taught America three very important lessons. First, while America may be a very diverse culture, it can be unified behind the men and women in uniform, particularly when they are in harm's way. But that support is not unconditional. The reason that American men and women are in harm's way is important. If Americans feel that the reason is bogus, fuzzy or a lie, their support will evaporate overnight.

Second, Americans expect clearly defined objects, even in brush fire wars. America's military history can be summed up in two words: "Unconditional Surrender." That is the legacy of America's military involvement. American military forces have a specific, identifiable mission that they usually perform well. But American involvement rapidly turns to chaos when the armed forces are ordered to perform functions not expected of the military: deliver mail, run railroads, stop looting, patrol streets, burn villages, kill civilians or confront mobs.

The Vietnam War was a conflict with no clearly defined objectives. And, disaster followed.

Third, since there were no clearly defined objectives, there was no exit strategy. If you take a trip, you usually know where you're going and what's going to happen when you get there. The moment the end of a project, trip or war is identified, time and task benchmarks can be established. Then, at any point in the process, everyone will knows where he or she is. If there are no clearly defined objectives, there is no end game, as they say in chess. If there is no end to the game, then it follows that there is no middle game, either. Thus, you have a start with no definable direction of travel.

Working backwards, a historian can map out the reasons that the Vietnam War was such a problem. Since there were no clearly defined goals, there was a catfight between the military authorities who were responsible for the combat and the politicians who were responsible for the reasons America was fighting. As the reasons for the fighting shifted—and along with it the funding—the military was forced to make strategic decisions based on politics. And, as more decisions were based on politics, Americans became confused as to why our military was over there with no identifiable objective. When the political rhetoric and the military campaigns did not coincide, Americans felt that they had entered a quagmire of double-talk and with each day of the war, more Americans were dying for no purpose.

Complicating the deteriorating situation overseas was the infuriating intricacies of the Selective Service System, commonly known as the draft. Military drafts are always difficult pieces of public policy. The biggest problems with the draft in the 1960s were that students could be deferred from military service, minorities and low income men were drafted in larger percentages than whites, and that there was no reasonable alternative to serving in the military once someone was drafted.

All of these problems could have been handled easily during the Vietnam War and could have made the American military a vibrant, representative tool of the American public. Many people advocated a universal draft where everyone had to serve. Choice would be given as to when and how that service would be given, but a deferment would have meant a putting off of the inevitable—not a means of dodging a commitment.

But the U.S. Congress was so frightened by the political fallout of draft protests during the Vietnam War that it chose a political response—ending the draft entirely. That bit of institutional stupidity had unintended effects on the U.S. military and American culture generally.

❧

The most important lesson to be learned from the Vietnam War, one America will re-learn in Afghanistan and Iraq, is that any military incursion must be preceded with a clear-cut reason for the action and a specific, identifiable goal that delineates the end of hostilities. Committing military forces to ongoing guerilla warfare has always been a losing proposition. American might is respected because we go into a conflict, settle it and then we go home. We may not be liked but we are feared and that, in itself, can force settlement of prickly issues.

The most important lesson we did not learn from the draft is that all of America must be protected by all Americans; men and women, white and ethnic, old and young, Christian, Moslem and Jewish. To be effective, the military must reflect the composition of America.

The best reason for universal service—military or a suitable alternative—is that the government gets quality work from quality people even if they do not like doing the work. At the end of a day, how competent an organization is will depend on how many quality people are working in the organization—not dodging it. And all Americans would profit from learning first-hand that the benefits of their citizenship come at a price.

Idealistic? Perhaps. But the bottom line is that the United States military is not getting any more qualified with the passing of time. This is a very dangerous state of affairs that is being ignored by Americans in general. The world is an unsafe place no matter how many cruise missiles you have and there is no guarantee that the United States military will be called upon to protect your city from flood, fire or nuclear terrorism. If that ever happens, your life is going to depend on the individual quality of the men with rifles on your doorstep. If they are the dregs of American society, you can expect America to go the way of the Roman Empire—which also did away with universal service at the peak of its economic and military power.

Once again, the key here is still the individual. Individuals make the difference in day-to-day life and individuals determine the course of history. Even more important, it is not any one individual here and there that makes the difference. It is *all* of the talented people. Consider the reference to Henry Ford in Chapter 3. For Henry Ford to have been successful there had to be myriad other successful industries already in place: glass, petroleum, steel, wire, rubber, switches, paint, horn, upholstery, air compression, brake, pedal, wheel and electricity. After his invention captured the American imagination, other industries developed: road development, insurance, hotels, restaurants, parts warehouses, repair shops, gas stations, parking garages and oil can makers, to name a few. Though Henry Ford may have been the seminal godfather, he's not the only giant of the era. Every industry mentioned above had at least one genius who moved his industry forward. The problem with how history is taught, is that students are left to believe that Henry Ford is the only man who deserves credit for the era. Wrong. Had *any one* of the industries listed above been immature, Henry Ford might not have been able to mass-produce his cars.

Technology and Individualism

The story of human ingenuity gets more complicated. Technology, the speed of communication and the growth of the Internet have irrevocably changed the landscape of human enterprise. In the 1950s and 1960s, a lead in technology meant something—an innovation—could be protected by patent and mass marketing was the key to financial success.

In the 2000s, marketplace leads have shrunk to months, and for many industries, weeks. Far from protecting an invention, patents are now used by competitors to see how the contraption was made and to brainstorm how to come up with a similar innovation just beyond the legal pale of copyright violation.

Even mass marketing is taking a technological hit. Under the combined assault of the ever-expanding number of channels on cable TV, easy access to buy and sell on the Internet and a growing number of specialized catalogs, mass marketing is under sustained attack. This is particularly true with the boutique stores. These institutions are seeing their customer bases whittled away by the discount stores on one hand and specialty catalogs on the other.

What does this have to do with the lessons of history and the individual? Quite simply, history is about to turn full circle. Mankind started as collections of individuals who eventually formed tribes that were organized by the force of personality. But each of these groups only had one leading personality. Everyone else was subservient. Throughout history this process continued.

Ideas that were not exactly in line with the ruler of the day were eliminated—and the people who came up with the ideas were eliminated from powerful positions. They were, in today's vocabulary, blackballed. That's if they were lucky. Death was often the price of being right when the ruler was wrong. What was important for survival in the Middle Ages was to do it the king's way, not the right way. What the pope did was important; what a scientist did was not. To stay alive, you did not postulate that to which the pope would not agree.

The Industrial Age did not change much. The talented tenth knows that every day is a hazard. Rather than having left the era of the divine right of kings behind, we now have the divine right of corporations. (A factory only has one personality even though there are 3,000 workers and 65 plants scattered across the country.) With no one person in charge, businesses have the ability to create good products and services yet, at the same time, the insidiousness to move the history of technology back to the stone age. Good policy in an office was often in direct contradiction with office policy. Good ideas were killed because someone higher up didn't like the concept.

The Information Age offers some more hopeful signs. Technology, which has been mitigating against the individual for centuries, is now coming to the individual's rescue. Suddenly, with the advent of cyberspace, businesses are growing smaller because people can work from home. Part-time workloads mean more people running small businesses in direct competition with big businesses. And, these smaller businesses will succeed because they can offer something their larger competitors cannot: individualized service.

Historical Movement as a Constant Flow

Historically speaking, we're not at the tail-end of any natural progression. There is only one rule for survival: change. For centuries, there have been discussions about the decline and fall of empires and nations. This, however, is rubbish. All of mankind is the same family and what historians mean by empires depends on the yardstick they use. What they really mean is that the dynasty that was in charge is no longer in charge.

The Roman Empire fell, but Italy is still a vibrant nation. Egypt is still a powerhouse in Africa. The powerful economic centers of the Ancient world—Athens, Istanbul, Rome, Paris and Cairo—are still with us today.

The speculation goes on. Writers and historians have made millions of dollars off dialectic hairsplitting analyzing the similarities between the United States and the Roman Empire. Scholars reach into the writings of philosophers Toynbee, Hegel and Marx to see if they can find the cracks in the historical foundation that indicate the start of the decline to oblivion. This is all superfluous. The rise of an empire comes about because of the dynamic individuals who harness the opportunities of the moment. Civilizations collapse because of a lack of dynamic individuals willing to make the sacrifices necessary to keep the institutions afloat. Yes, you need a critical mass of people to keep a civilization from disappearing off the face of the earth, but a culture will disappear faster without any qualified leaders than because of invasion or crop failure.

It's easier to study the rise of civilizations because dynamic individuals aren't bound by any rules of convention. Many revolutionaries had nothing to lose so they were confined by few principles. But once an empire is in place, the laws, rules, statutes, standards and amenities limit the options of dynamic individuals. But that is all they do: limit. History has shown that humans mature with their empires. The qualities of the shrewd, clever, sharp and astute change with the technology.

On the downside, humans plant the seeds of their own destruction. We are pretty good at watering the seeds as well. Populations that allow their leaders to wander into minefields, get what they deserve. We are all party to the destiny of our empires whether they be office dynasties or political majorities in the United States Congress. All societies waste their intellectuals, flick away golden opportunities, stumble into blind alleys and mistake charlatans for saints—all with good intention. This is nothing new. It's not terminal, either. Societies and empires live and die because of the actions of individuals, not rules etched in stone.

Franklin Roosevelt, in one of his great speeches, noted that his generation had a "rendezvous with destiny." Since then, politicians have talked about how Americans were on the "crossroads of the future." But we're now beyond both metaphors. We're in a new millennium of human existence that has nothing to do with numbers on any calendar. Using history as a guide, our future is clear because the answers of all our human dilemmas are already written in the pages of history.

Looking backward and forward at the same time, it is evident that the new millennium will be one that praises individuals more than any other age. We're entering an age of the small business, where quality and personal contact will be ever more important. Personality will be a major feature of this new age. No longer will an individual be able to be nothing more than a faceless cog in the mighty wheel of a corporate giant. The bureaucracy as we know it now will be disassembled in favor of smaller, more efficient units. Governmental services, corporate functions and office assignments will focus on smaller interest groups. Demand for quality will go up, mass production down.

Individual customization of mass products is the critical development of the Information Age. And it's the ultimate triumph of the individual over his or her surroundings.

Entertainment as a Historical Measure

Consider American television programs in the 1960s,. Back then, there were only three television networks. If you didn't like what ABC was broadcasting you could switch the channel to NBC. But the problem was that in order to make a profit, all three networks had to offer programming that had the widest possible appeal. To maintain that profitability, they had to keep increasing their audience size. At first it was easy. As more and more televisions were purchased and the U.S. population increased, there were larger audiences. All networks benefited as the pie size increased. But, gradually the increases in both slowed.

Then there were real programming problems. Since time was a limited commodity, there were only two ways to increase viewership. One was to steal program ideas from another network. This was marginally effective because all three were stealing from each other and unless there was an increase in the viewing population, the networks were simply trading patrons back and forth.

The other way to increase viewership, and, in turn profits, was easier: Identify and cater to common tastes. A broadcast of the New York Ballet did not attract as many viewers as *Gunsmoke*—so the New

York Ballet was off TV. Thus, began a three-decade rush to find larger and larger audiences willing to watch dumber and dumber programming. And remnants of this idea are still prevalent today. The late 1990s and early 2000s saw a mad rush to broadcast programs that were "reality" based—not scripted by Hollywood experts.

The other—and more important—development of TV programming in the 1990s was the explosion of networks and channels available to Americans. During the 1970s and 1980s, the collection of services known as "cable TV" refined their technology and business. For a monthly fee, a consumer could have his or her TV equipped to receive dozens—or hundreds of channels instead of a few. By the 1990s, mot U.S. homes had some form of cable TV. And the whole business model of TV programming changed. Instead of the widest possible audience, programmers wanted smaller *loyal* viewers. In the world of 100 choices, there was room for both *Gunsmoke* and the New York Ballet. Broadcasting gave way to "narrow-casting." And the many channels specialized as all-news, all-music, all-old movies programming.

As ever, there were a few individuals who led the move to specialty TV. Ted Turner was able to convert a motley collection of region TV stations into a global TV business that include CNN and half a dozen other networks. John Malone was able to build a Colorado-based cable company into one of the largest conglomerates in the United States.

As the 21st Century arrives, these established players are looking for ways to combine TV programming with the Internet—to create entertainment so customized and narrowly focused that it will be truly individualized.

Conclusion

What is happening to entertainment now will be happening to America over the next decade: a resurgence of individualism and quality. The era of forcing consumers to be satisfied with a mass-produced product designed to satisfy as many people as possible is gone. Locally produced, high-quality products will gnaw away at the foundation of the multi-national giants. High-quality, low-budget movies will successfully compete with television network specials. In the workplace, the emphasis will be on quality and personal contact, not generic products and services.

The destiny of mankind has already been written: you can find it in our past. Those people clever enough to use the lessons of history will leap to new challenges. Those who aren't will spend the rest of their days re-learning the lessons they should have learned in a high school history class. There is no tried and true method to move into the future, no guarantee of success. There is no crystal ball that will let us peer into the future. Things happen because individuals cause things to happen. The future is in the hands of the individual. All we can do is hope that people will use history as a tool to leap into the future with seven league boots rather than become mired in a swamp made centuries ago.

Conclusion

By now, you're probably thinking to yourself, *Wait a minute. I wanted to read a book about how to use history as a tool to my everyday life but I ended up with a book on sociology and a bunch of rules I already know.*

Well, if that's how you feel, congratulations, you've learned what history is. It's human interaction in action. There is no magic formula to predict the future—because human beings make the future.

Further, history is a complex subject. Even more important, it's not the lock-step progression of events your elementary school textbooks would have you believe. In fact, some of them are down right in error. Or important people and events are glossed over—or ignored altogether. There are many moments in which events could have taken an entirely different route.

America could have lost the American Revolution. The South could have won the Civil War. If Japan hadn't bombed Pearl Harbor would the United States have entered World War II? What if the Warren Commission had done a competent job in the investigation of the assassination of President John F. Kennedy? What if Galileo had received a science prize instead of being thrown under house arrest?

No book can give a complete list of historical events because no such list exists. This book touches on a few of the major ones. No book on history and historical processes would be complete without stating the obvious: There are so many factors that shape human behavior it's impossible to predict outcomes with a 100 percent accuracy—or even 75 percent accuracy for that matter. Humans can be difficult, confounding creatures. Vices can affect human activity positively; virtues can make some people behave badly.

If the lessons history has taught us could be condensed into a laundry list of items that can be used every day, the list would include the rules listed on the following pages.

Don't Fight Problems, Ride Them

Keep in mind that few "human" problems can ever be solved. Only the perception of those problems change. Abortion and family values were hot topics of discussion during the Roman Empire and they remain hot topics today. Prostitution, drug use, unwed mothers, rape, murder, counterfeiting and how to treat your mother-in-law are difficulties faced by every generation. You are not going to solve these problems no matter how moral your society is. History teaches us that problems are not resolved, they are just kicked around for a while and then into the next generation.

Your obligation is to see each problem as an opportunity. Since you cannot solve the problem, ride it. Figure out some way to take advantage of the situation. Profit from the misfortune. Shrewd people are those who come up with unique solutions to common problems. Develop some of your own. When you see a problem that you think cannot be solved, take advantage of it.

Instead of arresting drug dealers, for instance, why not just take their money and let them back on the street? You get their money and the drug dealer has to leave town because now his suppliers are after him.

In the long run, even the most well-meaning people will never be able to solve those problems that arise from being human. So try a new approach. Don't punish; profit. Don't punish stupid people; make them pay for the privilege of being stupid.

Use Common Sense

No matter where you work, there will be office politics. It's a given. Whether you are the president or a gravedigger, there's a certain amount of turf war you will have to wage. Yes, it's not fun, it's not enjoyable but it is part of life—get used to it.

But, what is important in the long-run is to use common sense. This is fairly easy to say, but in the long-run, no matter which side of the table you sit on, common sense will win. It may not be today, tomorrow or next week but, in the end, when a final decision is made, common sense will prevail.

Therefore, if you want to position yourself to win, use common sense and stick with your decision. You may not be popular with your colleagues—and you may not even be working at the same place when reason is finally established—but, in the long-run, you're better off being known as a person of common sense.

Trust Luck

Regardless of what anyone tells you, there *is* such a thing as luck. But it's not blind and it's not random. Thomas Jefferson said it best. "I am a great believer in luck," he noted. "And I find the harder I work, the more I have of it." Successful men and women plan for the future; they do not wait for it to arrive. They dream the future and it becomes a reality. They aren't content to swim with the normal flow of events.

One problem with trusting luck is that many people use it as an excuse for their own lack of achievement. They look at successful people and ascribe their success to luck. Jefferson's point was that successful people are hard-working...and hard-working people make their own luck.

If you wish to be a success, you have to get to the critical moment in your life before history does. Look into the future and see where your dreams and desires will intersect with the direction your company, state, industry or nation is going. Use every clue at your disposal. Know your market and plot your course. Adopt the strategy of a master chess player, think three, four and five moves ahead. Don't blunder into the future with your fingers crossed; plan.

Know How to Spot Talent

No matter how talented you are, you can't do everything on your own. As many a weekend gardener will tell you, even cutting the lawn can be a two-person operation.

In the long-run, every dream you have will depend on other people. Some of them will be working with you. Others will be opening doors for you. Some help will come from people you've never met. And, of course, you'll end up helping others on purpose, inadvertently, or because they were in the right spot when you failed.

To survive, much less prosper, you have to associate with talented people. The rich, well placed and connected come and go but talent lasts forever. Upward movement comes with the "talented tenth" of the population. Your rise to fame and fortune will depend on the team you have with you. If you know how to spot talent, you're already light years ahead of the game.

If you've never been good at spotting talent, take this simple test. Make a list of the three or four people in your office you like the least. These are the people who you think are, at best, a drain on the office. Over the next two weeks, ask each of them how they would solve a specific problem. Why? Because if you think these people are dolts, so does everyone else in your office. If they came up with a good suggestion, who would take them seriously? You are obligated to steal ideas from whatever source you can find them: magazines, industry literature, your spouse or from people you cannot stand to be around. Good consultants talk to everyone in the business because they are aware that no matter how complex the problem is, there is always someone on the floor who might know how to solve it. Just because that person is black, Mexican, female, fat, has pimples, votes Republican, worships Satan or is gay doesn't mean he or she is an idiot. Talent comes in all body sizes and races and talent, like gold, is where you find it.

Develop a Sense of Timing

One of the qualities of a great leader is a sense of timing. How did they know the time was right? There's no logical answer. It's like asking a football player after he tiptoed his way through the secondary how he "knew" which way to go. If he's honest he'll say he didn't; he just picked his way through the crowd.

The key to developing a sense of timing is not as mystical as it may seem. Leaders plan and then take advantage of the settings before them. That football player didn't plan for those holes to be in the line. They were just there. He was planning on running toward the goal line. The holes opened up where they did based on a wide variety of factors that had nothing to do with him. Their opening up was a random event. It took the skill of the runner to take advantage of them.

You should always be in the planning mode. What are you, your family, your office and your company going to be doing in six months, two years, five years. Do you have backup plans? Are you working on long-term plans? You cannot have a sense of timing if you have no plans. Long-term objectives like "I'll work here until I retire" is not a plan, it's a death sentence.

A sense of timing also comes with intimate knowledge of your ultimate goal. To write a best-selling novel, you have to understand how the markets work, what sells and why, what inroads are open to you, which publishing houses will handle the kind of book you write, etc. To be successful you have to plan. Like a good general, you study the terrain. You become one with your goal. When you have achieved this intimate connection, a sense of timing will be as natural as an open field scamper to the goal line.

In life, the most important requirement for success can be summed up in one word: finish. Nothing is more important than finishing. Nothing. What is particularly surprising is how few people actually finish. And, not finishing on time is as bad as not finishing as all. Unfortunately, people who finish on time or, God forbid, early are looked upon as aberrations of nature. Suppose you work in a bank and are assigned to pull together the marketing chapter for the annual report. The annual report is supposed to be out in December so you'll probably start working on it in September and, if your office is like every other office on earth, you will be burning the midnight oil to get the editing done the night before the annual Christmas party.

Now, what would happen if you went out and did the entire marketing chapter in September, right after the first meeting? First, no one would believe you had actually done it When they found out it was true, they would hate you—*really* hate you. Why? First, because you make the rest of the committee members look bad. If you can finish quickly, why can't they? Second, because you are finished you aren't part of the team.

In corporate America, being a "team player" is as important as breathing. It's not whether you win or lose, it's how you play the game. To play the game you must be a member of the team. There is no room for cowboys, hot shots, rogue warriors or loose cannons. You work with the team. If you have trouble with working in a team, your choices are leave the corporate world...or find a way to play through your trouble.

Another corporate reality: if you don't finish on time, you achieve nothing. Projects finished late are usually mediocre and hardly attract attention. Most people would say, if the annual report is mediocre, who cares? Annual reports are supposed to be mediocre. Yes, that's a fair assessment of most annual reports. No one reads those annual reports so they are a waste of time, talent and dollars.

Excellent annual reports are written, just like excellent books, newsletters and brochures. Excellence attracts attention in the positive sense of the word. Finishing on time means you have planned correctly. To plan correctly you have to think your way through the process. If you seek excellence in life, finish on time.

❧

Every family, business and period is shackled by its own myths. There are many things you probably believe that are just not true. Is this dangerous? Yes. Historically speaking, the key to success is realizing that perception is reality. It's not what you think that counts, it's how you think. Myths warp judgement.

Take politics, a field rife with myths. Staunch conservatives are a stumbling block to cultural advancement not because of the solutions they propose but because of their grip on old problems. They tend to want things to remain the same—or improve guided by the standards "we had in the good old days."

Extreme liberals, on the other hand, are stumbling blocks of another sort. Seeking change, they usually cannot connect the solutions we need tomorrow with the realities we are living with today. Both groups believe in myths that have no basis in reality. The good ol' days were never that good and there is no guarantee that any solution is going to make tomorrow any more enjoyable than today.

Using history as a tool, think through all of your problems completely. Do not just assume that everything simply will work out. Develop plans of attack as well as retreat. Never be afraid to admit you are wrong. And, once you discover that you are wrong, readjust your way of thinking immediately.

Beware of Who You Demonize

The only thing older than government is gossip. People love to gossip. Carrying tales is in our genes. It's fun, it makes fast friends and as long as you don't have to face the person you are talking about, it's a great way to pretend you have an intimate knowledge of things you know absolutely nothing about.

But there is a problem when you go beyond your own life. Making a claim that all union leaders are corrupt and all lawyers are crooked is irresponsible. No group is ever 100 percent everything. The moment you make the leap from attributing the characteristics of one person to the group, your mind lumps the entire collection as a monolithic unit. Then, whether you realize it or not, every time you see a member of that group, you unconsciously make the mental leap. That's the way the human mind works.

The whipping boys of the present generation are lawyers, union leaders and public relations spin masters. Lawyers are presumed to be sleazy and disreputable because if you weren't, well, how could you be a lawyer, right? Then there are the union leaders, carnivores who force management to keep on lazy people who should have been fired long ago. Then there are those disreputable PR spin masters, people who could make the devil a candidate for deification.

Nothing in the previous paragraph is true. It's all myth. All of it. Of course, there are some lawyers who are so crooked they have to screw on their socks. Some union leaders who couldn't fight their way out of a wet paper bag and some public relations people who are whores. So? What's the problem? Lawyers don't cause divorce or bankruptcy. Union leaders have to protect the rights of all workers, not just the ones you like. And when it comes to communication, just because you read something in the newspaper doesn't make it true.

The instant you demonize an entire group of people you have fallen prey to the evil of generalization. You are drawing conclusions that are not accurate. Worse, you are allowing yourself to think in terms of groups, not individuals. You choose a lawyer because she's good. You support union leaders who negotiate quality contracts. You listen to public relations people with high integrity because they will not lie to you.

Competent people understand that their quest in life is to find other competent people with whom to associate. History tells you this. Successful businesses are formed when two or more high-quality people find each other. Your quest is to find quality people, even if they are lawyers, union reps or company flacks. But the moment you demonize a profession, you cut yourself off from a source of competent people. If you won't hire a Jew, you are depriving yourself of the possibility of finding a competent worker who is a Jew. Be careful. There are not that many truly competent people out there. Every one you find is a jewel. Don't eliminate people you don't know based on a myth you've internalized since the age of three.

Read History

No book no matter how scholarly can give you a composite view of all the twists and turns of history. On the other hand, there has never been a book of history written that didn't carry some lesson you could apply to your own life. That's what the study of history is, in essence, the study of the past in order to help you solve your problems in the future. Mankind has produced very clever people and the stories of their lives will give you clues to make your life more successful.

Look for the movement behind the names and dates. If you're reading about a war, look beyond the military battles for *why* the fighting started. Look for the effects that people felt a year...and a generation...later.

Further, when you read history, don't be afraid to delve into original documents. Don't read a synopsis of the Declaration of Independence...read an actual copy of it. Far too often, people read general history books and get general information. These books are written from information contained in other books, thus the information offered is simply a rehash of myths of the era in which the book was written. But, the closer you get to the original source documents, the more valuable the history is. When in doubt, go back and read the original documents. Go to your library, your local courthouse or scour the Internet. The accurate information is out there.

Perhaps the most important lesson that history provides is to get involved in politics and public discourse. This doesn't mean you should run for public office—though if you're smart enough to read this book you might make a fine legislator. What it means is that you must involve yourself with the issues and personalities of your era. The only thing more important than politics is breathing. The men and women who sit on our school boards and assemblies or in the legislature affect our lives every day. Yes, *every* day.

Regrettably, few people realize just how important local government bodies and state legislatures are. Over the past few decades power has been relegated down from the United States Congress. Today, most of the important day-to-day issues of our lives are being legislated from the state capitols.

These issues include abortion, gay rights, the death penalty, drunk driving, teenage pregnancy, child molestation, the sale of drugs, AIDS and others. Local assemblies and state legislators exert a tremendous amount of influence over you. If they do not understand the lessons of history then they will be doomed to repeat the mistakes. That's going to be very expensive for you.

Appendix A

Ninety-Five Theses
or
Disputation on the Power and
Efficacy of Indulgences

The following is a list of the 95 Theses Martin Luther tacked up on the church door in Wittenberg on October 31, 1517 in his attempt to reform the Christian Church.

❧

Out of love and zeal for truth and the desire to bring it to light, the following theses will be publicly discussed at Wittenberg under the chairmanship of the reverend father Martin Lutther (*sic.*), Master of Arts and Sacred Theology and regularly appointed Lecturer on these subjects at that place. He requests that those who cannot be present to debate orally with us will do so by letter.

In the Name of Our Lord Jesus Christ. Amen.

1. When our Lord and Master Jesus Christ said, "Repent" (Matt. 4:17), he willed the entire life of believers to be one of repentance.

2. This word cannot be understood as referring to the sacrament of penance, that is, confession and satisfaction, as administered by the clergy.

3. Yet it does not mean solely inner repentance; such inner repentance is worthless unless it produces various outward mortifications of the flesh.

4. The penalty of sin remains as long as the hatred of self, that is, true inner repentance, until our entrance into the kingdom of heaven.

5. The pope neither desires nor is able to remit any penalties except those imposed by his own authority or that of the canons.

6. The pope cannot remit any guilt, except by declaring and showing that it has been remitted by God; or, to be sure, by remitting guilt in cases reserved to his judgement. If his right to grant remission in these cases were disregarded, the guilt would certainly remain unforgiven.

7. God remits built to no one unless at the same time he humbles him in all things and makes him submissive to his vicar, the priest.

8. The penitential canons are imposed only on the living, and, according to the canons themselves, nothing should be imposed on the dying.

9. Therefore the Holy Spirit through the pope is kind to us insofar as the pope in his decrees always makes exception of the article of death and of necessity.

10. Those priests act ignorantly and wickedly who, in the case of the dying, reserve canonical penalties for purgatory.

11. Those tares of changing the canonical penalty to the penalty or purgatory were evident sown while the bishops slept (Matt. 13:25).

12. In former times canonical penalties were imposed, not after, but before absolution, as tests of true contrition.

13. The dying are freed by death from all penalties, are already dead as far as the canon laws are concerned, and have a right to be released from them.

14. Imperfect piety or love on the part of the dying person necessarily brings with it great fear; and the smaller the love, the greater the fear.

15. This fear or horror is sufficient in itself, to say nothing of other things, to constitute the penalty of purgatory, since it is very near the horror of despair.

16. Hell, purgatory, and heaven seem to differ the same as despair, fear, and assurance of salvation.

17. It seems as though for the souls in purgatory fear should necessarily decrease and love increase.

18. Furthermore, it does not seem proved, either by reason or Scripture, that souls in purgatory are outside the state of merit, that it, unable to grow in love.

19. Nor does it seem proved that souls in purgatory, at lest not all of them, are certain and assured of their own salvation, even if we ourselves may be entirely certain of it.

20. Therefore the pope, when he uses the words "plenary remission of all penalties," does not actually mean "all penalties," but only those imposed by himself.

21. Thus those indulgence preachers are in error who say that a man is absolved from every penalty and saved by papal indulgences.

22. As a matter of fact, the pope remits to souls in purgatory no penalty which, according to canon law, they should have paid in this life.

23. If remission of all penalties whatsoever could be granted to anyone at all, certainly it would be granted only to the most perfect, that is, to very few.

24. For this reason most people are necessarily deceived by that indiscriminate and high-sounding promise of release from penalty.

25. That power which the pope has in general over purgatory corresponds to the power which any bishop or curate has in a particular way to in his own diocese or parish.

26. The pope does very well when he grants remission to souls in purgatory, not by the power of the keys, which he does not have, but by way of intercession for them.

27. They preach only human doctrines who say that as soon as the money clinks into the money chest, the soul flies out of purgatory.

28. It is certain that when money clinks in the money chest, greed and avarice can be increased; but when the church intercedes the result is in the hands of God alone.

29. Who knows whether all souls in purgatory wish to be redeemed, since we have exceptions in St. Severinus and St. Pashal, as related in a legend.

30. No one is sure of the integrity of his contrition, much less of having received plenary remission.

31. The man who actually buys indulgences is as rare as he who is really penitent, indeed; he is exceedingly rare.

32. Those who believe that they can be certain of their salvation because they have indulgence letters will be eternally damned, together with their teachers.

33. Men must especially be on their guard against those who say that the pope's pardons are the inestimable gift of God by which man is reconciled to him.

34. For the graces of indulgences are concerned only with the penalties of sacramental satisfaction established by man.

35. They who teach that contrition is not necessary on the part of those who intend to buy souls out of purgatory or to buy confessional privileges preach unchristian doctrine.

36. Any truly repentant Christian has a right to full remission of penalty and guilt, even without indulgence letters.

37. Any true Christian, whether living or dead, participates in all the blessings of Christ and the church; and this is granted him by God, even without indulgence letters.

38. Nevertheless, papal remission and blessing are by no means to be disregarded, for they are, as I have said (Thesis 6), the proclamation of the divine remission.

39. It is very difficult, even for the most learned theologians, at one and the same time to commend to the people the bounty of indulgences and the need of true contrition.

40. A Christian who is truly contrite seeks and loves to pay penalties for his sins; the bounty of indulgences, however, relaxes, penalties and causes men to hate them—at least it furnishes occasion for hating them.

41. Papal indulgences must be preached with caution, lest people erroneously think they are preferable to other good works of love.

42. Christians are to be taught that the pope does not intend that the buying of indulgences should in any way be compared with works of mercy.

43. Christians are to be taught that he who gives to the poor or lends to the needy does a better deed than he who buys indulgences.

44. Because love grows by works of love, man thereby becomes better. Man does not, however, become better by means of indulgences but is merely freed from penalties.

45. Christians are to be taught that he who sees a needy man and passes him by, yet gives his money for indulgences, does not buy papal indulgences but God's wrath.

46. Christians are to be taught that, unless they have more than they need, they must reserve enough for their family needs and by no means squander it on indulgences.

47. Christians are to be taught that the buying of indulgences is a matter of free choice, not commanded.

48. Christians are to be taught that the pope, in granting indulgences, needs and thus desires their devout prayer more than their money.

49. Christians are to be taught that papal indulgences are useful only if they do not put their trust in them, but very harmful if they lose their fear of God because of them.

50. Christians are to be taught that if the pope knew the exactions of the indulgence preachers, he would rather that the basilica of St. Peter be burned to ashes that built up with the skin, flesh, and bones of his sheep.

51. Christians are to be taught that the pope would and should wish to give of his own money, even though he had to sell the basilica of St. Peter, to many of those from whom certain hawkers of indulgences cajole money.

52. It is vain to trust in salvation by indulgence letters, even though the indulgence commissary, or even the pope, were to offer his soul as security.

53. They are enemies of Christ and the pope who forbid altogether the preaching of the Word of God in some churches in order that indulgences may be preached in others.

54. Injury is done the Word of God when, in the same sermon, an equal or larger amount of time is devoted to indulgences than to the Word.

55. It is certainly the pope's sentiment that if indulgences, which are a very insignificant thing, are celebrated with one bell, one procession, and one ceremony, that the gospel, which is the very greatest thing, should be preached with a hundred bells, a hundred processions, a hundred ceremonies.

56. The treasures of the church, out of which the pope distributes indulgences, are not sufficiently discussed or known among the people of Christ.

57. That indulgences are not temporal treasures is certainly clear, for many preachers do not distribute them freely but only gather them.

58. Nor are they the merits of Christ and the saints, for, even without the pope, the latter always work grace for the inner man, and the cross, death and hell for the outer man.

59. St. Laurence said that the poor of the church were the treasures of the church, but he spoke according to the usage of the word in his own time.

60. Without want of consideration we say that the keys of the church given by the merits of Christ, are that treasure.

61. For it is clear that the pope's power is of itself sufficient for the remission of penalties and cases reserved by himself.

62. The true treasure of the church is the most holy gospel of the glory and grace of God.

63. But this treasure is naturally most odious, for it makes the first to be last (Matt. 20:16).

64. On the other hand, the treasure of indulgences is naturally most acceptable, for it makes the last to be first.

65. Therefore the treasures of the gospel are nets with which one formerly fished for men of wealth.

66. The treasures of indulgences are nets with which one now fishes for the wealth of men.

67. The indulgences which the demagogues acclaim as the greatest graces are actually understood to be such only insofar as they promote gain.

68. They are nevertheless in truth the most insignificant graces when compared with the grace of God and the piety of the cross.

69. Bishops and curates are bound to admit that the commissaries of paper indulgences with all reverence.

70. But they are much more bound to strain their eyes and ears lest these men preach their own dreams instead of what the pope has commissioned.

71. Let him who speaks against the truth concerning papal indulgences be anathema and accursed.

72. But let he who guards against the lust and license of the indulgence preachers be blessed.

73. Just as the pope justly thunders against those who by any means whatsoever contrive harm to the sale of indulgences.

74. But much more does he intend to thunder against those who use indulgences as a pretext to contrive harm to holy love and truth.

75. To consider papal indulgences so great that they could absolve a man even if he had done the impossible and had violated the mother of God is madness.

76. We say on the contrary that papal indulgences cannot remove the very least of venial sins as far as guilt is concerned.

77. To say that even St. Peter, if he were now pope, could not grant greater graces is blasphemy against St. Peter and the pope.

78. We say on the contrary that even the present pope, or any pope whatsoever, has greater graces at his disposal, that is, the gospel, spiritual powers, gifts of healing, etc., as it is written in I Cor. 12 (:28).

79. To say that the cross emblazoned with the papal coat of arms, and set up by the indulgence preachers, is equal in worth to the cross of Christ is blasphemy.

80. The bishops, curates, and theologians who permit such talk to be spread among the people will have to answer for this.

81. This unbridled preaching of indulgences makes it difficult even for leaned men to reduce the reverence which is due the pope from slander or from the shrewd questions of the laity,

82. Such as "Why does not the pope empty purgatory for the sake of holy love and the dire need of the souls that are there if he redeems an infinite number of souls for the sake of miserable money with which to build a church? The former reasons would be most just; the latter most trivial."

83. Again, "Why are funeral and anniversary masses for the dead continued and why does he not return or permit the withdrawal of the endowments founded for them, since it is wrong to pray for the redeemed?"

84. Again, "What is this new piety of God and the pope that for a consideration of money they permit a man who is impious and their enemy to buy out of purgatory the pious soul of a friend of God and do not rather, because of the need for that pious and beloved soul, free it for pure love's sake?"

85. Again, "Why are the penitential canons, long since abrogated and dead in actual fact and through disuse, now satisfied by the granting of indulgences as though they were still alive and in force."

86. Again, "Why does not the pope, whose wealth is today greater than the wealth of the richest Crassus, build this one basilica of St. Peter with his own money rather than the money of the poor believers?"

87. Again, "What does the pope remit or grant to those who by perfect contrition already have a right to full remission and blessings?"

88. Again, "What greater blessing could come to the church than if the pope were to bestow these remission and blessings on every believer a hundred times a day, as he now does but once?"

89. "Since the pope seeks the salvation of souls rather than money by his indulgences, why does he suspend the indulgences and pardons previously granted when they have equal efficacy?"

90. To repress these very sharp arguments of the laity by force alone, and not to resolve them by giving reasons, is to expose the church and the pope to the ridicule of their enemies and to make Christians unhappy.

91. If, therefore, indulgences were preached according to the spirit and intention of the popes, all these doubts would be readily resolved. Indeed, they would not exist.

92. Away then with all those prophets who say to the people of Christ, "Peace, peace," and there is no peace! [Jer. 6:14]

93. Blessed be all those prophets who say to the people of Christ, "Cross, cross" and there is no cross!

94. Christians should be exhorted to be diligent in following Christ, their head, through penalties, death and hell;

95. And thus be confident of entering into heaven through many tribulations rather than through the false security of peace (Acts 14:22).

Appendix B

John L. O'Sullivan's Editorial

The following article appeared in the July/August 1845 edition of the *United States Magazine and Democratic Review*. Chapter 1 discussed Sullivan's concept of Manifest Destiny. The term, which John Louis O'Sullivan coined for a speech he made in 1839, basically meant that it was God's destiny that Americans should dominate the North American continent.

ᥱ᷉ᦞ

It is time now for opposition to the Annexation of Texas to cease, all further agitation of the waters of bitterness and strife, at least in connexion with this question, even though it may perhaps be required of us as a necessary condition of the freedom of our institutions, that we must live on for ever in a state of unpausing struggle and excitement upon some subject of party division or other. But, in regard to Texas, enough has now been given to Party. It is time for the common duty of Patriotism to the Country to succeed; or if this claim will not be recognized, it is at least time for common sense to acquiesce with decent grace in the inevitable and the irrevocable.

Texas is now ours. Already, before these words are written, her Convention has undoubtedly ratified the acceptance, by her Congress, of our proffered invitation into the Union; and made the requisite changes in her already republican form of constitution to adopt it to its future federal relations. Her star and her stripe may already be said to have taken their place in the glorious blazon of our common nationality; and the sweep of our eagle's wing already includes within its circuit the wide extent of her fair and fertile land. She is no longer to us a mere geographical space a certain combination of coast, plain, mountain, valley, forest and stream. She is no longer to us a mere country on the map. She comes within the dear and sacred designation of Our Country....

Why, were other reasoning wanting, in favor of now elevating this question of the reception of Texas into the Union, out of the lower region of our past party dissensions, up to its proper level of a high and broad nationality, it surely is to be found, found abundantly, in the manner in which other nations have undertaken to intrude themselves into it, between us and the proper parties to the case, in a spirit of hostile interference against us, for the avowed object of thwarting our policy and hampering our power, limiting our greatness and checking the fulfilment of our manifest destiny to overspread the continent allotted by Providence for the free development of our yearly multiplying millions....

Nor is there any just foundation of the charge that Annexation is a great pro-slavery measure calculated to increase and perpetuate that institution. Slavery had nothing to do with it....The country which was the subject of Annexation in this case, from its geographical position and relations, happens to be or rather the portion of it now actually settled, happens to be a slave country. But a similar process might have taken place in proximity to a different section of our Union; and indeed there is a great deal of Annexation yet to take place, within the life of the present generation, along the whole line of our northern border. Texas has been absorbed into the Union in the inevitable fulfilment of the general law which is rolling our population westward; the connexion of which with that ratio of growth in population which is destined within a hundred years to swell our numbers to the enormous population of two hundred and fifty millions (if not more), is too evident to leave us in doubt of the manifest design of Providence in regard to the occupation of this continent. It was disintegrated from Mexico in the natural course of events, by a process perfectly legitimate on its own part, blameless on ours; and in which all the censures due to wrong, perfidy and folly, rest on Mexico alone. And possessed as it was by a population which was in truth but a colonial detachment from our own, and which was still bound by myriad ties of the very heartstrings to its old relations, domestic and political, their incorporation into the Union was not only inevitable, but the most natural, right and proper thing in the world and it is only astonishing that there should be any among ourselves to say it nay....

California will, probably, next fall away from the loose adhesion which, in such a country as Mexico, holds a remote province in a slight equivocal kind of dependence on the metropolis. Imbecile and distracted, Mexico never can exert any real governmental authority over such a country. The impotence of the one and the distance of the other, must make the relation one of virtual independence; unless, by stunting the province of all natural growth, and forbidding that immigration which can alone develope its capabilities and fulfil the purposes of its creation, tyranny may retain a military dominion which is no government in the legitimate sense of the term. In the case of California this is now impossible. The Anglo-Saxon foot is already on its borders. Already the advance guard of the irresistible army of Anglo-Saxon emigration has begun to pour down upon it, armed with the plough and the rifle, and marking its trail with schools and colleges, courts and representative halls, mills and meeting-houses. A population will soon be in actual occupation of California, over which it will be idle for Mexico to dream of dominion. They will necessarily become independent. All this without agency of our government, without responsibility of our people in the natural flow of events, the spontaneous working of principles, and the adaptation of the tendencies and wants of the human race to the elemental circumstances in the midst of which they find themselves placed. And they will have a right to independence to self-government to the possession of the homes conquered from the wilderness by their own labors and dangers, sufferings and sacrifices a better and a truer right than the artificial title of sovereignty in Mexico a thousand miles distant, inheriting from Spain a title good only against those who have none better.

Their right to independence will be the natural right of self-government belonging to any community strong enough to maintain it distinct in position, origin and character, and free from any mutual obligations of membership of a common political body, binding it to others by the duty of loyalty and compact of public faith. This will be their title to independence; and by this title, there can be no doubt that the population now fast streaming down upon California will both assert and maintain the independence. Whether they will then attach themselves to our Union or not, is not to be predicted with any certainty. Unless the projected rail-road across the continent to the Pacific be carried into effect, perhaps they may not; though even in that case, the day is not distant when the Empires of the Atlantic and Pacific would again flow together into one, as soon as their inland border should approach each other. But that great work, colossal as appears the plan on its first suggestion, cannot remain long unbuilt. Its necessity for this very purpose of binding and holding together in its iron clasp our fast settling Pacific region with that of the Mississippi valley the natural facility of the route the ease with which any amount of labor for the construction can be drawn in from the overcrowded populations of Europe, to be paid in the lands made valuable by the progress of the work itself and its immense utility to the commerce of the world with the whole eastern coast of Asia, alone almost sufficient for the support of such a road these considerations give assurance that the day cannot be distant which shall witness the conveyance of the representatives from Oregon and California to Washington within less time than a few years ago was devoted to a similar journey by those from Ohio; while the magnetic telegraph will enable the editors of the "San Francisco Union, "the "Astoria Evening Post," or the "Nootka Morning News" to set up in type the first half of the President's Inaugural, before the echoes of the latter half shall have died away beneath the lofty porch of the Capitol, as spoken from his lips.

Away, then, with all idle French talk of balances of power on the American Continent. There is no growth in Spanish America! Whatever progress of population there may be in the British Canadas, is only for their own early severance of their present colonial relation to the little island three thousand miles across the Atlantic; soon to be followed by Annexation, and destined to swell the still accumulating momentum of our progress. And whatsoever may hold the balance, though they should cast into the opposite scale all the bayonets and cannon, not only of France and England, but of Europe entire, how would it kick the beam against the simple solid weight of the two hundred and fifty or three hundred millions and American millions destined to gather beneath the flutter of the stripes and stars, in the fast hastening year of the Lord 1845?

Appendix C

United States Constitution
Article I, Section 9, Paragraph 1

The following is an excerpt of the Constitution's Article I, Section 9, Paragraph 1. The excerpt demonstrates what politicians do with every hot issue they can't resolve: they foist it on to the next generation. Here, the hot issue is slavery. Under the United States Constitution, the original delegates agreed to dodge the issue by counting a black person as only three-fifths of a real person and then made it unconstitutional to prohibit the importation of slaves until 1808—nearly 20 years after the United States Constitution was ratified. This was the first compromise.

The migration or importation of such persons as any of the States now existing shall think proper to admit, shall not be prohibited by the Congress prior to the year one thousand eight hundred and eight, but a tax or duty may be imposed on such importation, not exceeding ten dollars for each person.

Appendix D

Gettysburg Address

November 19, 1863

Fourscore and seven years ago our fathers brought forth on this continent a new nation, conceived in liberty and dedicated to the proposition that all men are created equal. Now we are engaged in a great civil war, testing whether that nation, or any nation so conceived and so dedicated, can long endure. We are met on a great battlefield of that war. We have come to dedicate a portion of that field for those who here gave their lives that that nation might live. It is altogether fitting and proper that we should do this. But in a larger sense we cannot dedicate, we cannot hallow this ground. The brave men, living and dead, who struggled here have consecrated it far beyond our poor powers to add or detract. The world will little note, nor long remember, what we say here; but it can never forget what they did here. It is for us, the living, rather to be dedicated here to the unfinished work which they who fought here thus far so nobly advanced. It is rather for us to be here dedicated to the great task remaining before us, that from these honored dead we take increased devotion to that cause for which they gave the last full measure of devotion; that we here highly resolve that these dead shall not have died in vain; that this nation under God, shall have a new birth of freedom, and that government of the people, by the people, and for the people, shall not perish from the earth.

Appendix E

Your Vote Counts

You may not think your vote counts, but in many smaller states it's enough to tip an election. National elections, too. The following chart explains how this works and what happened to Al Gore in Florida in 2000. Remember, in a Democracy all you need to win is one vote.

❧

Don't Ever Think Your Vote Doesn't Count, Because in...

1776	ONE VOTE gave American the English language instead of German.
1845	ONE VOTE brought Texas into the Union.
1868	ONE VOTE saved President Andrew Johnson from impeachment.
1876	ONE VOTE gave Rutherford Hayes the presidency of the United States.
1923	ONE VOTE gave Adolph Hitler leadership of the Nazi Party.
1939	ONE VOTE passed the Selective Service Act.

1960   ONE VOTE per precinct elected John F. Kennedy President.

2000   No one knows who was actually elected President of the United States.

(The Division of Election in most states follows these with a list of local candidates who won by a gnat's whisker.)

Appendix F

The Lightbulb Hall of Fame[1]

Many people think Thomas Edison invented the light bulb in 1879, but there were working light bulbs as far back as 1802. And Edison didn't invent those. The following is a list of other inventors who created working light bulbs in the years between 1840 and 1879.

Edison's place in history is an example of economic progression. He was successful not because he "invented" the light bulb, but because he was able to make a profit on the invention. He managed to capitalize on his product.

☙

Date	Inventor	Nationality	Filament	Atmosphere
1802	Davy	English	platinum	air
1840	Grove	English	platinum	air
1841	de Moleyns	English	platinum	vacuum
1845	Starr	American	platinum	air
			carbon	vacuum
1846	Greener	English	carbon	air
1848	Staite	English	platinum	air

[1] Taken from *They All Laughed...* by Ira Flatow, HarperCollins, 1992, page 26.

Date	Inventor	Nationality	Filament	Atmosphere
1850	Shepard	American	carbon	vacuum
1852	Roberts	English	carbon	vacuum
1856	de Changy	French	platinum	air
1859	Farmer	American	platinum	air
1860	Swan	English	carbon	vacuum
1872	Lodyguine	Russian	carbon	nitrogen
1875	Woodward	Canadian	carbon	N/A
	Kosloff	Russian	carbon	nitrogen
	Konn	Russian	carbon	vacuum
1876	Fontaine	French	carbon	vacuum
1877	Maxim	American	platinum	air
1878	Sawyer	American	carbon	nitrogen
	Maxim	American	carbon	hydrocarbon
	Lane-Fox	English	platinum-Iridium	air-nitrogen
	Farmer	American	carbon	nitrogen
1879	Jenkins	American	platinum	air
	Hall	American	platinum	air
	Edison	American	carbon	vacuum

Appendix G

Language and Expressions

One of the most confusing aspects to learning history is understanding basic terminology. The words and terms used when talking about history or current events are not arcane or subject-specific. For example, you don't have to be reading a political magazine to come across the words *Republican* or *Democrat*. You'll find these words in any magazine or newspaper. And it's best to know these terms before reading far.

Throughout this book, historical terms have appeared that may seem confusing at first glance. In alphabetical order, the following terms and concepts will make your understanding of history more complete, as well as make sense of current events.

Anarchism. *Anarchism* is a state of no rules at all. Anarchists believe that all governments are bad and, since all humans are basically good, the lack of government will put humans on their best behavior and therefore no government would be needed. Every person would police himself, restrain himself from doing evil deeds and treat all others equally.

Anarchism doesn't work because humans need a form of government to regulate their behavior. Some community power has to be established to make sure that evil people pay for their deeds, that roads are constructed and children educated. Some power must create order. If not, the world would fall into chaos, or anarchy.

Babylonian Captivity. This means the removal of people for a political purpose. It does not mean killing them; it means kidnapping them and deporting them to a geographic area where they can be controled.

The first Babylonian Captivity took place in 586 BCE when Jerusalem fell to the Babylonians. Thousands of Jews were deported to Mesopotamia. It is believed that most of the Jews selected for deportation were either rich or influential. This meant that the deportations were as much to increase the wealth of Babylon as it was to neuter the Jewish state. The so-called captivity lasted until 538 BCE when the next ruler, Cyrus, allowed the Jews to return.

A second Babylonian Captivity occurred from 1305 to 1378, when the Papacy was forcibly moved from Rome to Avignon, France. While this Babylonian Captivity ended in 1378, the return of the pope to Rome created more problems than it solved. When Gregory XI returned to Rome and died, Romans rioted on rumors that the next pope might not be Italian. The Cardinals, fearing the mob, elected an Italian—Pope Urban VI—and then slipped out of Rome. Back in France, they elected *another* pope, Clement VII. (The French popes were known as "antipopes" and this era as "The Great Schism," a period during which there is the rupture of ecclesiastical union and unity.)

The mess was not resolved until 1417 when Martin V was elected and reunited the Italian and French factions.

Today, the term Babylonian Captivity implies that someone was removed from a position of authority and kept incommunicado. That person was not arrested and may not have lost any power, but he was removed. It would be like a company's Chairman of the Finance Committee being locked out of his office by feuding members and being forced to hold finance meetings in the Denny's across the street.

Capitalism. Stated as succinctly as possible, *capitalism* is an economic system whereby people have the right to make a profit. In broad terms, a profit is money earned over and above the amount of the original effort. If you spend $30 making an object and another $5 getting it to market and another $5 in sales expenses, you have to get at least $40 back to stay in business. Anything above $40 is profit. If you are providing a service—as most employees are—it's a little harder to calculate profit. Generally, service providers change how much they're paid for their services by choosing where, when and how those services are delivered.

The key to the entire system of capitalism is the word *choose*. You, individually, choose what you want to do. You, personally, will choose how enthusiastically you want to go after your own education, where you will work, where you will spend your money, how much you will pay for products and services you use and how you will vote for your local, state and federal representatives to spend your tax dollars. The total of all of your economic decisions added to those of everyone else in the nation make up the national economy. And this economy determines how much you are worth.

The upside of capitalism is that everyone has the right to choose to make a fortune—or at least a good living. If you choose to work hard and make the right choices, you can live on easy street. Just as there is a reward for success, there is also a punishment for failure. The downside of capitalism is that if you make the wrong choices, you could lose all your money and be forced to live on charity and welfare—or on the street. But the choice is yours, not the government's.

Collectivization. *Collectivization* is a term that has two meanings, one positive and one negative. Primarily, the term harkens back to the dark days of Stalin when Russian farmers were forced to "collectivize" and give up their private property. Less menacingly, *collectivization* can mean to work in unison, as in a union.

The negative connotation for the term comes from Stalinism. Realizing that the USSR—Russia and its satellite countries—was economically decades behind the West, Stalin began a program called *collectivization*. It was basically theft. What he did was order that all farm land be combined into collectives. Rather than have six wealthy farmers owning 20,000 acres apiece with a peasant population that worked the land, the six farmers would give their land to the collective so that everyone could farm all the land. In theory, by collectivizing, the combined farm would be larger and thus more efficient.

Collectivization sounded like a great idea if you were a peasant. But it was a terrible one if you were a wealthy farmer. When the wealthy farmers refused to give up their land, Stalin had them killed by the thousands. And, like so much of Stalin's murder, this turned out to be wasted. The collectives were less efficient than individual farms—not more so.

For Americans, collectivization is the term that has come out of the 1960s when communes were the rage. A "collective," it is important to note, is not the same thing as a "commune." A *commune* is where people live together with everyone sharing everything. A *collective* is when members of the organization pool their money and buying power for the common good, that good being lower prices. Many rural electric companies are cooperatives. Large discount stores like Costco are collectives because they distribute a share of their profits back to their card holders. Unions are collectives because they claim to represent all their members' economic well being. Companies that allow their employees to buy into the company with stock options are practicing collective principles.

It would be wise to use the term "cooperative" rather than "collective." Stalin's NEP failed because you cannot build an economy by taking wealth away from people. You build an economy by allowing people to earn their own wealth. A *cooperative* does exactly that. It is an organization that is founded on the principle that everyone's dollars together give everybody a better price, (i.e., a lower price).

Communism and **Socialism**. For any American born in the first half of the 20th Century, a big part of life was replete with warnings to fear communists and the Reds. Communism was the form of govern-ment that the Russians had; and most Americans taught that the Russians wanted to take over the world.

There was a bit of truth in that statement; but not much. First, the Russians were not communists. They were socialists and there is a great difference between the two. *Communism* is when everyone owns everything together. There is no "your car" or "my front yard." It's "our car" and "our front yard." True communism is a rare from of government and works well when there is very little to divide. The term *communism* comes from the French Commune of 1870-1871. German troops had invaded France and Paris was under siege. Be-cause the Germans had the city surrounded, no food was getting in so the people of Paris formed the Commune to maintain a defense of the city and divide the resources of the city among the people. But even the Commune was imperfect as a communist government. There was still a black market, restaurants for those with money, gambling and prostitution.

The so-called Russian communists sprang from the Bolshevik Party, known as the Red Russians and where we get the term *Red*. With the collapse of the Czar's government, the Russians established a consti-tutional republic headed by Alexander Kerensky. The Bolsheviks—a minority party—staged a coup that began what is known as the Rus-sian Revolution. The Bolsheviks established a new form of govern-ment by dividing Imperial Russia into province-like administrative units. These units, called *soviets*, were combined for the USSR, the Union of Soviet Socialist Republics.

Part of the organizing impulse of the new government and its Founding Father, Vladamir Lenin, was world domination in the sense that he felt the Soviet form of government—socialism—was so supe-rior to every other form of government that every nation would be-come socialist sooner or later.

Socialism, the form of government of the USSR, was not commu-nism. *Socialism* is a system where no individual owns anything but the state owns everything and everyone works for the state. Under socialism, in a perfect world, everyone's needs would be met by the state with everyone paying for the well being of everyone else.

The problem is that we don't live in a perfect world. Very few people are satisfied with what they have. They want more and most of them are willing to work for it. Under communism or socialism, the individual is forced to take a back seat to the state. This stifles private enterprise which, in turn, devastates the economy.

Bad economies undermine governments and political structures. Any system that can't deliver material comforts to those willing and able to afford them is destined for failure.

Constitution. One of the unquestionable virtues of living in the United States is that people live under a constitution, a written document that enumerates citizens' rights, the national government's rights and states' rights. While there is always a great deal of debate as to what the Constitution says, one of the reasons America has lasted as a Republic for so long is that it has a written code.

The Founding Fathers were well aware of just how important a written document was to the establishment of a society. That was the very foundation of a culture, from Hammurabi through the Roman Republic. Here, the key word is "written." That means that all of the rights delegated to the people, state and national government are enumerated. The United States Constitution is a document that can be touched. England, on the other hand, does not have a single constitution. The English have a collection of documents and rights that are called their Constitution.

Democracy, Representative Democracy and a **Republic**. The term *Democrat* or *Democratic*, indicating the political party, and the word *democracy*, a type of government, cause much confusion. Though all three words are derived from the same root, they are different.

While some Democrats would like the world to believe that they best represent democracy, this is inaccurate.

A *democracy* is a political system in which all the people make all of the decisions. Everyone has a say on every issue and the majority decides every issue. Democracy *can* work in small communities and organizations but in the application of its true form it is flawed. Even in a very small community, not everyone will show up to vote. Some people cannot make it because they are sick, they don't care about the issue, don't care about participating in the community or have better things to do with their time. A true democracy only exists when everyone votes on every issue every time—and, frankly, this system begins to look a lot like anarchy when put in practice.

Because a democracy is unwieldy, representatives are elected who represent the people. In the United States Congress, for example, every American is represented by a member of the House of Representatives who is chosen from the district in which he or she lives, and a Senator who is one of two statewide office holders. These men and women vote for the people of that district. America is known as a representative democracy because every eligible voter has his or her say through an elected representative. Americans live in a *republic*, a government in which they have supreme power because they vote for the people who will represent them.

Democratic and **Republican**. Two of the most widely used and most misunderstood words in American English are *Democrat* and *Republican*. Americans use the terms but, if pressed to specifically define them, most get tongue-tied. Some people say there's not much of a difference between the two while others say they are worlds apart.

Generally speaking, the Republicans represent business interests. They feel that the future of America is best left to the private sector and, while they understand that government regulation is necessary to maintain a level playing field, too much regulation will stifle business. Since the private sector provides the revenue to run federal, state and local governments, Republicans feel that an expanding private sector is the best way to keep the economy stable.

Republicans also believe in cash flow in the purest sense of the word. What makes a culture vibrant is the amount of cash the people have in their pockets. They will spend that money on products which, in turn, stimulate the economy. The government is not a good investment for money because it doesn't add anything to the economy. The bigger the government, the less money there is to circulate in the private sector.

Democrats view the world differently. They view government as a service provider. Welfare, for instance, is looked upon as a way to help people who have had problems get on their feet. As far as a government is concerned, a Democrat would say, government is designed to service the private sector. It provides services that the private sector should not, cannot or will not do—like deliver the mail, protect the country, regulate utilities, pave the roads, educate the children.

Republicans historically charge Democrats with spending too much tax revenue on social services that are not necessary or economic, like welfare, economic development aid to rural residents and paving of roads that few people use. Democrats counter by stating that all the money of the United States belongs to *all* the people and everyone deserves a fair share of the services.

In the 1990s and 2000s, a growing portion of American voters have been turned off by the partisan squabbling of Democrats and Republicans. They have become Independent or No Party registrants. In the early 2000s, more new voters were registering without choosing a political party than either the Democrat and Republican party. If this trend continues, America will be ripe for a Third Party that represents the disenfranchised voter who is unhappy with the Republicans and not pleased with the Democrats.

Diaspora. The term *diaspora* was traditionally used in terms of Jewish history but today has a much more secular meaning. Diaspora comes from Greek and means "exile." Around 70 CE Jews in what is now Israel fled or were deported out of the Middle East. Either by force or choice, they were scattered all over the known world. Over the centuries, some of these Jews melded into the cultures of their adopted countries while others established ghettos. Today, *diaspora* is a scattering of something that is not tangible from a central location, like an idea or a cultural impulse. An example: a columnist might write of the diaspora of frustration over the federal deficit that has made it from Wall Street to Main Street, implying that the fear over too much federal spending is finally reaching the "man in the street."

Hegemony, Imperialism and Colonialism. As the United States continues to involve itself in wars around the world, some terms from the first half of the 20th Century are making a reappearance. The three most common terms being bandied about, usually by critics of the U.S., are *hegemony*, *imperialism* and *colonialism*. All three carry a negative connotation to developing countries but each is part of a natural political process—and the three are easily confused.

Hegemony is the process of absorbing a land mass into the embrace of the single country. The history of the Untied States is replete with hegemony. As the American population moved west, whenever the population of white males became large enough for a state to be formed, a state was formed. That was because there were far more benefits to being part of the United States of America than not. (Only three of the current 50 states did not become absorbed as territories first. All three were independent nations or republics. Texas was the Lone Star Republic, California was the Bear Flag Republic and Hawaii was a monarchy.)

What made and makes American hegemony different from that of other empires is that new states become part of the United States with the same rights as all other states. Hawaii and Hawaiians have the same rights as New York and New Yorkers. Territories absorbed by other nations have not been so lucky.

Imperialism is when a nation takes over another nation or area and then exploits it for every natural resource possible. This process thrives in the form of colonies; so the most common form of imperialism is *colonialism*. Businesses from the mother country—with or without the explicit blessing of the mother country—simply arrive and start extracting natural resources. The local residents are treated like peasants and only hired for menial labor while their wealth drains out of their country. If the locals put up a fight, troops from the mother country arrive and re-establish order. When the natural resource is gone, so are the businesses.

Over the long-run, colonialism doesn't work. It makes enemies of those who could be friends, involves the military in guerilla wars that never end and gives the mother country a proverbial black eye in the international community. There is nothing wrong with helping a country give its right wing dictator the boot; but there is something wrong with stealing a natural resource from a country that another country has helped liberate.

Icon and **Iconoclast**. An *icon* is a symbol. Originally it meant a religious symbol and the *iconoclast* was someone who broke the symbol. With the passage of time, an icon has come to mean anything that symbolizes an era, school or movement. France's King Louis XIV was the icon absolutism while American President Ronald Reagan was the icon of Supply Side Economics.

An *iconoclast* is someone who is against the established political, cultural or social order. It means someone who is rebelling against the conventional. A painter with a new art form is called an iconoclast. An iconoclast is not trying to establish a new order or a new political reality, simply charting his or her own way in a new and different manner from the established order.

Liberal and **Conservative.** In American politics, you can understand the difference between a Democrat and Republican, but still be confused by the terms *liberal* and *conservative*. These two words are often used in correlation to each other. In other words, a conservative may call another conservative a liberal because the two have conflicting views on the same issue.

Generally, a *liberal* is in favor of changing cultural and political standards while a *conservative* is not. The liberal looks at the culture and sees that it is flawed. To correct those flaws, the liberal suggests changes. If the change is modest, the liberal is called a liberal. If the change is extreme, the liberal is called a *radical*.

Conservatives, on the other hand, understand that the culture is flawed but that there is no guarantee that changing anything will make it better. In fact, they believe that change could make the situation worse. An extreme conservative is called a *reactionary* because he or she reacts to any suggestions of change rather than suggesting a better way.

Liberals are more likely to view human rights as being more important than property or business rights. Conservatives feel the opposite way. This is not to imply that these always result in opposing points of view. A liberal might be in favor of legalizing marijuana because he/she believes that all humans should have the right to choose what they put into their body. A conservative might be in favor of the legalization because the government has no right to restrict someone from selling what another person wants.

It is also unwise to draw any sweeping conclusions as to liberal and conservative views. Most people are liberal on some issues and conservative on others. Only a small percentage of people are liberal or conservative on *every* issue.

Libertarian. A *Libertarian* is someone who believes that all humans have a free will and can choose their own destiny. While a libertarian is in favor of as little government as possible to allow humans the widest range of options, this does not mean a libertarian is an anarchist. He or she believes in very little governmental control.

An extreme libertarian could be called a *libertine* but the term carries with it some odious connotations. A libertine is usually someone who does not feel bound by any moral, religious or ethical restraints. It is most frequently used to describe someone who is living a dissolute life with lots of wine, women and song.

Mandate. *Mandate* is a misused term in American political vocabulary. The actual definition of the term is an order or issuing of authority to complete an action. A superior court may mandate an inferior court to perform an act and the inferior court has no choice but to comply.

However, in politics, successful politicians talk about a "mandate of the voters." In other words, because people voted for a particular candidate, they are giving that winning candidate the green light to implement his or her view. A pro-life candidate that wins might say the people of the district had given him or her a mandate to push for the pro-life position.

You should be skeptical of people who use the term *mandate*. Be wary of its use in a political sense. Because someone gets elected for a political position doesn't mean he or she is the best candidate for the job. He or she may have gotten the most votes, but it shouldn't automatically mean he or she has a mandate to do whatever he or she wants while in office.

When you hear the word *mandate*, step away from the person making the claim so you don't get hit with the lightning bolt that voters usually send such an individual.

Monarchy and **Dynasty.** A *monarchy* is a form of government where there is a king in charge. Usually the king was born into the position and his son or daughter will succeed and then a grandson or granddaughter thereafter. The progression of power in a single family means that a *dynasty* has been created.

Paradigm Shift. One of the historical catchphrases that began in the last decade of the 20th Century was the term *paradigm shift*. The term is a fancy way of saying a complete and total change to the current state of things. An extreme example of a paradigm shift would be if a spaceship of Martians landed on the White House lawn and demanded to see the President. In that one instant, everything that Americans believed to be true would change. That change would permeate religion, art, culture, technology, business and human relations.

An example of a paradigm shift in recent years is the exploding popularity of the Internet. All aspects of human existence have been affected. Communication at the speed of light has made us better informed, opened doors of opportunity that had not existed before and made billionaires out of people who could not finish high school. On the flipside, it has become a pasture for sexual predators and spam heaven for lowbrow products and services. American culture before the Internet was significantly different than American culture after the Internet. This is a *paradigm shift*.

Polarization. *Polarization* is not healthy to the body politic. It means that a single issue that cannot be resolved is being pushed to center stage and taking time and energy. A good example is abortion in the U.S. There are many people who feel that abortion under any circumstances is murder. Others feel that abortion is a bad idea but, under certain conditions and circumstances, it should be legal. Since there is no identifiable middle ground, the issue polarizes Americans. This means that you have to be either *pro-choice* or *pro-life*. Instead of having a spectrum of opinions, there are only two choices and people cluster around the two poles: the position of the pro-choicers or the position of the pro-lifers. As more and more people are attracted to one pole or the other, there are fewer and fewer people left in the middle. If a political campaign ends up being a fight between a pro-choicer and a pro-lifer, all other issues disappear. The candidates spend their time talking about abortion—not lowering the deficit, getting computers into schools and changes in the administrative code.

In U.S. history, the most polarizing issue has been slavery. It became the political pretext of the Civil War. If there should ever come another issue that polarizes all Americans to the point where there is no middle ground, there will be some kind of cataclysmic event because, paraphrasing Abraham Lincoln, "no nation can exist half slave and half free."

Progressive. *Progressive* is the term used to describe someone who wants to change things for the better. When someone is called a *progressive*, it means he or she is pushing for a change, no matter his or her party affiliation. Usually the term is used in connection with reforming corrupt or ineffective governments. The term was coined by the Progressive Party in the early decades of the 20th Century to describe their political agenda. In the early 21st Century, it is used by some political liberals who worry that the term "liberal" has developed a bad meaning to voters who are tired of partisan bickering.

Quorum. Without a doubt the most important word in the United States Constitution is *quorum*. The actual use of the word can be found in Article I, Section 5, paragraph 1, which reads, "Each House shall be the Judge of the Elections, Returns and Qualifications of its own Members, and a Majority of each shall constitute a Quorum to do Business." The word refers to a select group of competent people that can transact business or make laws.

The reason the Founding Fathers wanted to make absolutely sure there was a specific statement as to the size of the *quorum* was to make sure that a collection of congressmen did not slip away to a tavern and pass whatever law they wanted. With a quorum that required a majority of the chamber in question, to pass any law there was going to have to be some opposition. There was also going to be the scrutiny of the press.

The right to free speech is very precious to Americans in general and the press in particular. Implicit in the American system is the belief that good ideas will prevail and bad ones will go away. The U.S. Constitution's quorum requirement reminds everyone that it is a bad idea to enforce good ideas by railroading a decision and not letting the opposition time to speak.

Realpolitik. *Realpolitik* is one of those words that has a specific meaning for the person using the term but to anyone else, the definition is nebulous. It's a term like "reasonable" or "soon." What is reasonable to a man might not be reasonable to his wife. Promising to pay a bill "soon" has no meaning at all.

The term *realpolitik* was coined by Otto von Bismarck, the Iron Chancellor of Germany in the 1870s. Bismarck, intent on unifying Germany, was determined to use every weapon at his disposal to achieve that end. He would enter alliances for momentary gain and then disavow the policy to take advantage of an ally's weakness. He would support democracy one day and be its sworn enemy the next.

Today, *realpolitik* has a softer meaning. Generally it is used to describe a reality that has come to pass. In days when money is tight, a congressman may tell a constituent that funding for his pet project would have to be cut because of *realpolitik*. That is, the reality of the situation required me to do something that I do not agree with but "that's the way politics is."

You should be suspicious of people who use the term *realpolitik*. More often it is used as an excuse to do something unpopular or unethical. It's another way of saying, "it's not my fault, the system made me do it."

Sacrosanct. *Sacrosanct* is a term that loses most of its impact on Americans. A general dictionary definition for sacrosanct is "sacred" or "inviolate." The term comes from Latin and originally meant "consecrated with religious ceremony." The Caesars used the term to their advantage by declaring themselves gods and thus sacrosanct. To the Roman citizens, this meant that to kill a Caesar was to kill a god—and those who did so would pay for their sin in both this life and the next. Some of the emperors, like Julius Caesar, were deified after their death. Others, like Nero, declared themselves living gods.

Today, sacrosanct means something you cannot touch. In state politics, for instance, education funding is sacrosanct. That is because Americans view education as the single most important function of state spending. Balancing a budget by cutting educational funding is political suicide...and, in some states, it's actually illegal.

Strict vs. Liberal Interpretation. There is an old expression that says while great ideas may be god-sent, the devil is in the details.

Generally speaking, when you delve into the details, there are two ways of looking at them: strictly or liberally. A *strict* interpretation means that you examine the exact words that were written and base any interpretation of the document on the exact meaning of the word. For instance, since the Bible states that the world was created in seven days, a strict interpretation would be that the world was created in seven, 24-hour time periods.

A *liberal* interpretation, on the other hand, would define "day" with a number of interpretations. "Day" doesn't have to necessarily mean an exact 24 hours; the meaning of the line in the Bible is more about the Earth being created than the amount of time it took.

It's easy to nit-pick the Bible because it is a collection of documents written, edited and translated by an array of scholars over two millennia—so one has to expect some changes in tone, style and even literary intent.

The United States Constitution, on the other hand, was written by a select number of men over a short period of time who knew *exactly* what they were doing. Even more important, these men understood that they were creating a document that had to have the ability to expand for new times but was still specific enough to serve as the bedrock of American civilization.

Vague spots in the Constitution can be frustrating for those that try to find a definitive meaning. Consider Article II, Section 4, which reads: "The President, Vice President and all civil officers shall be removed from office on impeachment for, and conviction of, treason, bribery, or other high crimes and misdemeanors." Looking at the "high crimes and misdemeanors" part of this phrase, you can see how complicated interpreting can get—especially since there's no definition of "high crimes and misdemeanors."

A strict interpretation of the passage might eliminate the term *high crimes* because there is no specific definition as to what the term means. A strict interpretation would also require proof of the commission of at least two misdemeanors. This is ridiculous, of course, because if a President were guilty of treason, who cares how many misdemeanors he committed?

A liberal interpretation of *high crimes and misdemeanors* would allow Congress to determine what this phrase means. The United States Congress is not bound by any law concerning impeachment other than what the Constitution says. Because the Constitution does not specifically define "high crimes or misdemeanors," Congress has the right of interpretation.

However, this is a minor sentence in the Constitution that has only been examined seriously three times in U.S. history. But how about a sentence in the Constitution that affects the lives of all Americans every day?

A good example of such a line is Amendment 10 of the Bill of Rights: "The powers not delegated to the United States by the Constitution, nor prohibited by it to the states, are reserved to the states respectively, and to the people." What this appears to mean is that if it is not listed as a power of the federal government in the Constitution and not specifically given to the states, then that right belongs to the people. Sort of.

An income tax, for instance, was not enumerated in the United States Constitution. A strict interpretation might be that income tax is not constitutional as it was not in the Constitution. A liberal interpretation would be that the Constitution, like other documents, must change over time and any amendment must be viewed as an addition, correction or interpretation and thus part of the original document.

Index

20% Off Silver Lake Publishing books

Silver Lake features a full line of books on key topics for today's smart consumers and small businesses. Times are changing fast—find out how our books can help you stay ahead of the curve.

[   ] **Yes.** Send me **a free Silver Lake Publishing catalogue** and a 20% discount coupon toward any purchase from the catalogue.

Name:_____

Company:_____

Address:_____

City:_____ State:_____ Zip:_____

Phone:_____

Silver Lake Publishing • 2025 Hyperion Avenue • Los Angeles, CA 90027 • 1.323.663.3082

slpbb

Free Trial Subscription

Silver Lake Publishing introduces **True Finance**, a monthly newsletter dedicated to money and its management. **True Finance** offers more than dry lists of mutual funds or rehashed press releases. It focuses on the trends—technological, economic, political and even criminal—that influence security and growth. It includes columns from the authors of some of Silver Lake Publishing's bestselling books, including **The Under 40 Financial Planning Guide**, **Insuring the Bottom Line** and **You Can't Cheat an Honest Man**.

[   ] **Yes.** Please send me **a free trial subscription to True Finance**.

Name:_____

Address:_____

City:_____ State:_____ Zip:_____

Phone:_____

Silver Lake Publishing • 2025 Hyperion Avenue • Los Angeles, CA 90027 • 1.323.663.3082

slpbb

BUSINESS REPLY MAIL
FIRST-CLASS MAIL PERMIT NO. 73996 LOS ANGELES CA

POSTAGE WILL BE PAID BY ADDRESSEE

SILVER LAKE PUBLISHING
2025 HYPERION AVE
LOS ANGELES CA 90027-9849

NO POSTAGE
NECESSARY
IF MAILED
IN THE
UNITED STATES

BUSINESS REPLY MAIL
FIRST-CLASS MAIL PERMIT NO. 73996 LOS ANGELES CA

POSTAGE WILL BE PAID BY ADDRESSEE

SILVER LAKE PUBLISHING
2025 HYPERION AVE
LOS ANGELES CA 90027-9849